*Seeds*

Also by Richard Horan

*Life in the Rainbow*

*Goose Music*

One Man's Serendipitous Journey

to find the Trees That Inspired

famous American Writers

from faulkner to Kerouac, Welty to Wharton

# *Seeds*

## RICHARD HORAN

HARPER ◖◗ PERENNIAL

NEW YORK • LONDON • TORONTO • SYDNEY • NEW DELHI • AUCKLAND

HARPER ● PERENNIAL

FIRST EDITION

*Tree seed illustrations by Debbie Ferrer and Matthew Ferrer*

Library of Congress Cataloging-in-Publication Data is available upon request.

ISBN 978-0-06-186168-0

11 12 13 14 15    OV/RRD    10 9 8 7 6 5 4 3 2 1

This book is dedicated to the people of the island

nation of Kiribati, who have lost

all of their trees due to the rise in sea level,

which has contaminated the groundwater.

*I never saw a discontented tree.*

—JOHN MUIR

# Contents

# Part Three

# Part four

# Part five

# Part Six

# Part Seven

# Seeds

I GREW UP IN SUBURBIA. I remember the houses and the people and the schoolyards, but I remember the trees most of all. I remember the smell of them in spring, redolent of pollen. I remember them in summer, plump and green, large as churches. I have visions of them in fall, brilliant with color, as dazzling as the circus. I see them standing still in winter, somber but steadfast.

I remember the red maple tree out in front of my own house, more a playmate than a plant. I used to sit up in the topmost branches and look out over the world like a crow, imagining infinite forests, unbound freedom, and life before cars and cities.

I have come to believe that where we played as children, so utterly consumed in the moment, is intricately woven into our emotional and intellectual circuitry and we carry the leafy landscapes and odors in our souls throughout our journey on earth. Even if we don't encounter trees early on, we find them around us at critical points in our lives—when we are in love, in turmoil, at peace.

In so many yards and parks across America, ancient trees have stood proud, watching all like gods. They are both the silent witnesses of and active partners in our personal history.

During college—the last rite of childhood—I had a philosopher/naturalist friend who had gone to forestry school before transferring to Boston College. He knew the names of all the trees. Oftentimes we would ramble through the neighborhood, near St. John's Seminary or around the great reservoir at Cleveland Circle, discussing Thoreau, Emerson, and Nietzsche. And as we strolled along, he would occasionally stop to identify a species and talk about its uses and outstanding characteristics. It was a perfect complement to our inspired ramblings, like a good bottle of wine with a gourmet meal. Ever since then, I have always stopped to notice the trees.

TREES ARE THE PLANET'S most precious resource. They provide us with our life-giving breath. They are home and harvest to so many creatures of this green earth. Together they form the wild jungles and dark forests that embody our sense of awe and wonder. As a species, we are but children, and not too long ago our ancestors climbed down from the safety of the trees' arms to walk the earth on two legs. But we seem to have forgotten our arboreal origins.

More often than not, trees are seen as just being in the way; we are destroying them at a catastrophic rate. Where are we growing to? I wonder.

Thankfully there is hope, with organizations and initiatives such as the Sierra Club, the Arbor Day Foundation, The TREE Fund, the Tree of Peace Society, The Nature Conservancy's Wildlife Corridor project, and the Billion Tree Campaign.

As a writer, I have made a solemn oath to the trees to write only what is necessary, for every page of printed material is a precious piece of wood flesh. There is no other art form that is so dependent on a living species.

There is much to be written, but there is far more to be revered.

*There he began thrusting his iron rod into the earth, making a hole in which he planted an acorn; then he refilled the hole. He was planting oak trees. I asked him if the land belonged to him. He answered no. Did he know whose it was? He did not. He supposed it was community property, or perhaps belonged to people who cared nothing about it. He was not interested in finding out whose it was. He planted his hundred acorns with the greatest care.*

—JEAN GIONO, THE MAN WHO PLANTED TREES

# Lincoln, Twain, Presley, and Faulkner

SWEET GUM

DURING THE SPRING BREAK OF 2001, my wife, our two daughters, and I went on a vacation to the Gulf of Mexico. Destination: Dauphin Island, Alabama. We drove from our home in Wisconsin, covering more than a thousand miles of interstates and back roads. To break up the drive, we put together an itinerary of historical places to visit along the way.

First stop: Springfield, Illinois, and Abraham Lincoln's home. Originally just a cottage, the place was expanded by the Lincolns into a two-story, twelve-room house soon after they moved in. When we visited it, the saltbox colonial had an overabundance of creaking stairways, paisley wallpaper, crimson carpets, and primitive-looking furniture. And it smelled funny.

My youngest daughter, just seven at the time, was dazzled by it. I felt it lacked all "freedom of interior and exterior occupation," to borrow a phrase from Frank Lloyd Wright, but then again, the young Lincoln was not noted for his architectural contributions to the house, just his legendary prowess there with an adz.

In the living room, a photograph caught my eye: a picture taken in May of 1860 of Honest Abe standing out in front of the house next to a young basswood tree. Coincidentally, there was a fully mature basswood in that same spot just outside the window.

"Say, is that the same tree as the one in the photograph?" I blurted out.

"I believe it is," the docent replied.

I felt a thrill run down my spine.

It was the perfect excuse to escape, so I left the family behind to continue the malodorous tour while I went outside to take a closer look at the ancient hardwood that had known Lincoln personally. There was nothing special about the tree—no patina-proud plaque pointing out its pedigree, no initials carved into the bark, no tattered rope swing. It looked like any other tree. On the ground and underfoot were scads of golden pea-size seeds. I don't know what possessed me, but I reached down and picked up a handful and jammed them into my pockets.

This tree had known one of the greatest and most complex figures in American history. Had Lincoln even leaned against it and pondered his future? Surely he must've dreamed under that tree, dreamed of a better life for his family, for his fellow citizens, black and white. Suddenly those seeds in my pocket from that touchstone felt like pennies from heaven.

NEXT STOP: HANNIBAL, MISSOURI, on the western banks of the Mississippi River, just an hour and a half from Springfield. At Mark Twain's childhood home, we were disappointed to learn that we had missed the last guided tour of the day. I searched the yard for old trees and seeds. Nothing. But Hannibal itself was old and seedy, surprisingly untransformed by its one-time resident's fame. Later that evening, while my brood swam in the indoor pool at the hotel, I decided to have a look around town in the waning sunlight.

Because I have been a transient most of my life, I have a knack for bonding quickly with any given locale. I need only wander around a place for a little while to feel a keen sense of belonging. As a teacher, I've learned that someone's environment has as much to tell us about that person as does his or her friends and family. So, within the hour, *Ich bin ein Hannibaler.*

I came to the base of Cardiff Hill, that illustrious playground of Tom Sawyer and Huckleberry Finn. A rusty sign modestly boasted of the site's place in literary history. As I made my way up the steep incline along a narrow dirt path, I half expected two waifs to come bouncing out of the bushes in rolled-up dungarees, wooden swords in hand, battling make-believe pirates.

Standing there atop the hill, looking down at the broad, muscular river below, I suddenly realized I was breathing in Twain. In that sublime vista drenched in the heavy, ionized air of the river valley, his worldview revealed itself to me in one wet respiration. A crow called out behind me as if to clear its throat. I turned to follow it and found myself gazing upon, for as far as the eye could see, a proud stand of hardwoods—locusts, box elders, elms, maples, oaks—running north to south along the ridge behind me. These were the offspring (there were no ancients among them) of trees that had once watched little snot-nosed Sam Clemens at play. This time I had a pouch strapped around my waist; rummaging around the area, I gathered up what seeds I could find and deposited them in it.

NEXT STOP: MEMPHIS. The magic of Graceland is not found in the memorabilia sold at the gift shop, or in the heady opulence of His private plane, or in the less-than-grand entrance to the ersatz plantation, or in the cheesy sixties décor, or in the "chicken-fried" trivia, or in the Safari Room, or in The Hall of Fame, or in the jumpsuit shrine, or even in the divine bathroom where he expired. No! The magic of Graceland is found in the people's reaction to it.

So while my wife and kids listened to the guide, I people-watched behind dark sunglasses. In fact, I was so thoroughly entertained by the kaleidoscope of rapture that I'd almost forgotten about my new hobby: collecting seeds from the trees that once knew historically significant people. That is, until I found myself outside, between the Hall of Fame and the jumpsuit shrine. And there, on the lawn, scattered like tiny Elvis capes, was a sea of maple seeds. At first I was worried that the security folks might intervene, but no one paid me any mind as I knelt down and excitedly scooped up the little key-shaped pods and placed them in my pouch.

Sated, I wandered over to the line of people waiting for their turn to stand in front of the King's grave. It was while standing in that line, fingering my waist pouch as if it were filled with gold doubloons, that I had my epiphany: I would travel across America to gather the seeds from the trees of great Americans who had influenced my life or influenced the course of American history.

I would visit their hometowns in search of the trees that may have played a part in their early development and helped form their views. I'd look into their lives and works for references to trees. I would also seek out trees that had witnessed great historical events.

The names came flooding in. First, the champions of nature:

Thoreau and Emerson, Carson and Muir. Then the novelists whose words were succor to me, as a student and then a teacher: Kerouac, Wharton, Shirley Jackson, Henry Miller, Vonnegut. The great poets, too, and American places: Gettysburg, Mount Vernon, Wounded Knee. The deluge of names and places cascaded through my brain for some time before it ebbed to a trickle.

FINAL STOP: OXFORD, MISSISSIPPI. I don't think there is a place on the surface of the planet that feels more uncomfortable to a native New Yorker than the Deep South. The air, the architecture, even the trees exude a sort of Yankee repellent. For some odd reason, it doesn't work in reverse; that is, Southern boys such as Truman Capote, Willie Morris, and even the late, great New York City chronicler Joseph Mitchell, felt right at home in a Manhattan clam bar or on an East Hampton beach. I wonder why that is.

The city of Oxford is the quintessence of Southern gentility. At its center is a classic square around which sit antebellum structures made of fiery red brick trimmed out with white columns, iron-railed porches, and ornate roof moldings. We arrived, all of us jam-packed into a late-model Olds 88, during a torrential downpour. If the sun had been shining, I'm certain pedestrians would have halted in their tracks and kids at play in the square would have missed catching the ball as they all turned to watch the silver sedan with the Wisconsin license plates entering the scene.

Faulkner's home, which he named Rowan Oak, wasn't easy to find even with directions, but I spotted it at the end of a residential street: well hidden behind a thick grove of pines. There was a hand-written sign on the gate: "Closed for Repairs." Hell, we'd driven sixty miles out of our way to get here; no stupid sign was going to keep me out. It was still raining, so my family happily stayed behind in the car with the radio on while I hopped the fence and entered the property.

It was spooky in there. The majestic plantation-style mansion, with its giant white columns and large shuttered windows, eyed me suspiciously as I diffidently approached. There was no one around. Everything was still. The ample yard and the numerous living quarters of the once un-free help were well maintained, but there was a tragic, severe feeling to the place. The trees completely surrounding the property had an immuring edge to them. Illness lingered. I could imagine Faulkner's dark, rummy eyes watching my every move, his lips pursed around the mouthpiece of a bulbous-headed pipe, as I splashed around the outside of the house, peering in all the windows.

It had stopped raining and was misting; everything was steamy and gray and damp. My umbrella was of little use, so I pulled it closed and hung it from my belt. Completely drenched, my wet, tangled hair covering my face, I felt squalid. In a sudden act of exuberance, I sprinted across the lawn and did a feet-first slide up to the base of an old maple tree at the far end of the yard. And as I lay there, soaked head to toe and looking up into the matronly branches of the tree, my epiphany back at Graceland began to play through my head again: I would be sure to spend significant time on a Southern writers' tour—Eudora Welty, Carson McCullers, Richard Wright, Flannery O'Connor, Truman Capote, Harper Lee, and Tennessee Williams—and wouldn't miss a non-literary hero of mine, Muhammad Ali.

I could feel the girls' impatience pulling me back through the dampness, so I gathered what maple seeds I could find and sprinted toward the car, vowing to revisit Faulkner.

**I** TOOK MY COLLECTION of famous tree seeds back to Wisconsin and planted them in our yard. A few sprouted, but most didn't make it, and the rabbits ate those that did. I managed to salvage a few saplings, and gave them out as presents to friends and family. But that's as far as it ever got.

A few more trips ensued: unplanned family events. A few years later, I visited Ellis Island for the first time. There stood ancient sycamores, still greeting all who stepped off the ferry. Imagine the millions who saw those trees at the start of their new lives? I collected pocketfuls of the seeds and stored them in my basement.

When my father passed away in the spring of 2005, I returned to my childhood neighborhood to drive by the house where I had grown up. I just wanted to make that connection before we put him into the ground. It was early spring, and the buds were beginning to bulge out on the trees. The blush of color to the scenery made everything look like a Seurat painting. Behind my old house, the tall, intertwining cherry trees from my youth were still there, but out in front, my great playmate, the red maple, was gone.

I drove down the block to the site of my elementary school. The building had been torn down decades before and turned into a small park, but behind it stood the same grove of hardwood trees I used to play among at recess. I parked the car and entered the four-acre woods. Nothing had changed but me. Standing there beholding the same wonderful trees of my childhood, I felt a glow of belonging, of embrace. I remained in those woods for a long time. When I returned to the car, my heart was full to overflowing with the seeds idea once again.

THAT WAS FOUR YEARS AGO. Since then, we'd moved from Wisconsin to upstate New York for my new teaching job. I compiled a list of dozens of great American writers whose homes I wanted to visit. Friends and colleagues, upon hearing of my idea, urged more names upon me, and I happily, if also anxiously, added them to my notebook. How would I possibly find the time to make these trips? No matter. I had to take action, to take the first step.

On an unseasonably warm day in March, I set out from my new home on the southern shores of Lake Ontario to collect seeds. Unlike John Chapman, a.k.a. Johnny Appleseed, I had no business plan and no gospel; and I would be taking seeds, not giving them. But like him, I was on a mission. I would start nearby and work my way out: short trips, then long trips out West, down South, and over to New England.

According to season and location, be it during summer vacations or on long weekends, I would go with family and friends or on my own. But bit by bit, I would gather the seeds, bring them home, and grow them, and then tell my family and friends the stories of the trees from which the seeds came and the lives and literature they touched.

## Northern red oak (*Quercus rubra*)

RED OAK ACORNS

## North Syracuse, New York

The Wizard of Oz Memorial Oak Grove in North Syracuse, New York, is purported to have been the playground of young L. Frank Baum and the inspiration for the enchanted forest described in his books. It was the perfect place to start my odyssey, not just because of its proximity to my own home, but because my very first memory in life is of watching The Wizard of Oz on television. I can remember vividly those belligerent trees, with their tragedy mask faces and guttural voices, throwing apples at Dorothy and Scarecrow. Seeing them for the first time, I became so hysterical that my dad had to remove me from the room and put me to bed. It wasn't until graduate school that I finally read the book, which is just as powerful as the film. The Cowardly Lion became one of my favorite literary heroes of all time because, in the end, he defeats the greatest enemy of all: his own fear.

A little about L. Frank Baum: He was born in Chittenango, New York, in 1856. His first name was Lyman, which he hated, preferring to use his middle name, Frank. He was a sickly kid, with a bad heart. Because he wasn't allowed to play like the other boys his age, he turned to his own imagination for entertainment. When he was twelve, the Baum family moved to Roselawn Estate in what is now the town of Mattydale, New York, just north of Syracuse. Frank loved it there.

The estate was situated along the first plank road built in the United States. Made entirely of wood, the Plank Road in New York was more than sixteen miles long and was used to transport salt from Onondaga Lake to parts south. The boards were made of hemlock and had, according to those who drove over them, a distinctive golden hue.

During those youthful, imaginative years at Roselawn, young Frank and his brother Harry wrote and published a young person's newspaper called *The Roselawn Home Journal*, a common enterprise for kids back in those days. Perhaps the most well-known piece he wrote for the publication was about the infamous Cardiff Giant. In 1869, a man named George Hull deceived the public by making a twelve-foot-tall giant out of gypsum and buried it on a farm south of Syracuse. Its "discovery" made quite a stir around the nation. The giant was later put on display in a museum, and it is conjectured that the image of the Cardiff Giant inspired Baum's description of the great hairless head of the Wizard of Oz: "There was no hair upon this head, but it had eyes and a nose and mouth, and was much bigger than the head of the biggest giant."

Later in his life, Baum didn't just write wondrous tales for children; almost at the same time he promoted pogroms for adults: "Having wronged them [Native Americans] for centuries we had better, in order to protect our civilization, follow it up by one more wrong and wipe these untamed and untamable creatures from the face of the earth."* Shocking and heartbreaking as it was to find this out about him, I can blame the man and not the artist. There are those who achieve greatness on paper or canvas, with celluloid or brass, but whose lives are wretched failures. There are only a rare few, such as Thoreau or Krishnamurti, whose lives are their art. I suspect Baum, coddled and sickly as he was as a child, grew up to become a sort of literary Cowardly Lion himself.†

TWO MILES FROM ROSELAWN ESTATE was a thick wood owned by friends of the Baum family. A vestige of that land remains and is now called the Wizard of Oz Memorial Oak Grove. It is situated right alongside North Syracuse Junior High School's football field, behind a strip mall and two subdivisions. It is a sublime oasis, and it reminded me of the grove behind my old grade school. Relatively small, just seven acres in total, the grove is acknowledged as the

---

* As the editor of the Aberdeen (S.D.) *Saturday Pioneer*, Baum ran this heinous missive on January 3, 1891, in response to the Wounded Knee Massacre.
† From *The Wonderful Wizard of Oz*, chapter 6: "'What makes you a coward?' asked Dorothy, looking at the great beast in wonder, for he was as big as a small horse. 'It's a mystery,' replied the Lion. 'I suppose I was born that way. All the other animals in the forest naturally expect me to be brave, for the Lion is everywhere thought to be the King of Beasts. I learned that if I roared very loudly every living thing was frightened and got out of my way. Whenever I've met a man I've been awfully scared; but I just roared at him, and he has always run away as fast as he could go.'"

most historic old grove forest in the eastern United States. Apropos of everything, *Baum* in German means "tree."

I parked the car and slid out, slung my backpack over my shoulders, and grabbed my five-gallon bucketful of small tools and a golf club to clear away leaves. I casually walked over the semi-frozen turf of the playing field and toward the trees. Only one person was running on the track. A young boy was walking his dog along the outside of the grove, but he was heading away from me, back toward the subdivision to the north. Off in the distance a truck engine rumbled. To my right, the L-shaped strip mall complex stood with its back turned toward the grove. Amazingly, it was graffiti-free.

As I entered under the thick canopy of hardwoods, I imagined hearing a *Peter and the Wolf* bassoon begin to play. There were no exotic birdcalls, just the happy-go-lucky *deet deet deet* of a chickadee flitting about in the branches above. I trod softly, listening to every sound, eyeing every tree, allowing the essence of their sylvan souls to enter into me and lighten my load. It was amazingly quiet in the old grove, despite the nearness of school, highway, and shopping mall. I walked on expectantly.

Suddenly there was a terrific explosion. I nearly jumped out of my boots. The roar of jet engines made the sky ring. I turned in time to see, through the branches of the trees, the sleek steel shaft of a 727 nosing forward into the wild blue yonder. Within seconds the clamor dissipated, leaving me to contemplate the oceanic contrast of yesterday and today. Little Frank Baum had to conjure up the scariest noise he could think of to break the lambent quietude of the woods: a mighty lion's roar.

Moving on down the path, I came upon the first giant tree: a red oak. The fluted base was like nothing I had ever seen before. It had three times the normal girth of a fully mature oak. According to my notes, this red oak stood over 100 feet tall and was more than 150 years old. A plaque nailed to the trunk about fifteen feet up displayed the name of Walt Disney and the words "Imagination, Inspiration, Animation." I took out my notebook and scribbled down the name and epigraph, adding another celebrated person to my overgrown list of places to visit.

In this memorial grove one can find eighteen plaques on eighteen ancient oak and maple trees. In addition to Disney, there are dedications to familiar heroes from the past: William Shakespeare, Mother Teresa, Mahatma Gandhi, Jackie Robinson, Martin Luther King, Jr., John Muir, Edgar Allan Poe, Nelson Mandela, Albert Einstein, Harriet Tubman, John F. Kennedy, John Lennon, Rosa Parks, Anne Frank, and, of course, L. Frank Baum. Additionally, there's a new plaque for the 9/11 rescue workers, with the words "Always Remember," and one for a Matilda Joslyn Gage, who turns out to be Baum's mother-in-law and a women's rights advocate. I didn't know about her, and felt the trees had brought me new knowledge. (I had no idea at this time how often I would have these little gemlike discoveries over the next year.)

I wondered who had picked these names. Who was on the selection committee? No matter: it was an honor roll of greatness, not to mention the fact that the plaques proved to me that I was not alone in my desire to connect great human lives to trees.

I found Baum's tree at the far north end of the woods. It was a gigantic red oak more than a hundred feet tall. The roots leading up to the trunk arced out of the soil like the claws of a skyscraper-size pterodactyl. I tried reaching my arms around the tree trunk, in an effort to get close. It wasn't much of a hug, more like a bug on a windshield. The hard, rutted bark left dents in my cheek.

I put my gear down and removed a digital camera from my backpack. I searched around for a spot on the forest floor to lie down and take a picture, in order to capture the sublimity of the monster. It was futile. Every angle I tried failed to capture its full size. In lieu of awe, I just snapped a couple of pictures of the plaque. Crows began to caw in a tree close by, warning one another of the odd human at large acting suspiciously.

Finding viable acorns in early March would be no small task. What squirrels hadn't buried or eaten, worms and Mother Nature had. With my seven iron and plastic bag at the ready, I began my search. I had chosen a seven iron because I figured a seven would give me enough angle and leverage to slice into the leaves without leaving a divot, but it wasn't working out that way. The two-inch-thick carpet of leaves was packed so tightly that I found myself sawing into it as if cutting cornbread. After a while I refined my technique—it was more chip than putt—and found the best stroke to enter the soft, chocolaty loam underneath. Unfortunately, all I found upon entering that zone were acorn tops. The damn things were everywhere.

An odd noise startled me. To my utter surprise, an old world little man dressed in a black suit, white shirt, no tie, leather shoes, and jet-black hair was walking briskly toward me along the path. I stopped chipping as he drew abreast of me. I was so startled by his appearance that I couldn't help staring. He was carrying a white shopping bag out of which a French baguette protruded like a giant's thumb. His head was bent down as he hurried along, avoiding eye contact.

"Beautiful day," I cock-a-doodle-dooed.

He just nodded, peeking up for an instant to offer an enigmatic little smile, before he bent farther forward to distance himself from the guy with the golf club. After a few moments, I turned back down to my work, cutting at the carpet of leaves in search of the sacred acorns. As I chipped and pulled, I wondered about that man, how long had he been walking here, the things he'd seen. I glanced back up a few moments later only to find that he had disappeared from sight.

I chipped around for about half an hour and still found nothing but tops, which looked like miniature brown berets. I pictured the mice and voles of the grove wearing them to parties and talking with fake French accents. Perhaps I was a fool to think I could find viable acorns in March, yet how many thousands upon thousands of them had rained down on that very spot the season before? What biologists call propagule pressure. As John Fowles wrote of trees in his masterpiece *The Tree*, "Their main evolutionary defense, as with many social animals, birds and fishes, lies in their innumerability, that is, in their capacity to reproduce—in which, for trees, longevity plays a major part."

It was that book, an encomium to nature and a warning to mankind, that made me realize as a college student the dangers inherent in our obsession with naming and taming the natural disorder of our planet. I was bound and determined not to make that mistake with my seed gathering. I'd be careful, reverential. I would listen and learn.

After another half hour of continuous searching, I did not find a single complete acorn. I was running low on patience and had to take a break. I walked out of the woods to feel the warm sunshine on my face. The rays were hot, even for March. I was contemplating switching to a nine iron next time out when I shifted my weight and felt a crunch underfoot. I looked down. All along the grassy strip lay dozens of acorns bulging up out of the buckled ground. The recent thaw had unearthed a lode.

I fervently bent to the task, and eventually found seven viable acorns. I stopped at that lucky number and, using a trowel, filled two double plastic bags of dirt, about ten pounds' worth. And as I walked back toward the parking lot through the grove, a bird sang a sweet song, with repeating notes that sounded exactly like "Seeds, seeds, seeds." I wasn't sure of the species, so I took out my binoculars and zoomed in on it. It was a titmouse, the ancient symbol of poetry and success.

THE DAY WOULD NOT HAVE BEEN complete without a visit to the spot where Baum's home once stood. The house burned down back in the 1950s; today an indoor roller rink stands in its stead along the bustling four-lane State Route 11.

Route 11, the Plank Road in Baum's time, has, unfortunately, lost its golden hue. It is now a paved highway, and "a tragic sprawl-scape of cartoon architecture," to borrow the phrase James Kunstler used to describe suburbia in *Home from Nowhere*. On either side of the highway, fast food joints, shopping centers, office parks, and car dealerships abound. The busy road rushes headlong toward an intense delta of merging and deviating thoroughfares, crowned by the overpass of Interstate 81, which connects Canada to the Smoky Mountains of Tennessee. There are myriad signs overhead, too many to read safely while driving. I stayed in the middle lane, carried along by the current of traffic. I floated directly under the overpass, then coasted out from under its shadow and came to rest at a traffic light. From there I could see the roller rink up on the right.

The parking lot was a quagmire of ruts, rubble, and potholes. I bumped, dipped, and splashed through it all and parked the van facing the rink, a windowless, concrete-block structure the length of a football field. On the spot of the once bucolic setting of Baum's beloved Roselawn Estate, with its "wide porches and . . . lovely patches of green sward all about, with stately trees bearing rich and luscious fruits . . . gorgeous flowers . . . birds with rare and brilliant plumage . . . a small brook, rushing and sparkling along between green banks,"* sat a cinderblock gob of spit, a far cry from the brilliant architecture and wondrous sights of the 1893 World's Fair in Chicago that was the model for his Land of Oz.† For the second time in one day, the pleasant past and the pernicious present stood in earth-shattering contrast.

At the tinted-glass entrance doors, I paused. Like the Cowardly Lion, I was afraid to move forward. Only lunatics and maniacs would go inside a place like this on such a beautiful day. I encouraged myself with thoughts of a souvenir, pulled back the heavy door, and walked in.

I had my sunglasses on, which I had to remove immediately in the gloomy cave. The window booth in front of me was so dirty it was almost opaque. The woman sitting inside was clothed in a lurid pink-terrycloth outfit. All around her was a menagerie of multicolor stuffed animals and kitschy bric-a-brac. She was talking on her cell phone and didn't bother to acknowledge me as I stepped directly in front of her. Finally, she looked up, holding the phone away from her mouth and challenged, "What do you need?"

"Can I go in and look around? I just want to take a look inside. I'm not going to skate or anything." I had the urge to tell her more, but I stifled myself.

She shook her head and paused for a long moment. "Okay. Go

---

* Available at www.syracusethenandnow.net/History/LFBaum/WizardofSyr .htm. Page 2–3, 2/28/2006.

† For more on that fair, read Erik Larson's bestseller *The Devil in the White City*.

ahead, but don't take too long," she warned with narrowed eyes before returning to her phone conversation.

I was daunted by the drabness of the interior. This was not the dazzling Emerald City; rather, it was painted indigo blue, and it smelled horrible. The odor was like a toxic mix of rug cleaner and synthetic popcorn butter. I had the urge to hold my breath. Straight ahead was the roller rink. Everyone was moving about as if infected with melancholia.

I drifted to the edge of the rink and leaned on the rails. The vast floor was made of dark hardwood, the rich timber locked up under a thick, dull coating of aged polyurethane. The floorboards may have been milled from those same stately trees that had once constituted the road in front of Roselawn Estate. Overhead, the roof looked tenuous. Kids wobbled unsteadily around the rink on Rollerblades. Baum described the denizens of Oz as "happy and contented." Indigo City was the diametric opposite; the people here were dismal and dispirited.

I HAD SEEN ENOUGH. Back outside, the sun, sky, and air all rushed forward to support me, grabbing me under the arms as they carried me over to my car. I leaned against the hood and gingerly ran my finger along the jagged edges of my experience. The stunning justice of it had cut me deeply: Writing books for little children "in which the wonderment and joy are retained and the heart-aches and nightmares are left out,"* while at the same time exhorting their parents to commit genocide by calling for "the total extermi-

---

* L. Frank Baum in the introduction to *The Wonderful Wizard of Oz*.

nation of the Indians."* Perhaps omniscient fate had deigned to reward his hypocrisy by preserving a sliver of his beloved enchanted forest while perverting his beautiful Roselawn Estate into a nightmarish heartache. Serves the bastard right.

I climbed into the car and sat, feeling quite satisfied with the results of my adventure. I had collected seven viable seeds, passed unscathed through the enchanted forest, had been allowed to enter Indigo City, and had even seen a titmouse. It was a great start.

As I headed for the parking lot exit, I noticed two lines of old maple trees running off into the distance, directly across the six-lane highway. It was possible that they had once stood as sentinels along the driveway leading up to Roselawn Estate. Trucks and buses whizzed by, momentarily spoiling my view.

I wondered how long those trees would be there before condos or an office park eliminated them.

What more could possibly be built along this Yellow Brick Road?

* Baum, *Aberdeen Saturday Pioneer*. January 3, 1981.

**Silver maple** (*Acer saccharinum*)

SILVER MAPLE SEED

## Lowell, Massachusetts

"There is something brown and holy about the East," Kerouac said in *On the Road*, as he stood in San Francisco looking back across the continent he had just traversed. He was, of course, describing his hometown: Lowell, Massachusetts. Catholic churches are everywhere; one is never out of sight of them. The innumerable steeples crowned with crosses rise above the rooftops like God's craning neck, watching all, protecting all, forgiving all. Kerouac's was a spiritual quest; Lowell is the source of that spirituality.

The city is surrounded by water. To the north and east is the churning, mass-producing engine called the Merrimack River. To the south is Thoreau's Concord River. And circling the entire city like a medieval moat are numerous canals. But the ubiquitous waters of Lowell are not for show or entertainment. Water means work in this brawny city. And though the textile mills remain as glaring reminders of an exploitative past, the Popsicle-red factories abide the world's indignation in order to dote on their beloved citizens with grandmotherly pride.

At the downtown bookstore, I bought a fresh copy of *On the Road*. Just holding the book in my hands and looking at its cover with his name in capital letters, I got all weepy and full of anxious love and sentimentality for America, soaring America, and crazy friends, and everything joyous and free, lonely and sad. From that moment on, I felt his presence close and sympathetic.

My first stop was the Jack Kerouac Commemorative Park, just around the corner, along the canal way. What a disappointment. Excerpts from his novels were inscribed onto large glossy granite columns, laid out in a lame replica of a mandala. The columns felt ridiculously arbitrary. There was nothing Kerouacian about the park, other than the drug deals that no doubt take place there at night. All the trees were newly planted. I felt him urging me away.

I walked up the street a couple of blocks and found the National Historical Visitor Center housed within an old brick mansion. Inside was an impressive nineteenth-century hallway of massive oak doors on either side, punctuated by antique wall sconces of the same period. No one was around. One of the great doors at the end of the hall was ajar, so I let myself in.

The august Victorian room had rich, handcrafted wood paneling all around and an ornate mantelpiece topped by a dynamic painting of a merchant ship nobly adrift on the tumultuous green Atlantic. It was all very mayoral. Behind a large, cluttered desk was a diminutive woman from another era working at a computer. There was something vaguely familiar about her, sitting there in her outdated dress, with her tightly coifed hair and India-ink eyes.

"May I help you?" she asked. I was surprised to hear English come out of her mouth.

I delivered my spiel: "I'm looking for Jack Kerouac's childhood homes. I'm doing some research on them, and I haven't been able to find any information about them."

She nodded pleasantly and, without a moment's hesitation, picked up the telephone to inquire from others. She made three separate calls; the first two yielded nothing. On the third call she got hold of someone who had plenty to say about it. She stood there for a long time getting an earful. At long last she hung up, shaking her head apologetically.

"I'm sorry, but there really isn't anything like that to be found other than the Commemorative Park and his grave site out at the Edson Cemetery."

"I've just visited the park. It's the houses I'm interested in, not the grave. So there are really none to see?"

"No, I'm sorry. There are houses, of course, but people live in them. They prefer not to be disturbed."

Now my interest was really piqued. I was convinced it was a ploy of some kind. With an amiable but utterly professional tone, she directed me back down around the corner to the Boott Cotton Mills Museum, to pick up a map that would provide directions to the cemetery where Kerouac was buried. I thanked her and left. Of course, I didn't tell her that I had no intention of visiting Kerouac's grave or anyone else's, for that matter. Mine was a quest to connect with life, not death.

Back outside, I took a deep breath, looked around, and saw a line of schoolchildren at the entrance to an old brick building across the way. I headed over to check it out. A sign that read "The Working People's Exhibit" hung over the entrance. Inside was bedlam. The beleaguered teachers were having a heck of a time keeping the kids quiet enough so that the docent could do her job. It was a pretty lame museum, with mannequins in various states of rigor mortis, dressed in the incredibly drab styles of the Civil War period. No wonder the kids were mutinous.

I noticed what looked like an archive in the back of the place, so I waded through the crowd. Indeed, there was an archive there, neatly tucked behind a wall of plate glass. A woman sat at a desk, oblivious to the commotion beyond. I tapped on the glass door. She looked up, smiled, and waved me in.

"Hello. I'm in town doing research on Jack Kerouac's childhood homes, and I'm having a heck of a time trying to locate some of the houses where he lived." My spiel was starting to sound a little desperate.

Her eyes danced. "Kerouac's homes? We have that."

She pushed her chair back and walked purposefully over to a line of file cabinets in among twenty-foot-high shelves of books and documents. The town's archive was as tall as it was wide. Lowell was quite proud of itself, and why shouldn't it be? She riffled through several drawers before extracting a neat stack of folded papers from one. She leafed through them, nodded, pushed the drawer in, and headed my way.

"It should all be in here." She handed everything to me.

I was stunned. "Can I just take them?"

"Yes, they're yours. I've got duplicates."

Pictures, names, numbers, and addresses—it really was all there.

Then I noticed her reddish hair. All she needed was a wand and a silk dress.

"Thanks," I said, my face lighting up with a boyish grin.

"You know, they have his rucksack on display upstairs," she said to me as I was reaching for the door handle.

"Really?"

"If you go up the stairs, you'll find it."

Sure enough, the green canvas rucksack was there, encased in a cube of Plexiglas. The wrinkled sack looked withered and feckless, like an eagle with clipped wings enclosed in a tiny cage. I wanted to liberate it, bust it out, put it on my back, and run out of that sterile environment. Then my eyes shifted to the right: he was standing there in that famous photograph on a Lower East Side balcony, smoking a cigarette, with a book under his arm. *Saint Jack*. I stared and stared at the photograph for a long time. All went quiet and out of focus for me except for his black-and-white profile. I watched in rapture as he exhaled a puff of smoke and turned toward me with a frown: *They've missed the point*, his eyes cried out.

"But I didn't," I replied to myself, which must have reassured him, because he immediately turned back to his determined gaze beyond the cigarette and toward the open road. The world began to hum again. A young boy standing next to me was looking up at me with a big question mark on his face. I smiled and left.

CROSSING OVER THE PAWTUCKET FALLS on the University Avenue Bridge into Pawtucketville, I was delighted to see a profusion of trees covering the steep slopes down to the edge of the rushing waters of the Merrimack. This side of the river is where Kerouac was born and raised. It was called Little Canada in those days; French Canadians were the main immigrant force working the mills. Amazingly, it hasn't changed that much since the 1920s and '30s, when Jack was running around speaking joual, or Canadian French, with a football under his arm and his knees all scraped up. The tenement houses still line the streets that now percolate with rich and varied scents and complexions.

I didn't need to walk around a lot to fall in love with the area; I was a native son the moment my feet hit the pavement. Voluptuous black women in exotic tops and pants strutted by on high-heeled shoes. Men in white shirts and dark pants loitered in front of convenience stores, gesticulating with thick, muscular fingers. I think Jack would have felt right at home in his old neighborhood today. Hell, his former house at 118 University Avenue had a For Rent sign out front. He could probably have slept in his old room.

I stood looking up at Kerouac's old tenement house to the fourth floor, where the pamphlet said he used to live, trying to picture it as it was when he was a kid. I imagined hearing his mother's voice calling him in for lunch, yelling out the window, *'Ti Jean, viens déjeuner! Cours vite avant que la bouffe ne devienne froide.*

Cops in blue uniforms were everywhere directing traffic. A team of utility workers in Day-Glo hardhats was up on cherry pickers replacing power lines. There was even one worker peeking out of a manhole in the middle of the street. Everywhere there was movement and color, sound and life. I stood for a while staring at the building, incredulous that there was no acknowledgment of its former tenant. It was still just a dingy old tenement house. I became aware of one of the traffic cops eyeing me suspiciously. It was time to move.

Right behind me was a short, squat brick building: the Pawtucketville Social Club. In the packet that Glinda had given me, it told of how Kerouac and his friends used to shoot pool there, and how Jack's father, during the Great Depression, had been the manager of the place. The door was open, no doubt as it had always been. An odor of stale beer and tobacco greeted me the moment I entered.

It was dark and fetid in there, a perfect refuge from the noise of the streets. There was one man seated at the long bar, his back to me. Another man sat drinking a bottle of beer at a round table in the middle of the room, watching one of the television sets mounted to the wall. Behind him was a large pool table bathed in a pool of holy light. This was a place that time had forgotten. I could feel Jack's presence everywhere.

I wandered slowly along the walls in search of Kerouac memorabilia, but I didn't get very far before I was accosted:

"You need something, pal?" It was the guy sitting at the round table. He was a certified tough guy. He had the requisite tattoos, facial scars, and lack of a dental plan to prove it.

"I'm doing some research on Jack Kerouac, and I know that his family was affiliated with this place. I was just wondering if you had any old photographs or anything like that in here?"

He eyed me suspiciously, searching my face for signs that I might be a narc or, worse, a comparative literature professor. With his mouth slightly open, his head thrown back at a provocative angle, and his eyes squinting menacingly, he let loose a grunt: "Nuhn-un." The guttural sound was quite articulate. What he had actually communicated in that grunt was: *This is Lowell, Mack, and you don't go around askin' questions about people, dead or alive.*

"Well, I'm glad to see the building is still here and in good shape," I responded.

My words seemed to soothe the savage's breast, because his eyes softened. "Yeah, you know he used to live across the street, above the cop station." I waited for more details, but that was the extent of his information.

"Mmm, hmmm" was all I could come up with. I was going to have a beer, but I didn't want to taint the purity of it all. We stared at each other for a long moment. It was time to collect the seeds.

BACK OUTSIDE AND JUST UP THE STREET, I found two huge silver maples with voluminous shade-providing canopies. They were spectacular. Both were probably a hundred years old, growing right up out of the sidewalk and in perfect health. Even better, under both trees were large puddles of recently fallen seeds. And best yet, many of the seeds had already begun to sprout. Maple keys are one of the plant kingdom's most prolific crops. In the spring, their round little ends swell with green fertility before their little white tongues sprout out of their protective folders in search of nutrients. Underneath the tree, I helped myself to a newly fallen batch. Unlike oaks, which can live for a thousand years, maples are not as long-lived, but they're perfectly at home along a stream, in a thick wood, or in the middle of Pawtucketville, so long as there's a good supply of water.

I couldn't believe my luck. With great alacrity, I scooped up heaping handfuls of maple keys and placed them into Ziploc bags while the neighborhood houses, with their happy window eyes and smiling porch mouths, looked on. The sun was shining on everything.

Carefully stuffing the Ziplocs in my backpack, I took out Glinda's notes again. There was a passage about the Kerouacs having lived on Phebe and Hildreth streets. I didn't have a map; I just supposed the two streets were somewhere in the neighborhood, so I began to walk around. I didn't find them, but what I found made my heart sing. Everywhere I looked, a jackpot of trees. On the front lawns and in the backyards of most houses were outrageous oaks, mammoth maples, wondrous willows, colossal cottonwoods, and Brobdingnagian basswoods. They stood there like fabulous antiquities. In fact, they reminded me of the giant, mythic statues in the Piazza della Signoria in Florence. At the Wizard of Oz Memorial Oak Grove I had expected to find trees, but in Lowell I had had no such expectation. It was thrilling to know there were so many still left.

IN REVISITING KEROUAC'S WORK, I found that whenever he mentions trees, his haunting sadness vanishes, replaced by a sense of lyrical happiness. In *On the Road*, bound for Denver and not having slept for many days, he finds a spot "Under a tremendous old tree . . . [and] fell asleep for two delicious hours." In the *Dharma Bums*, he confesses: " . . . in the shade of the trees I rested well." And in his sublime collection of Buddhist poems *The Scripture of the Golden Eternity*, he apotheosizes: "The secret God-grin is in the trees." I felt certain that the majestic array of Pawtucketville's hardwoods had played a role in his healthy reverence for arboreal splendor.

After about a half hour of wandering, I came upon a smiling, grandfatherly crossing guard, proudly attired in the uniform of his before-school and after-school avocation. His circular cop's hat was covered in plastic, even though it had stopped raining many hours before. I think he liked the added ornamentation. I asked him where Phebe and Hildreth streets were located. Relishing the question, he crinkled up his brow, massaged a temple, and rubbed his chin.

"Now I'm thinking that Hildreth is on the other side of town," he mused in a musical New England accent. "But Phebe . . . Phebe is around the corner, just down the block. If you follow this road here to the bottom of the hill, you'll come to it."

I thanked him cordially and followed his pointed finger. Sure enough, I found Phebe, a very neat little street of single-family houses, tucked one block east of University Avenue. It was probably two hundred yards as the crow flies to Kerouac's previous home. I fell instantly in love with Phebe Street. It reeked of happy homes, pleasant people, and well-cared-for children. There was the most wonderful perfume of cherry blossoms, too.

I walked the length and breadth of it twice but could not find where Hildreth Street intersected it. I stood in the middle of the sidewalk, looking both ways. Then, as if on cue, a nun approached, dressed in whites and grays, her pendulous silver cross looking so heavy it didn't even move as she walked toward me.

"Hello, Sister," I said. "I wonder if you can help me?" I was holding my historical packet out in front of me as if to show her my only weapon was paper, not steel.

"Yes?" She had such an at-peace air about her, I could have been holding a beer and a revolver and I believe she would have responded in the same manner.

"I'm looking for Hildreth Street."

"Oh, that's on the other side of town. If you take the VFW Highway . . ."

"But it has to intersect with Phebe. See, it says right here that Jack Kerouac lived on Phebe and Hildreth streets."

"Well, this is Phebe." Then she tilted her head and glanced down at my finger, reading what was written on the page sideways. "What they probably mean is he lived on both streets at different times. They don't intersect."

"Oh my. Whaddaya know." The puzzle had been solved by someone much more literate than I. For some reason, the thoughts in my head came racing out of my mouth without my consent, and I spat out, "This is such a nice neighborhood. It's more . . . more up-scale than I expected. I guess I always imagined Jack Kerouac living in abject poverty."

"Yes, it is a very nice neighborhood. Of course the university has grown a lot. Poverty often gives rise to great riches." She stood in profile to me, speaking metaphorically and gesturing at the nearby University of Lowell campus buildings as if they were mountains off in the distance. Her hand movements seemed to describe the magical transformation of the long-ago normal/textile training school into a magnificent shining university on the hill, with all of the honors, rights, and immunities thereunto appertaining.

"Yes, I believe that's true. Thank you." If I had been wearing a hat, I would have doffed it.

"My pleasure. God bless you."

I did feel blessed.


A SPIRITUAL JOURNEY is not a self-centered act; rather it is a self-less act, done for the sake of others. Like the Papago Indians, who journey alone a hundred miles across the perilous Southwestern desert to the shores of the Gulf of California to cleanse themselves in the magic waters and acquire healing powers to bring back to the tribe, Jack Kerouac took to the open road for the same purpose. His beatified mission in peregrinating and putting his thoughts and deeds down in words was not to preserve those memories but to glorify them, sanctify them; and not just for his sake but for the sake of others. That's what saints do. He often referred to the Dean

Moriarty character in his books as a saint. Moriarty was no saint; he was a punk.

The saintliness he believed he saw in Dean was the very same he believed he saw in his older brother, Gerard, who died at nine. Kerouac limned his brother in his short novel, *Visions of Gerard*, as a veritable little Saint Francis who loved God and all the small creatures of the kingdom. It's easy to see the connection in *On the Road* when he first describes Dean Moriarty: "He reminded me of some long-lost brother; the sight of his suffering bony face with the long sideburns and his straining muscular sweating neck made me remember my boyhood in those dye-dumps and swim-holes and riversides of Paterson and the Passaic." But neither Dean nor his brother was a saint. The saint he saw was really a reflection of himself. Subconsciously, he knew it! Why else would he have given himself the name of Sal Paradise in *On the Road*—Paradise, the abode of the righteous after death, abode of God and the blessed?*

In the Catholic religion, before beatification and ultimately canonization can occur, there must be at least three miracles attributable to the person in question as proof of his extraordinary holiness. In addition, the person's religious qualities, his love of God and neighbor, and his writings are also extensively examined. I believe Jack Kerouac is a saint. How many countless miracles must he have performed? How many lost and hopeless souls have been saved through his sacrificial life and words? How much more love of God and life and neighbor could one possibly inspire in words and deeds?

Somewhere down the road, with the sun sinking low on the horizon, casting biblical shadows across the rolling continent from end to bittersweet end, when I know where I am going at long last,

* *On the Road*, Penguin Classics, New York, 1991, page 7.

I'll think of Jack Kerouac, young Jack Kerouac, with a football under his arm, a rucksack on his back, and the holy glow of a saint; I'll hear his deft and desperate fingers playing Bebop on his tattered typewriter—*ticka ticka tacka ticka tacka ticka tick*—the keys chipping at petrified pages forming immaculate images of sweet-sad yesterdays and longed-for tomorrows, I'll think of Jack Kerouac, the brother I never had, I'll think of Jack Kerouac.

## Edith Wharton and Esther Forbes

White pine *(Pinus strobus)*
Sugar maple *(Acer saccharum)*
American beech *(Fagus grandifolia)*
Mountain silver bell *(Halesia tetraptera)*
Japanese maple *(Acer palmatum)*
Tulip poplar, a.k.a. tulip tree *(Liriodendron tulipifera)*
Lilac *(Syringa)*

BEECH NUT CASE AND BUDS

### Lenox, Massachusetts

There are chateaus in America! I had no idea. Edith Wharton personally designed and built one in 1902 with her husband, Teddy, and architect Ogden Codman, and called it The Mount. The Mount is located in the midst of the beautiful Berkshire Mountains, at the extreme western end of Massachusetts. It was home to Mrs.

Wharton from 1902 to 1911—that is, when she wasn't gallivanting around New York, London, or Paris. Exquisite pine and hemlock forests, an Italian walled garden, a formal flower garden, a rock garden, a lime walkway, and terraced fields of bluegrass surround The Mount, all of these extravagances sitting on a rocky knoll overlooking a cool mountain lake. Edith Wharton was filthy rich, and she sure could write one hell of a story.

My youngest daughter and I were on our way to a college interview at Holy Cross and had planned a tour of The Mount, right off Exit 2 of the Mass Pike. We parked next to an old stable in dire need of a paint job and repairs, and walked a quarter mile along a winding driveway through an Enchanted Forest look-alike to the main house. Towering hemlocks and white pines filled the dark woods on either side, while hundred-year-old maples marked the way along the edge of the drive. In contrast to the stable, the main house was impressive, very impressive.

A tour had just started as we paid the admission fee and took our place among the other dozen tourists. I knew the place was hurting for money and had been on the edge of foreclosure until just recently, so I didn't mind paying the twenty-dollar admission. (My kid was free.) That said, the place was only half-restored. The front hallway and the second floor had all been redone, but the rest of the first floor consisted of bare plaster walls, scratched-up wainscoting, and treadbare tiles. There was an elevator, but we were told it took fifteen minutes to go from the first floor to the second.

In all four corners of the Versailles-imitation gallery on the second floor, large mounted photographs set on easels showed what the interior of the house looked like when the Whartons lived there. It was pretty damn sumptuous, what with all the bronze statuary and oil paintings and French furnishings. The names of the rooms alone (boudoir, drawing room, library, and gallery) and the views of the property were enough to give us a sense of what it must have been like to live like a queen, before taxes, at the beginning of the last century.

Standing in Mrs. Wharton's bedroom, we learned that she worked on her fiction and nonfiction in bed, while leaning on her little dog. She wrote *The House of Mirth* there. Her drawing room, right next door, was plush, with a huge Garden of Eden painting on the wall and French doors leading out to the terrace. The docent pointed out the fact that the circular table in the middle of the room, permanently set for high tea, sat only eight. Apparently Mrs. Wharton didn't have more than six friends worth seating. I took this to mean that a high-society gal like Wharton, who wrote culturally honest books, was not the kind of company her social equals dared or cared to keep. The feeling was likely mutual.

The tour lasted just fifty minutes, and we were delighted to get outside into the fresh mountain air and the sunshiny day to walk among the trees. *Symmetry* was the key word here, and one reiterated by the docent during the tour. Everything was geometrically perfect: the gardens and walkways and terraces formed squares and rectangles; the bushes, and fruit trees, and the flowers were the exact same height and shape. The eye was intentionally steered along straight lines that led to right angles or circular vertexes.

Few people knew that Wharton considered herself a better landscaper than a novelist. She said of her work at The Mount in 1911, "This place, every line of which is my own work, far surpasses *The House of Mirth*." Unfortunately, all of those gardens she doted on were destroyed by neglect over the years. Then in 1999, Edith Wharton Restoration (EWR) came to the rescue. The landscape contractors did an admirable job of reviewing the original list of plants and putting in place as many original varieties as they could. According to the literature I read, boxwoods have been planted to replace the large sun-shading hemlocks that once lined the lime walks and walled gardens but are now endangered due to the wooly adelgid blight. Much of the rock garden, the green terraces, the two fountains, and the paths are restored, and a new irrigation system is in place. The last phase of EWR will take place in the coming years: the replanting of the flower garden.

We walked the limestone path until the monotony overwhelmed us, and we took flight. Tripping the lawn fantastic, we tumbled out of the labyrinthine gardens, literally over shrubs and down the many-tiered lawnscape toward the trees and the lake below. In no time, we were almost out of sight of the tour group and even of the house itself. There were some old trees back in the woods that merited investigation, so I got my baggies out and entered under the bowers while my daughter settled herself on a rock with her apple and her book. I came upon two amazing trees nearly side by side: a white pine and a sugar maple.

The white pine had two trunks, each the size of a normal trunk, exploding out of one nucleus from the ground. It was like a spiral of antiquity, but healthy as hell. There was an old, rusty ladder, like the kind found at the bottom of a fire escape, leaning against the trunk, so odd and out of place. I sprang up the rungs, quick as a whip, away to the top.

Back on the ground at the base of the great tree, I couldn't find even a single sapling. There were, of course, no viable pinecones, it being mid-spring. But right next door was the mammoth Sugar maple, the biggest I'd seen on the property. All around it grew tiny saplings the size of my pinky, growing up out of the leaf-covered ground. I dug up a dozen. My bags replete, I stopped to look around.

The woods were thick and dark, and the land undulating. All was lush and primordial. I stood facing into the forest, and I felt a rush of certainty that what I saw and felt was an accurate representation of what had been there when the Whartons first came to the land before building The Mount.

I caught up with my daughter, who was sitting on a bench along the perimeter of the symmetrical gardens reading the copy of *Ethan Frome* I had bought for her. She was sitting prettily, directly in line with the middle of the great mansion, a youthful, modern-day version of Edith Wharton herself, dressed in T-shirt, sneakers, and jeans.

EDITH WHARTON WROTE more than forty books, her first at age eleven. She was an aristocrat, and she is often described as the last Victorian writer. She received the French Legion of Honor for her help during the First World War, housing homeless women and feeding refugees and orphans. Her novels were enormously popular when they came out because not only were they superbly written and highly entertaining to read, but they challenged the conventions of her class. It's no surprise that many of her stories were made into movies, most of them in recent years.

Anyone visiting The Mount who hasn't read her books might get the wrong idea about her. She was not an aristocrat of the Gilded Age who was out of touch with real life and real people. She, like the characters in her stories, was victimized by her bad marriage, by her oppressive social class, and by the restrictions placed on her because of her gender. Edith Wharton might have been the last writer of the Victorian era or the first of the modern era—either way, she was way ahead of her time.

## Worcester, Massachusetts

There is nothing left of Esther Forbes's house except the trees. Today the houseless city lot faces the campus of the Worcester Polytechnic Institute. Where once sat a grand Tudor-style mansion, built in 1898 by Ms. Forbes's father, now only spectacular arboreal specimens remain—yet what perfect representations they are of such a delightful talent.

When I pulled up to the chained-off driveway, I let out a shout. "Yow!" The car came to rest directly below the most spectacular American beech tree I'd ever seen. Its silvery trunk was broad and gnarled, with Herculean musculature sufficient to support an extraordinary array of low-lying, long-distance branches. In fact, a few of its bow-shaped appendages reached all the way to the hood of the car, extending some thirty feet from the bole, the part of the trunk beneath the point where branching commences.

I had learned from a conversation with Esther Forbes's grand-nephew that this great weeping beech, a cultivar of the American beech, was planted somewhere around 1840 or 1850 by Esther's grandfather William T. Merrifield. It was actually grafted (attached) to a small and hardy species, probably an ash, because beeches are very hard to plant and have a low survival rate. There is still a clear demarcation where the graft took hold a century and a half ago.

A bronze plaque set in stone next to the tree informs all visitors that the property was once the home of Esther Forbes, Pulitzer Prize–winning author of the immortal children's classic *Johnny Tremain*.

My youngest daughter and I were in Worcester to settle a score. Well, not really, but in my mind we were. Thirty-five years before, I had driven to Worcester for an admissions interview at Holy Cross

College. I was just a junior in high school at the time, and at 5 foot 10 and 175 pounds, with a not-so-blazing 5.2 time for the 40-yard dash, I had come to the realization that I wasn't going to play tight end for Notre Dame. So I had set my sights on Holy Cross, another highly esteemed bastion of Catholic higher education, only with a less formidable football program.

Once on campus, I met with the football coach, who encouraged me to "walk on" if and when I got accepted. He promptly directed me to the Admissions office with a light-hearted "Good luck," as he gently but firmly closed the door behind me. At Admissions, I had a one-on-one session with a particularly hard-to-impress counselor. He was thin-lipped and stern-faced. My father advised me to mention the fact that I had been an altar boy. I did, but the counselor didn't seem to want to hear about that. What he did want to hear about were the books I was reading.

"So, what books have you read recently?"

"*We Die Alone*."*

"Can you summarize it for me?"

"Sure. It's a true story about an Upper Norwegian Resistance fighter that takes place during World War Two in Upper Norwegia, which is occupied by the Nazis at the time."

"Upper Norwegia?" He coughed.

"That's right. The guy and a bunch of other Resistance fighters launch a surprise attack on a German air base somewhere in Upper Norwegia. But it doesn't go as planned, and he gets wounded and left behind on a freezing island off the Upper Norwegian coast. He manages to evade his captors and escapes by hiding out in a snowdrift. It's a pretty dire situation: he's wounded; he doesn't have

* By David Howarth, Macmillan Publishers, 1955. An excellent read.

enough clothes on; he's hiding in a snowbank in the frozen tundra of Upper Norwegia . . ."

"In Upper Norwegia?" he asked, sighing.

"That's right."

Anyway, you get the idea. The worst part about it was I didn't realize my mistake until I was in the car driving home. Why the guy didn't correct me, I'll never know. But the scratches made by "Upper Norwegia" caused me a great deal of distraction in the ensuing months as my brain continuously replayed the record of that conversation and those two stupid words over and over again. In fact, the whole college admission process was ruined for me after that. Needless to say, I didn't bother to apply to the College of the Holy Cross, so it was sweet redemption to hear my kid say, as our feet hit the pavement after her interview out in front of Admissions, "I told her your stupid Upper Norwegia story."

"You didn't."

"I did."

"What did she say?"

"She just laughed."

"Did you tell her I was an altar boy?"

"No. I think one story's enough to let them know how big a loser my dad is."

IT WAS MID-AFTERNOON and the sun was high and mighty as I prepared to traipse around the Forbes property (now a public park) and glean seeds from under the trees. Back in the car, my wee one sat in the backseat reading, with the door open and one foot resting cavalierly on the dirt driveway. Three male students from WPI were playing Frisbee on the little patch of lawn beyond the great beech tree. A female student with a basket was gathering lilacs and other flowers, while a neighborhood woman was walking her dog. As I stood looking around, it occurred to me how familiar the neighborhood seemed. It was exactly like all the upper-class neighborhoods I had walked through over the years, but there was one big difference: I was actually *on* the property looking out. It struck me from that angle just how rich the rich are: they can build these monstrous homes on a single acre of land, arrange the trees and gardens, shrubs and buildings, in such a way that simulates a country setting, though they are in the very midst of a metropolis.

Beechnuts, like balloons, aren't viable unless inflated. I found scads of deflated beechnuts, but what I was after had long since been chomped, stored, or eaten by those little gray devils. It was hopeless; there were no viable seeds, so I gave up after about ten minutes. Behind me, along the street, was an always-accommodating tulip tree, under which I found as many samaras—the dry, winged, often one-seeded fruit of the ash, elm, or maple—as I cared to collect. I stood along the sharply angled road pinching the little yellow blades between thumb and forefinger and delivering them into a baggy.

The house that Esther lived in from 1898 until her death in 1967 was called Merrifield, in honor of her grandfather. "It cost $10,000 to build the house and $15,000 to landscape it, but that house was a juggernaut," Esther's grandnephew Matthew Erskine told me over the phone, describing his childhood at Merrifield. "It leaked and burned a thousand gallons of heating oil a month. It was never a comfortable house. It had twenty-eight rooms. It was like living in a museum." Merrifield was torn down in 2002. It certainly must have been something, judging by the trees alone.

Back on top of the property, I became dazzled by what I found. The land had two levels, and at the edge of the upper level was an old metal arbor that leaned well off kilter but still managed to form a square walk-through tunnel about forty feet long. Morning glory vines and other wind-abouts wove through the mesh along the sides and top. This was a remnant from Esther Forbes's garden, no doubt. Closing in on all sides of the arbor way were unwieldy bushes and weeds and vines that, I was told, were most likely planted by Esther.

At the far end of the arbor, I came upon a rare treat: a mountain silver bell in full bloom. The flowers look like little white chimes, with an orange clapper inside and a creased waist outside. This species of tree is native to the southeastern United States, with a few uncommon specimens found north of Maryland. They rarely grow to above forty feet, but this one was close to seventy feet or more. Unfortunately, the four-sided pale green seed, like a little square puffball, doesn't appear until fall, and since it was early May, I resolved to come back later to collect a few baggies' worth.

The Parks Department has a storage shed at the opposite end of the lot, to the north of the silver bell. Directly behind it I found two humongous Japanese maples. It wasn't that they were tall, although they were a good forty feet high; rather, it was their girth, their round canopies, and the straight-up-and-down-ness that distinguished them from the average specimen. Japanese maples are noted for their contorted trunks and their zigzag layers of leaves and branches. Not these two. Their trunks looked like those of cottonwoods, with their thick ridges of faded brown bark full of insect holes. I was fortunate enough to find a few clumps of their seeds in the grass beneath them, which must have fallen prematurely during a rainstorm.

Between the Japanese maples and the mountain silver bell were lilac bushes in full bloom. All the varieties were purple and smelled exquisite. The smell of lilacs is, for me, one of the most wonderful aromas in all the world, and forever reminds me of Whitman's elegiac poem to Abraham Lincoln, "When Lilacs Last in the Dooryard Bloomed," from *Leaves of Grass*. I made the rounds and filled my head with that intoxicating perfume, sticking my mangled nose in a dozen clusters of flowers. I did manage to find a few crusty seeds, but most had long since turned to dust and fallen to the earth. Nearby was a dogwood tree in bloom as well, but it didn't look old enough to date back to 1967, the year Esther Forbes passed away.

My baggies in hand, I stood next to the great beech tree for one last look around. What a beautiful yard; what a beautiful woman. I believe I was in love with her because her story of a young boy living in Boston at the start of the American Revolution had turned my world upside down. When I read the book at age ten, I experienced envy for the very first time. I moped around for weeks afterward, feeling deprived that I hadn't been born, like Johnny Tremain, during a more exciting period of American history. For many years afterward, during the summer months, I would don a tricorn hat, a puffy shirt, roll up my dungarees to my knees, pull on white baseball socks, shoulder a toy musket, and pretend I was living in the Revolutionary period. All the kids in my neighborhood thought I was loony. But when my elementary schoolteacher announced the Daughters of the American Revolution essay contest, I wrote about the American Revolution as if I were Johnny Tremain, and I won!*

---

* The DAR sponsors an American history essay contest each year for elementary school students. A topic is selected and contest instructions are then sent to schools by participating DAR chapters. Essays are judged for historical accuracy, adherence to topic, organization of materials, interest, originality, spelling, grammar, punctuation, and neatness.

I WAS MADE AWARE of a family rumor. The story goes that Houghton Mifflin asked Esther to write *Johnny Tremain* as a sort of patriotic tribute to the troops during the Second World War, since she was hard at work researching her Pulitzer Prize–winning biography of Paul Revere at the time. It's easy to discern the sedulous research because the book is loaded up with extraordinary details of daily life just prior to the Battles of Concord and Lexington.

"Envy and wrath shorten the life," says Ecclesiasticus 30:24.

However, envy of a fictional character must certainly lengthen life—be it a small boy from Connecticut or a dying man lying inside a snowbank in Upper Norwegia.

# Gettysburg

**American sycamore** (*Platanus occidentalis*)
**Tulip poplar, a.k.a. tulip tree** (*Liriodendron tulipifera*)

CALIFORNIA SYCAMORE
SEED POD

**MY LIST OF VITAL WRITERS' NAMES** kept growing by leaps and bounds, but there was one famous *place* that called to me louder than all the others, the place where Americans slaughtered one another in the name of states' rights (the South) and equality for all (the North): Gettysburg, Pennsylvania.

The National Park Service, in its infinite wisdom, recently decided to administer a historical haircut to the Gettysburg battlefields. They have designated some 575 acres of trees that didn't exist during the battle (at least not in their present state) for removal. NPS's intent with this "forest canopy reduction program" is to give visitors to the park a more authentic view of how things looked on July 1–3, 1863.

Many like me, however, think this is a ridiculous idea, mainly because cutting down those trees represents the final chapter of the story: how nature, in its infinite wisdom, tried to repair the wounds of those bloody three days of battle. Besides, if the NPS truly wanted to turn back the clock to the way things looked 150 years ago, then the sidewalks, tour roads, monuments, shops, and the tourists in town should also get the axe.* Perhaps most unforgivable of all is that mistakes have been made in the program, and some of the precious few remaining witness trees have been felled.[†] But the blasphemy doesn't end with the trees. Recently, the Park Service tore down the old Cyclorama and Visitor centers on Taneytown Road and built in their stead a new $135 million complex it is billing as "The New Visitor Experience Center." When I visited, I found the admission fees had increased, while the number of viewable artifacts had decreased. In my opinion, the new building is nothing more than a boondoggle of a movie theater/gift shop. Why on earth do we need a New Visitor Experience Center when we already have six thousand acres of the actual preserved battlefields, complete with historical markers, statuary, panoramas, maps, observation towers, and more? (Next thing you know, they'll be selling off parcels of the battlefield, building condominiums, and filming reality shows on what's left of the sacred grounds.)

* For a thorough examination of this issue, read the transcript of Brian Black's December 1, 2010, lecture at Shippensburg University titled "Contesting Gettysburg: Preserving an American Battlefield Shrine," which was sponsored by the South Mountain Speakers Series: southmountainspeakers.blogspot.com/2010/04/contesting-gettysburg-preserving.html.
† To see the mistakes, check out www.gettysburgdaily.com/?p=1808.

THE LARGEST SYCAMORES I've ever seen stand along the Old Baltimore Pike, two hundred yards north of the National Cemetery, at the entrance to the Gettysburg Middle School. I came across the two colossuses one unseasonably warm night while out strolling the sanctified streets. I was driving my oldest daughter down to Washington, D.C., to attend a high school leadership conference, and because we had gotten a late start we decided to stop for the night in Gettysburg. While she finished her takeout meal back in the room, I decided to stretch my legs. Not more than hundred yards from our hotel, I came upon the two giants. With the aid of the surrounding streetlights, I was able to find a dozen or so of the golf-ball-size seeds in the landscaped shrubbery around the trees. I did not bring any Ziploc baggies with me on my evening stroll, so I just jammed what I found into my pockets. Most of the seeds crumbled to mush in my hands, but in no time, my pockets were full. The little seedpods will dangle in the trees all winter until the wind and rain break them down to mush and fluff.

In the gloaming that evening, the sycamores appeared otherworldly. Their mottled bark reminded me of earth tone camouflage fatigues. There is a plaque beside the more southern sycamore, validating its attendance at Lincoln's parade on November 19, 1863, the day he came to town to deliver the Gettysburg Address. A scene of the parade is etched into the plaque's metal. I stood next to the tree, trying to measure its girth. It would have taken two people to join their arms around it. George Washington once came upon a sycamore in the middle of an Ohio River island that measured forty feet in circumference, and that same sycamore was measured a century later at forty-four feet in circumference. But most sycamores that big and old are hollow on the inside and likely full of chimney swifts and little brown bats.

In America's primeval forests, sycamores, a.k.a. buttonwood, a.k.a. plane trees, were the girthiest hardwoods among all the giants that reigned there. History books documenting the early exploration of America's wilderness are peppered with noteworthy encounters with these sycamore behemoths. The sycamore's use throughout the ages is a grab bag of specialization. Because of its girth, cross-sections of the trunk were cut and holes drilled to make oxcart wheels. Hollow sections of trunk of three to four feet, with a flat panel nailed to one end, were used as large storage barrels for grain. And later, when America went wild for three-dimensional viewing with stereoscopes, sycamore was the wood of choice for Sir Charles Wheatstone's invention. Today sycamore is used mostly for shipping crates and chopping blocks, as the wood never cracks or splits. And because the sycamore is the only common tree (along with field maple and lime) with insect-pollinated flowers, it is a vital source of pollen and nectar for bees—and a major allergy season irritant.

THE NEXT MORNING I got up and dressed before the teen awoke and set out for the East Cemetery Hill Battlefield, which was mere yards from our hotel. Also adjacent to the hotel was the Jennie Wade House, a small brick building with a life-size bronze statue of the eponymous Jennie out front. Jennie Wade was the only civilian casualty of the great Battle of Gettysburg. Apparently she had been baking bread for the soldiers when a Confederate sharpshooter holed up in an attic three hundred yards away decided to use the bright red side door of her home for target practice. His bullet pierced the door and struck Jennie, killing her. Encounters with her ghost are legion.

There is a very old tulip tree growing out of the algae-covered rocks of a low-lying stone wall at the apex of the East Cemetery Hill Battlefield. Tulip seeds are hardy little blades, incredibly numerous, and though they usually fall as a cluster still attached to the husk, they will scatter far and wide when the wind blows. Even the most fastidious grounds crews cannot clear away all of the seeds of a tulip tree.

The tulip tree is the foil of the sycamore. Where the sycamore is wide, the tulip tree is tall. In every eastern hardwood forest, the highest canopy will invariably be that of a tulip tree. It is often miscategorized by many as a poplar, but it is no poplar. Actually it is a member of the magnolia family, and proudly displays its redolent flowers in spring. Its four-lobed leaves often remind me of webbed hands. The battlefield tulip tree, because it has had no competitors throughout its existence, has expressed its growth outwardly as well as upwardly, and is as broad as it is tall. The billowing branches of the tree are as impressive a sight as the august equestrian statue of Major General Oliver O. Howard, just yards away, sitting tall and regal in the saddle.*

After filling an entire Ziploc bagful of seeds—I was prepared today—I stood for a while in the early morning light, looking out over the East Cemetery Hill Battlefield. Standing there among the company markers, I could feel the history oozing out of the ground. This was the crucial spot where both armies bungled their respective advantages on that first day. Ultimately the Union troops prevailed, and one doesn't need to be a military strategist to get a sense of how great a purchase that real estate provided the defending Army of the Potomac. Standing there under that majestic tulip

* From an op-ed piece published in the *New York Times*, September 7, 1974.

tree, I couldn't help but reflect on how it had witnessed those horrific three days of fighting, just a sapling peeking up through the
stones of the wall. This thought gave rise to the idea that there
are certain places on this earth destined for infamy. I wondered if
such places have within their bedrock or topsoil some malignant
magnetism that induces men to commit atrocities. And what do
the trees feel having stood witness to such horrific events? Do they
retain within their cellulosic fibers a mark or memory of the horror? Is the terror and fear retained like air bubbles in the heart of
glaciers?

It took my breath away to think that the tree was there on that
final day of the great battle, July 3, 1863, to hear the spine-tingling
rebel yell as twelve thousand men in a line a mile long came screaming and charging across the fields below, bent on their own immola-
tion. It was there to suffer through the never-ending frenzy of sulfur,
smoke, and bullets as the maniacal wave of murderous humanity
raged ever closer, horses whinnying and rearing, mini-balls blurring
the air, and men screaming, dying, crying out for loved ones. It was
there for all of that lurid horror, and yet to look at it today—an ex-
emplary specimen, symmetrical and stately, pristine and pure—is to
see proof that nature's influence is above all inviolable.

Down at the bottom of the Cemetery Ridge, within sight of the
tulip tree and the imposing bronze equestrian statues, there is a cow
pasture. Amazingly, the Park Service allows local farmers to graze
their cattle there. A stone wall separates the pasture from the access
road. Just behind that wall I found an ancient mulberry tree that
had fallen down, bent in two, but very much alive. Its trunk was
well over two meters wide, and its branches, many of which were
dead, were as fat as the boles of most mature mulberry specimens.

(Why is it that mulberries have forever been associated with blood and death instead of joy and sweetness? For example, "The White Mulberry Tree" is the name of the crucial chapter of Willa Cather's 1913 novel, O Pioneers!, because under the branches of a mulberry tree two star-crossed lovers are killed, a reference to the stories of Pyramus and Thisbe and Romeo and Juliet.)

This fallen warrior must have been there that day as wave upon wave of Confederate soldiers, many dressed in the homespun butternut yellow uniforms their own wives had made for them, met their maker as they tried to charge up the steep ridge toward the Union stronghold. No doubt it, too, was a mere sapling when that event took place, somewhat protected from the bullets raining down from above. On its bifurcating branches, within arm's reach, I found just a few shriveled berries that had not fallen during the summer. The scabrous fruit was the color of dried blood.

I put the precious few berries in a Ziploc bag and made the sign of the cross.

**MY COCKAMAMIE SCHEME,** to restate it loosely, was this: I would go around the country collecting tree seeds at the homes of famous peoples I admired, grow them into saplings, then buy a cheap parcel of land and plant them there. If all went well, within a few years I would start giving the trees to my book-, nature-, and history-loving friends. With each sapling, I'd include an artsy-fartsy card describing each species' name, its history, and how it was connected to the person or place.

I live in a rambling old house built in 1861 in the faraway canal-, college-, and lakeside city of Oswego, New York. At the back of our house there is what's called a Florida room, which the former owner added on for God only knows what reason. The room is roughly three hundred square feet, with slatted windows that open with a hand crank. The huge windows span the entire width and breadth of the south-facing wall. We keep the heat down real low during the winter months. I set up two rectangular, cafeteria-style tables along the windows for the potted saplings to sit in over the winter, to soak up the sun's rays. I use the word *sun* loosely here, because during an Oswego winter, the sun is more like a will-o'-the-wisp. With a couple dozen half-gallon milk cartons cut in half for cheap planters, and filled with potting soil bought from the local nursery, my little indoor grove was well on its way.

One day a publishing friend of mine was up for a visit. I had invited him to speak to my college class of English majors about the book world landscape. That evening, back at the house, with my wife's new CD playing (my wife, Mary, is a professional jazz vocalist, and both of our daughters are musicians, so our house is always full of music; I'm a lucky man) and before a few bottles of wine, some fresh-baked bread, and bowls of pasta, I gave him the obligatory house tour.

I took him into the Florida room to show off my collection of saplings, their names and affiliations printed neatly on white index cards in my very best penmanship. He was smitten. He laid his glass of red wine down and reverentially picked up one of the Kerouac maples, holding it up to his face and twirling it around to examine all sides.

"Little Jack Kerouac probably climbed in the branches of that tree's parent," I boasted.

"What's this all about?" he asked, lowering the little silver maple, his eyebrows scrunched tightly together, and scanning the row of pots.

So I told him my plan.

"Nunh-unh," he said, shaking his head from side to side. "You're going to write a book."

THAT WAS A YEAR AGO. The description of the travels I'd already completed—plus an outline for more people, places, and trees—was submitted and accepted for publication. I plotted out a patchwork travel plan for the coming year, squeezed in between teaching assignments and family commitments. My scheme had suddenly sprouted from a cock-eyed literary treasure hunt into something much bigger. I couldn't wait to get started again. There was one problem, however: it was winter.

I'd have to wait for spring, unless, of course, I started in California.

# Part Two

*In the shade of the house, in the sunshine of the riverbank near the boats, in the shade of the Sal-wood forest, in the shade of the fig tree is where Siddhartha grew up . . .*

—HERMANN HESSE, SIDDHARTHA

## Henry Miller

Eucalyptus *(Eucalyptus robusta)*
American sycamore *(Platanus occidentalis)*
California redwood *(Sequoia sempervirens)*
Black locust *(Robinia pseudoacacia)*

CALIFORNIA
REDWOOD SEED

## Pacific Palisades

To a New Englander, Southern California is terra nova. It has the look of a land that has just had the cellophane removed. Under the sunbaked landscape, where the warm, pleasant air and magnificent blue ocean surf provide constant solace and companionship, everything sparkles. Everything glistens. Everything dazzles. Noticeably, there are no lichen-stained stone walls. No morose gray churches. No gloves, sweaters, or woolen socks needed. It's like the world placed on a masseuse's table being soothingly kneaded and rubbed and pampered.

I flew into LAX on a Thursday afternoon in late January to attend my cousin's wedding in nearby Orange County. I had planned out a weeklong itinerary to visit the residences of some of my Californian idols. No sooner was I behind the wheel of my compact rental car than I was headed straight to Henry Miller's former home, high above the blue ocean waters at Pacific Palisades.

I had no preparation whatsoever for what I would find in the way of flora at any of the places on my Golden State list. Pacific Palisades, three hundred meters above the sea, is a veritable jungle nursery, lined with all manner of bushdom and treedom. I had never, for example, seen a eucalyptus before. They are a spectacular sight, with their long strips of vertically peeling bark in varied shades of skin tones up their never-ending trunks, taller than any tree back east. (I would later learn about these exotic imports and the deadly role they play in the unprecedented wildfires that are the scourge of Southern Californian and many Australian communities. They are powder kegs.) There were giant redwoods, too, and weird, misshapen trees with "pollarded" branches that I would learn about shortly. Everywhere I looked I saw something I had never seen before.

Ogling the arboreal splendiforae towering above my clown-short car, I forgot to pay attention to street signs, so I pulled over and parked to consult a map. As fate would have it, I discovered, after checking my printed directions, that I was sitting directly in front of Henry Miller's old home. Dumb luck. I turned off the engine and sat for a moment in silence, staring wistfully at the house, my mind having a difficult time assimilating the reality, that I was, in fact, sitting in front of Henry Miller's. Henry Miller in exile from Brooklyn.

Henry Miller was the writer who took the literary world to

task. He saw the truth of life that all the dour-faced dullards were pussyfooting around, and he blew smoke at them. He understood how "silly it is to go on pretending that under the skin we are all brothers. The truth is more likely that under the skin we are all cannibals, assassins, traitors, liars, hypocrites, poltroons." He tried to live mundanely at first. He went to grammar school and high school, and took a wife. They had a child. He got a job in an office. He commuted to work and wore a suit, tie, and hat. But the truth plagued him. He couldn't sleep, he couldn't eat, he couldn't fornicate . . . Well, maybe he could fornicate, but he couldn't play chess very well. So one day he made a break for it and found his way to Paris. It was the height of the Depression and the Jazz Age. He had "no money, no resources, no hopes." And yet he was "the happiest man alive." From his mind erupted a paradigm shift in literature. No longer were the words on the printed page a "chthonian world [where] the only important thing is orthography and punctuation." No more. Literature was gloriously transformed into one "prolonged insult, a gob of spit in the face of Art, a kick in the pants of God, Man, Destiny, Time, Love, Beauty . . . what you will." * At long last, life became art, and not the other way around.†

I GOT OUT OF THE CAR and stood in the middle of the road looking at the house straight on, camera in one hand and notebook in the other. Miller's former house is a dwarfed version of an English manor home, square, with huge windows, ornamental shutters, and

* Miller quotes are from his *Tropic of Cancer*. Grove Press, New York, 1961.
† He had numerous watercolor exhibits throughout the world; the film adaptation of *Tropic of Cancer* was in production, and his opera, *The Smile at the Foot of the Ladder*, was produced in Germany and Italy.

an impressive front door. Not old. Thirty or forty years, I'd guess.
Glancing around at the other houses on the street, I saw that most
were multimillion-dollar replicas of Mediterranean mansions. Not
at all what I had envisioned for Henry.

But all the houses in Pacific Palisades are mere terracotta pots
in comparison with the incredible fauna that grow in front of them
and along the margins of the intersecting roads. Every ten yards one
finds a masterpiece of verdure. Eucalyptuses soar more than a hundred and fifty feet in the air. Redwoods, like sentinels of a gigantic
realm, tower over some of the houses near which they stand. And
then there are those weird trees, their trunks and bulbous branches
gnarled and hunchbacked, standing along the well-manicured curbs
like garden gnomes. I began to snap photographs of the trees, or at
least I tried to; the damn batteries on my digital camera had died.
I put the camera back in the car, reassuring myself that I would
return with a nephew and a working mechanism.

The lone tree in the small front yard of Miller's home held nothing of any interest to me. It was an exotic little cultivar of some kind
but was probably less than twenty years old. The lots upon which
each house was built are small, and it was easy for me to see what
was behind the house from where I stood. I could see no expansive
canopies, no soaring trunks or billowing branches of any kind in
the backyard; the trees that delighted and inspired Henry were definitely not in his yard.

Henry Miller moved to Pacific Palisades in 1962, and it is where
he died in 1980. By the time he moved to the house on Ocampo
Drive, he'd accomplished, in my opinion, his best writing, so he
began to dabble in other art forms. Also during this period, in 1964,
the U.S. Supreme Court declared that *Tropic of Cancer* was not ob-
scene and that its publication and sale were protected by the U.S.

Constitution; Miller was vindicated, and the sale of his book in his own country was finally permitted. However, he also continued to write, finishing his *Nexus* series of books (*Sexus*, *Nexus*, and *Plexus*) and, in 1972, his autobiography, *My Life and Times*. Still, this was where Miller sat back to rest on his laurels. The lush affluence of Pacific Palisades certainly must have massaged his state of repose.

Because it was January, I held out little hope of finding any viable seeds, but to my amazement, everywhere I looked—under the soaring eucalyptuses, the gnarled locusts, the sky-scraping redwoods—a smattering of seeds, *in January*. Amazing how different a world it was out here from the frozen stillness of northern New York. Under the eucalyptuses, I found little green capsules, like tiny teacups the size of thimbles. In no time I had filled an entire Ziploc bag. Then, as luck would have it, while I was standing there trying to figure out what the heck was up with the barkless tree with the bobbed and knobbed branches, along came an elderly lady out for her daily constitutional. She leaned on a cane with one hand and a Latina aide with the other, and promised years of memories for me to harvest. I wet my lips and hummed a few bars to myself to make sure the equipment was working.

"Pardon me, but would you happen to know what kind of tree this is?" I asked her, hamming it up with my hands on my hips and my head askance with exaggerated befuddlement.

The old dame planted her cane in the grassy median and came to a halt. Then, with perfect grace, she turned and glanced back up at the tree, proclaiming, "This is a sycamore." The *r* at the end of the word sounding like "aw."

"A sycamore? But the branches . . . they're . . ."

"Pollarded." Again the *r* almost nonexistent.

"Pollarded?" I had never heard the term before.

"Yes, they trim them back to get that heavy effect on the ends. They're wonderful to see in the spring. But why do want to know?" she asked, looking me in the eye.

So I told her about my quest. A smile lit her patrician face. "Henry Miller! Why he lived here for many years. I used to see him all the time riding his bike around the neighborhood."

I couldn't resist commenting: "He loved to ride his bike. He wrote a book about it. My *Bike and Other Friends*."

"But if you've come here to collect seeds, young man, this is not the right time of year for it. You have to come in the spring, when everything is blooming, or in the fall, when the seeds are dropping."

"I know. I'm out here from New York for a wedding, so I thought I would visit and see what I could find. This is kind of a scouting expedition."

"From New York, are you?" A conversation ensued about The City and her family connections there. I tried to get her back onto the topic of Henry Miller, but the conversation never turned back in that direction. Finally, we exchanged names and parted ways. It was a fruitful encounter: she had given me the image of Henry Miller on his bike, cruising the neighborhood under the loving branches of the trees that watched him at adult play.

I scanned the curb area and gleaned dozens of locust pods full of seeds from a very old and exotic-looking specimen. I took them in my hand and shook them. They rattled happily, beating a scratchy fertility beat. I stood and ran my eyes over the gnarly old locust, and as I did, I felt a pang of certainty pulse through my veins that Henry Miller passed by this tree daily, breathed in its seasonal aromas, and admired it for all its charms.

Loaded down with swollen bags of seeds, I bid a contented adieu to the Palisades. On the way out, I drove along the edge of the cliffs and got out of the car to see the view afforded from up there. *Spectacular* does not adequately describe it. Standing that high above the ocean, and with a straight-on view of the horizon line, one has the sensation of flight. I believe that, for the creative soul, a horizon line is a psychological imperative, the physical embodiment of the infinite expanse of all things. No doubt Henry Miller craved it, since he chose seaside homes.

## Big Sur

I motored on to Miller's other California home, far to the north, in Big Sur, that mythic landscape where mountains meet ocean, but now I had my nephew Matthew with me. At twenty-two and six foot four, with a lanky swimmer's build, Matthew was just the right addition. He added the heavy dose of innocence that I sorely needed. In this day and age of tabloid psychotics, a swarthy, pony-tailed male stranger (me) creeping around asking you if he can pick things up off your lawn begets phone calls and alarm bells. But supplement me with a cool young guy with doe eyes and a casual updo, and I am suddenly looking a lot more legit. Also handy with a camera and an apt phrase, Matthew would be a great addition to my California expedition.

Driving along the Pacific Coast Highway, a half mile straight up from the smashing waters on the coastline, is no doubt an awe-inspiring activity in the light of day, but to do it at night is merely death-defying. After we crossed the dramatic Bixby Creek Bridge, all 280 feet high and 320 feet long of it, we stopped to look back from whence we came. An amazing sight: the soft green humps of land rising in front of the foaming waters at the edge of the continent like the toothless gums of an ancient jaw. We limped into Big

Sur groggy and hungry. We found a room across the street from the restaurant where we ate, and then went right to bed.

The following morning I was up with the birds. As I stepped outside, I found a thick mist all around, erasing all above fifty feet. The air was quite chill and damp. Ravens barked overhead. As I stepped farther from the motel room I became aware of the trees behind me. Great wonders of joy! Not ten feet behind our motel, the largest organisms on earth towered over me. The huge black bases of the coastal redwoods looked like the footless legs of Titans. Their girth was so vast that I envisioned them supporting cities five thousand feet above me. Suddenly there was Matthew standing sleepily behind me, his updo more like an updon't. He looked at me looking at the trees. Then he followed my gaze upward. We both smiled. I like to think he was imagining what I was: the tree cities.

Like Lilliputians, we ambled along the highway and across the road to a general store, where we bought some coffee and breakfast burritos and discussed our plan for the day. I laid out a map of the area on top of a blue U.S. Post Office box and we stood studying the names of the mountains and roads. I realized that we had passed Miller's home on Partington Ridge Road the evening before, some six miles south of our present position, back along the highway. We'd try to get there on the way back out, but nearby were two notable Miller-related places. We set our sights on them.

AT A SHARP BEND in the road, we came to the famous Nepenthe Restaurant, site of Miller's original crash pad at Big Sur. The story goes that when the writer moved back to the United States from Paris in the 1940s, he pined for the landscapes he had experienced while traveling through Greece shortly before the outbreak of World War II. In 1944, completely penniless as usual, he paid a visit to a novelist friend, Lynda Sargent, who was living in a log cabin on the edge of eternity at Big Sur. Sargent let him crash there until he could find a house of his own. He ended up staying only two months, because along came Orson Welles on some whimsical weekend tour of the area. Welles saw the cabin and bought it as a wedding present for his then-wife Rita Hayworth. They named it Nepenthe, from the Greek word in Homer's *Odyssey* that means "the one that chases away sorrow." Miller had to rent a room from the mayor of Big Sur until he found another place to live. He ended up staying in Big Sur for the next eighteen years.

Nepenthe sits on the cliffs eight hundred feet above the Pacific, with iconic Big Sur vistas running off into the infinitude to the north and south. Wide, sprawling decks jut out over the abyss. The former Welles/Hayworth house is now a restaurant/bar built into the center of the decking, high among the trees. We climbed up the wooden stairs and followed the deck until we got to the restaurant; it wasn't open yet. The structure itself is a one-story, four-sided affair, with glass walls running the length and breadth of three of the four sides. There are cool concrete steps on the south deck, with pastel-colored pillows laid out for people to use to sit and meditate. There is a large live oak growing up next to the restaurant and the deck. I searched but could find nothing to take away. We looked out over the scenery for a spell, smiled at each other again, and then moved on to our next stop.

The Henry Miller Memorial Library is just across the street. Built in 1966 by Miller's close friend and a fellow painter, Emil White, after Miller moved to Pacific Palisades, this adorable little cabin in the woods sits nestled in the elbow of the Pacific Coast Highway underneath a copse of giant redwoods. The library isn't a library per se; rather, it is a bookstore/performing arts center/ cultural center. White dedicated the library to Miller in 1981, as a place where local writers, artists, and musicians could perform and display their works.

The day we were there was a Tuesday, and the library was closed. However, the gate wasn't locked and there were no "No Trespassing" signs (not that that, as you'll come to learn, would have stopped me anyway). We let ourselves in and walked unabashedly up to the cabin. An old typewriter peered out at us from inside the sliding glass doors. No one was around.

The little library sits in the crotch of a deep canyon, with redwood trees close by on three sides. The place is oriented toward the Pacific, three hundred yards straight ahead. There's an outdoor stage for events to the south of the building and a hodgepodge of abstract sculptures littering the grounds all around it. But my attention was drawn back to the three massive coastal redwoods in front of the cabin, which formed a triad. Under those prodigious specimens, the human world is negligible. I walked over to them, leaned back, and looked up. The bottom of my stomach dropped out. Redwoods are the tallest trees on the planet, and the tallest ever recorded, up the coast a ways, was measured at over 375 feet. They have a life expectancy of a thousand plus years, and the oldest one found was dated at well over two thousand years. The trees in the Big Sur area are among a small settlement of redwoods far south of the great stands that still remain in vast stretches of Northern California and southern Oregon. It is highly likely that, standing next to those three that day, I was in the company of the oldest organisms I'd ever laid eyes on. Looking at them, I found it amazing that a human could come along and have such a lack of poetry in his heart that he would even consider cutting them down, let alone the conceit to carry through with it. It's even more amazing to think that a former governor of California (think *Bedtime for Bonzo*) once said of a very old grove of redwoods, "I saw them; there is nothing beautiful about them, just that they are a little higher than the others."

The history of the redwood runs parallel to the story of Western Hemispheric expansion. About the time our forefathers were signing the Declaration of Independence, Spanish explorers were documenting their sightings of redwoods. The tree that I beheld that day in Big Sur probably predated the Pilgrims' landing at Plymouth Rock, and more probably witnessed a vigorous migration of Native Americans, going and coming, and blissfully ignorant of the lethal invasion manifesting from the East. The majestic redwood forests along the western coast remained essentially untouched until the 1850s gold rush, when the California government began to give away huge tracts of land to homesteaders, who gratuitously chased away the natives, and cut, cut, cut. And once the chainsaw was invented, forget about it. Only about 5 percent of the original redwood forests remain.*

THERE WAS A SMALL PLYWOOD platform set up under the three-pronged giants, and I stood in the middle of it looking up the endless trunks, feeling the most overwhelming sense of awe and humility. I am quite certain that Henry sat out in front of what at the time was a mere cabin and stared up at the giant trees in Zen meditation. Only positive energy exists around the redwood.

* For more about the extraordinary redwoods, read Richard Preston's *The Wild Trees: A Story of Passion and Daring*.

While Matthew photographed the objets d'art beside the library, I got to work collecting cones, hoping to find some with viable seeds still inside. Redwood cones are a contradiction: they're tiny. I've read that redwoods reproduce primarily through vegetative reproduction, a process by which a rhizome or stem on the root grows up to become a new tree. Lots of trees reproduce in this manner. What I like about this reproductive process is that the new tree is genetically the same as the old tree. In fact, the Latin name *Sequoia sempervirens*, "always alive," describes this process perfectly: it is the tree of immortality.

Time was running short. We had another author's home to get to. There was nothing more I could do but answer nature's call and skedaddle. Directly behind the library, an outbuilding fits in perfectly with the rusticated fêng shui. The bathroom was jammed full of pictures of the old fudster, including an eerie life-size bust just inches from, and at eye-level to, the toilet's user. Whoever put that there was hip to Miller's humor. On the back of that door, under the large poster of a smiling octogenarian Miller were these words, written in big bold print, "Always Merry and Bright" (with the word *merry* crossed out and replaced with the word *regular*). I closed the door and paid my respects to the man who had expanded my *Weltanschauung*.*

It was Henry Miller who gave me my direction in life. At age twenty-one, I had no idea what I wanted to do with my life. I'll never forget the day I was lying on my bed quietly reading a paper-

---

* One of Miller's favorite words, meaning "view of the world." Freud defined the word in *The New Introductory Lecture on Psychoanalysis* as "an intellectual construction which solves all the problems of our existence uniformly on the basis of one overriding hypothesis, which, accordingly, leaves no question unanswered and in which everything that interests us finds its fixed place."

back copy of *Tropic of Cancer*. Suddenly hands reached out from the pages and grabbed me by the scruff of my neck, a big foot kicked me in the groin, and a cranky voice with a Brooklyn accent called me every name under the sun, before he proceeded to point out the sublimity of the world around me, e.g., the finger-stained glasses, the just-washed dishes, the freshly squeezed enhancements, the piss-poor workmanship, the all-inclusive rates, the fucked-up faiths, the broken-down spirits, the all-out violence, the fancy pants romances, the last-best chance, the one-and-only copy, the gone-but-not-forgotten what's his name. . . .

In sum, Henry Miller lit my world on fire, and that fire is still raging.

# Krishnamurti

**Pipul, a.k.a. bodhi** (*Ficus religiosa*)
**Lemon eucalyptus, a.k.a. naked lady** (*Eucalyptus citriodora*)
**California pepper** (*Schinus molle*)
**Coast live oak** (*Quercus agrifolia*)

BODHI LEAF and BUDS

THINK TOO MUCH and you'll miss the point; that's what Krishnamurti taught me. Thought, like time, is constantly moving, but instead of moving linearly, it jerks forward and backward, violently, forever upsetting our balance. Thought is an imp. It plays constant tricks, and won't and can't and never will be tamed. Even thinking about thought sends it reeling. Krishnamurti, who dedicated his life to observing thought, sedulously studying its insane fragmentations and psychotic repetitive patterns, discovered that thought is time and activity is not. Thinking and acting are two separate realities.

As for this tree journey of mine, I didn't think about what I was doing until after I had started doing it.

The Krishnamurti Foundation of America's Pepper Tree Retreat and Education Center, in Ojai, California, lies in a sun-baked valley 745 feet above sea level, ten miles as the crow flies from the Pacific Coast, surrounded by the Los Padres Mountains. Only about fourteen acres in total, the humble little retreat of the deceased philosopher/saint has just a handful of buildings, all well shaded by a mix of citrus trees, mature live oaks, ornamental cypresses, ancient California pepper trees, eucalyptuses, and one holy specimen of the ancient fig tree known as the bodhi tree, an offspring of the very same one under which the Buddha meditated.

I had contacted Michael Krohnen, the archivist of the Krishnamurti Library, a month before, and he was waiting when Matthew and I pulled into the parking lot two minutes ahead of schedule. Herr Krohnen is a sweet-smiling man with a risible German accent.

With his hands held comfortably in place behind him, he took us on a tour of the grounds where Jiddu Krishnamurti strolled from 1922, when he first came to Ojai, until his death in 1986. The first tree we came upon was the sacred bodhi. Procuring a nearby plastic chair to be used as a ladder, Krohnen gave me a nod, and I placed the chair against the tree and stepped up on to it. He held the chair steady for me as I reached up into the tree to try to pull seeds off its sacred branches. And while I grunted and pawed, he explained the tree's history.

"This tree is called the pipul tree [pronounced *people*] but it's also known as the bodhi tree because legend has it that the Buddha sat under one of these trees in about five hundred B.C., when he gained enlightenment. Ever since, it is called the bodhi tree, the 'tree of awakening.' The original tree is in India, in a place called Bodhgaya, in northern India."

I was having a heck of time trying to remove the tiny green balls, about the size of BBs. They were stuck hard and fast to the branches' sticky bark, as if deliberately trying my fine motor skills, which are about as well refined as an arthritic orangutan's.

Our earnest guide placidly continued: "In the course of the spreading of Buddhism all over India under the emperor Ashoka, it spread out to Sri Lanka and parts of Asia, to Thailand, Burma and so on, and a cutting of that original tree was taken to Sri Lanka, or Ceylon, as it was called at the time. And there, in a place called Anukapora, they have a big tree that is supposed to be the offspring of the original bodhi tree. This tree here is in turn an offspring of that tree in Sri Lanka."

"I hope you don't mind," I said, "but I just broke off a small branch. Sorry, I'm not very good at this." I held up the mangled bit of the sacred specimen.

"No, no, it's fine, you keep going. See, you have got some seeds there."

The leaves of the bodhi are a wondrous shape. The round broadleaf describes an almost perfect circle, with the midrib extending way down into a long thin lobe, forming a tail like a stingray's. The leaves, I was told, are suggestive of the Buddha's ears. In Western culture, small, lobeless ears close to the head are considered beautiful, but in Oriental cultures, large, pendulous earlobes are admired; the bigger the ear, the more wisdom and compassion the person is reputed to possess. I love how cultures contrast; what I don't love is being from the culture that admires beauty above wisdom. Nonetheless, just to look at the leaf, one can divine something special about the tree from whence it came.

I was able to break off several small branches full of leaves with a few seeds stuck fast to them, and as I stepped down from that wobbly chair, my fingers were tingling from contact with the venerable organism. I gingerly slipped the leaves, branches, and seeds into two large Ziploc bags, feeling that I had in my possession a magical talisman of infinite goodness and power.

Krohnen led us around to another tree, called the lemon eucalyptus, or naked lady. He demonstrated the name for me by grabbing a handful of its long, finger-size leaves, rolling them together in his palm, and holding them up to my nose: they had a decidedly lemony aroma. He then insisted that I feel the smooth, fleshlike quality of the barkless trunk—with my eyes closed, I felt what seemed exactly like the spectacular skin of a woman. And then, with a twinkle in his eye, Krohnen began to relate one more unusual quality, like a gourmet chef revealing the pièce de résistance of a rare dish he had just prepared.

"But there is another characteristic which makes this tree quite different from the other eucalyptuses. A lot of ordinary eucalyptuses shed their bark as they go along, bit by bit. But not this one. The bark sheds when it's hot, all at once, so suddenly you get—*woop*—and off it comes."

"Like a prom dress."

"Like a prom dress?"

"It's an expression. Not a particularly appropriate one, either," I tried to explain.

"Oh?" His eyes were still twinkling.

Standing there looking at the sensuous musculature of the naked lady, with Krohnen twinkling alongside her, I had this sudden warm sensation, like good Karma. Here I was, visiting the home of the greatest of all observers, who had taught me that the meaning of life is life itself. I began to think about the man with whom I had come to make contact: Jiddu Krishnamurti.

He was born into a Brahmin caste near Madras, India, in 1895. As a young boy, he was thought by his teachers, the other children, and even his own father to be mentally retarded, and was often beaten. He loved nature and would sit all day long on the banks of a river in quiet meditation. Then, at age thirteen, he was discovered by Annie Besant and C. W. Leadbeater, members of the Theosophical Society, a group of eccentrics who believed that humanity was descended from seven root races, and that these races were ineluctably evolving toward one spiritual race. The Theosophists believed that they had to prepare humanity for the coming of the World Teacher. A year after meeting Krishnamurti, in 1909, Leadbeater, who claimed to be a clairvoyant, declared that Krishnamurti was the World Teacher they had been looking for. With his younger brother Nitya as his companion, Krishnamurti was then taken from his family and educated abroad in order to be prepared, and to prepare the world, for his "coming." After living a relatively opulent life in British high society, while also enduring an exhaustive daily regimen of exercise, hygiene, classical studies, and meditation, he traveled to California, staying in Ojai. There, on the retreat grounds, he underwent a spiritual awakening, just like that of the Buddha, but instead of it happening underneath a bodhi tree, it occurred beneath a California pepper tree. Finally, on August 3, 1929, during a speech he was giving in Holland, he renounced his affiliation with the Theosophists, proclaiming, "Truth is a pathless land, and you cannot approach it by any path whatsoever, by any religion, by any sect."

I REALIZED THAT KROHNEN was waiting for me to finish my thought.

"Oh, well, yes," I said, struggling. "Prom dresses are what high school girls wear to the end-of-the-year dance, you know, and the boys try to take them off afterward, and those who are successful, well . . . *woop*, off they come, real fast."

"I see, ha, ha, ha. *Woop*! They come off all at once, like the bark."

"Legend has it." I liked this man very much.

This time I didn't need assistance to gather seeds. I had only to forage for the naked lady's woody fruits, called gumnuts, on the ground at her feet. The eucalyptus tree is an import with not a particularly good reputation in this country. It has created a great deal of havoc in areas prone to wildfires. Because the tree's crowns have high concentrations of flammable oil, eucalyptuses can literally explode when ignited. In the Oakland and Berkeley Hills wildfire of 1991, which burned more than three thousand houses and claimed twenty-five lives, eucalyptus trees were primarily to blame. Today many communities in California have set up fire-mitigation programs to suppress the spread of eucalyptus seed sprouts. Doing what I was doing—gathering eucalyptus seeds for planting—would have been considered tantamount to arson in some Californian communities.

In no time my baggy was full, and we were walking slowly across the grounds, Krohnen relating stories about the early days when Krishnamurti and his brother Nitya first came to the Ojai Valley from India in the 1920s. We soon arrived at the back of the archive building, where a large California live oak stood by itself, its massive branches splayed out in whirlybird fashion, shading a circle fifteen meters across. It was dark under the tree. The oak's round-lobed leaves were like the stunted fingers of dwarves and the color of dark green army surplus gear. The tree exuded a serious and contemplative aura that seemed to weigh down and quiet my thoughts. Krohnen had a story about it:

"It was already a fairly large size in 1953 when K"—he referred to Krishnamurti as K—"started writing *Education and the Significance of Life*, which formed the foundation for all of the schools that he founded both in India—there are about seven schools, and then the one in England, Brockwood Park—and also the one here in California called Oak Grove School. Yes, he had a real fondness for this tree."

It was while I was enrolled in graduate school studying education that I first read Krishnamurti's writings on the function of education. He wrote, "We are turning out, as if through a mold, a type of human being whose chief interest is to find security, to become somebody important, or to have a good time with as little thought as possible . . . Education should awaken the capacity to be self-aware and not merely indulge in gratifying self-expression." * Ironically, shortly after reading his writings on education, I began to suffer from panic attacks. It was as if my subconscious mind knew that what I was preparing for was contrary to my nature. While his other writings helped me deal with my anxiety, I went on to teach all over the world at various levels, and I have seen firsthand to what degree the educational systems of the planet inculcate conformity and encourage competition while destroying compassion and decimating creativity. But that's another matter.

Matthew and I gleaned the area for the bullet-shaped acorns of the live oak. Viable acorns out of season are notoriously difficult to find. Once the seeds are on the ground, the squirrels and weevils

* From "The Function of Education," the first chapter of Krishnamurti's *The First and Last Freedom*, Harper and Row Publishers, New York, 1975.

take immediate advantage. One has to get up pretty early in the season to beat those ever-vigilant foragers to the task. I held out little hope at this time of year of finding anything. Most of the acorns we found had the telltale hole of weevil infestation, but amazingly, we did find a handful that held some promise.

We walked back around to the front of the archive building. Where the walkway begins, tipped completely on its side but still very much alive, was an ancient California pepper tree. The trunk was a mass of knobs and knurls, lumps and burls. Krishnamurti had a low stone wall built around the tree to honor it, because this was the tree under which he had had his breakthrough, as he himself referred to it. Today, the heavy part of the trunk rests on the top of the wall. The trunk's innards are fully exposed to the elements, and the sensitive wood pulp has faded to gray, having somehow assimilated to the open, albeit mild California elements. Lying bent over like that, the tree reminded me of a mythic creature standing guard outside a forbidden vault. Matthew began snapping away with his thirty-five-millimeter camera. Then Krohnen, smiling at the tree beatifically, began to tell us the famous story:

"I don't know how to quite describe that type of an experience. You might call it a sort of breakthrough, you know, an epiphany or a spiritual experience. If you read up on it you will find, just shortly after they had come here in 1922, he was sitting under this tree when this thing happened. And there are a number of descriptions of that experience described in books. Krishnamurti's brother Nityananda describes it later on, K himself describes it, and then there were one or two other people who were present and who also attest to something extraordinary happening, and so, you know, I don't know what to make of it. It was always thought of as something out of the ordinary. It, of course, is all too easy to get into clichés about it and say that, oh, it was like the Buddha's enlightenment. And I don't want to go there . . ."*

But I wanted to go there. I was a pilgrim, far afield, visiting a holy land in order to physically connect my wonder to his wonder. And there it was, the tree under which the wonder had all taken place. I wanted some of that wonder! Yes, I knew all about his visions, all about how he underwent a series of painful convulsions he termed "the process," which culminated in his feelings of "compassion, which heals all sorrow and suffering." † The visionary journey is the QED of sainthood, and Krishnamurti, like Saint Francis, like the Buddha, like Christ, had his epiphany.

When I began to suffer from the panic attacks, I had the opposite of a visionary journey. Instead of being suffused with light and compassion, I felt overwhelmed by confusion and far removed from myself and the world around me. Then, somehow, amid the immense fear and anxiety, Krishnamurti's words began to take effect. He talked me through the ordeal. His insistence on the now made a deep and lasting impression on my mind; his idea that "the time process cannot bring the new; time is not the way of creation" ‡ helped me understand the immediacy of life and action and the futility of self-centered activity and thought.

Unfortunately, there were no seeds ready for harvesting from the pepper tree. Fortuitously, the sister tree or its clone was just fifteen feet away. It held plenty of ripe seeds. I plucked what I could in the way of peppercorns.

---

* For the most detailed account, read Mary Lutyens's biography of Krishnamurti called *The Years of Awakening*, Shambhala Publications, Boston 1975.
† This was how Krishnamurti described his feelings after his "breakthrough" under the pepper tree.
‡ From *The First and Last Freedom*.

From there, we ended our seed gathering and entered the half-century-old archive building, designed by the famed architect Charles Willard Moore. We went directly into the large meeting hall, painted entirely white. It had a surprisingly homey fêng shui, despite the soaring ceiling and triangular trusses overhead and the opulent fireplace and mantelpiece against the eastern wall. There were several sheepskin rugs on the tile floor, and two massive south-facing windows, where the sunlight poured in, swathing the room in soft, tender radiance. Krohnen recited a list of famous people who had sat in this very room: Aldous Huxley, Greta Garbo, David Bohm, Dr. Jonas Salk, D. H. Lawrence, Jackson Pollock, Igor Stravinsky, the Beatles, and many more.

We filled the room as best we could. Matthew sat on one of the plush chairs next to the fireplace, Krohnen on another, while I sat on a huge couch. I began a conversation about Krishnamurti's most compelling subject: the observer is the observed. I asked Krohnen about David Bohm, a name I did not initially recognize. Bohm was the famed quantum physicist who had worked with Robert Oppenheimer and Albert Einstein on the Manhattan Project, and who was blacklisted during the McCarthy era as a Communist. He met Krishnamurti in England. Krohnen told the story:

"Sarah Bohm, David's wife, was with him in the library in England, and David was doing some research on activities involving the observer and the process observed, and she was going through books and she came upon a book by K, and as she opened the book she saw this thing saying that the observer is the observed. So she went over to David and gave him the book and he started reading it, and he became all enthusiastic, exclaiming, 'This is exactly what I am talking about, what I am studying!' And so they wrote to the publisher and eventually got a response, and the publisher informed them when K was going to be in the country. So they arranged to meet. Bohm and Sarah went to his hotel and they introduced themselves and David started explaining his work very slowly and then, apparently, K was listening to all of this and he said, 'YES! YES! YES!' They hugged, and you know it was the beginning of this long friendship."

I, too, was excited, and broke in with: "I've read about how quantum particles act differently when they are observed. They have taken measurements of their interactions over a membrane, but when they try to film this interaction with a camera, the results are always much different."

"Exactly," Krohnen agreed. "You know it's not unlike when you observe a woman walking across the room. She acts differently than if you do not observe her."

We all smiled foolishly at each other. Three generations of boys smitten by the fairer sex.

I had a flashback, to wit: "I went snorkeling in Mexico last year and it is the most liberating experience to float on the surface and watch the rainbow-colored fish swim by. You become so totally consumed in viewing them that you forget yourself. The observer is the observed."

"Exactly."

"Do you know if Krishnamurti ever went snorkeling?" I asked with a smile.

"Snorkeling? No, I don't know that," he said, rubbing his chin.

"Can't you picture him in big Hawaiian swim trunks, flippers, mask, and snorkel?"

His eyes twinkled at the image. Then he came out with the closest analogy he could find: "You know, K was pretty good at throwing a football."

I WAS FIGHTING BACK TEARS as I shook Krohnen's hand. He is the perfect spokesperson for Krishnamurti. As we got in the car and closed the doors, sealing ourselves off from the sanctity of the retreat, Matthew looked at me with those big doe eyes and said, "Thank you, Uncle Ricky, for that experience."

"Don't thank me, thank him," I said with a lump in my throat the size of a grapefruit, looking at Michael Krohnen, who stood with his hands in his pockets, whistling now to himself. I began backing out of the driveway, rubbing my eyes with the back of my wrist. I beeped the horn once before putting it into Drive and heading out for the open road, tears now tumbling down my cheeks.


WE KEEP MISSING THE POINT, despite divine intervention from our patron saints. On the well-paved road to life, we're all hunched over the wheel, traveling at a high rate of speed, following the red taillights of the cars in front of us, hell-bent on some distant destination. Life is not up ahead of us in the windshield; nor is it behind us in the rearview mirror. It's here and now, in the car, on the road as we go, fast or slow.

**California redwood** (*Sequoia sempervirens*)
**Big-leaf maple, a.k.a. Oregon maple** (*Acer macrophyllum*)

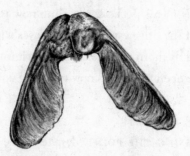

OREGON MAPLE SEED

AFTER VISITING KRISHNAMURTI'S retreat, I wanted to quit. It wasn't the seed gathering or traveling that had me flummoxed; it was the scope of my conceit: How could I possibly write about these legends? Somewhere in the tangled neuropathology of unpaid bills, I was thinking way too much. Fortunately Matthew snapped me out of my funk with an absolutely perfect suggestion:

"Maybe tomorrow, on the way to San Francisco, we can stop in La Honda." He was studying the road atlas in his lap.* "It won't be that far out of the way at all. If we take Route 84, at San Giorgio,

* It was the 1964 second edition from Riverside Press.

of the Pacific Coast Highway, it's like nine miles. From there, San Francisco is an hour away."

"La Honda? What's in La Honda?" I was clueless.

"That's where Ken Kesey lived. You know, the Merry Pranksters and the psychedelic bus? Remember we were talking about that at the wedding reception?" He was surprised that I didn't remember.

"Ken Kesey!" In my anticipation of the Henry Miller and Krishnamurti visits, I had completely forgotten about Ken Kesey. What an idiot!

After college I wandered around the country for over a year—hiking the Appalachian Trail, living with a friend in Miami, working on a ranch in Texas, running out of money and work in Seattle, before settling in Milwaukee. For two years I lived there like a recluse, reading four-inch-thick books and writing a seven-hundred-page novel that will never be published. To pay the bills, I found a job working as a nurse's aide in a mental hospital close to my apartment. That experience would become the subject of a novel that eventually *did* get published, by Steerforth Press: *Life in the Rainbow.*

While *One Flew Over the Cuckoo's Nest* remains one of my all-time favorite books, it did not match my own experiences working in a nuthouse. Kesey opens with Chief Broom describing the "Black boys in white suits . . . sulky and hating everything, the time of day, the place they're at here, the people they work around . . ." I was one of those "black boys in white suits," albeit more of a white boy in a white suit (all of my fellow aides were black), but we definitely weren't sulky; nor did we hate everything, least of all the people we worked around. To the contrary, we conspired strategically to help them out. Nonetheless, both novels express equal outrage at a system run amok. When *Life in the Rainbow* was released in 1996, I wrote Kesey to tell him all about the book and to ask for his endorsement. He never did respond, but his good friend Larry McMurtry did, and with a flattering letter.

Late in the afternoon, under a bright California sun, we turned off the Pacific Coast Highway onto Route 84 at San Giorgio and headed for Kesey's Merry Prankster house at La Honda. Matthew had researched it on Wikipedia and had a printout with a photograph and a write-up on the place spread out in his lap. Of course we drove right by it. But the printout had a picture of another famous La Honda venue: Apple Jack's Saloon.

Apple Jack's is an old-time roadhouse saloon that time seems to have forgotten. Built underneath a stand of towering redwoods, it sits in between the legs of the giant trees, attracting dyed-in-the-wool hippies, weekend frat boys, and Harley dudes like flies to flypaper. It is an old place in the classic cottage style, with a steep-sloped roof and faded gray clapboard siding, yellow trim around square windows, and a droopy pinewood porch. It is, for all intents and purposes, the psychedelic's version of the Gingerbread House. We pulled up in front and hopped out. I half-expected Kerouac, Kesey, Cassady, and Company to come stumbling out of the place.

Instead, there was Terry.

He sat by himself out on the front porch, like a mangy old crow, drinking a Heineken and smoking a cigarette. He was a small man, gray-haired with glasses, very thin, and shaky as hell. He was pleasant, nonjudgmental, happy as a lark to be sitting there watching the blurry world go by, with malice for none (except cops, as it turned out) and charity for whoever would buy him a beer.

"Welcome to Apple Jack's," he hiccupped. Drunk as he was, he could still see the stars in our eyes. "Visiting?"

"We are," I responded.

"Let me tell you a little story about this place."

"Do you mind if I record it?" I had my handy-dandy Sony microcassette recorder out of my pocket like a shot, my finger on the Record button.

"No, I don't care, you go ahead. I'll tell you a story; then you can buy me a beer, how's that?"

"Great." I moved in closer, smiling at him, the cassette leading the way. He was relishing the attention, I could tell.

"I moved here in '73. Now in '73 when two A.M. came, it didn't mean it's over. It meant all nonlocals get out. And they locked the door here; then the drugs would come out and the poker chips and the—huh? Oh wow!" He suddenly stopped talking and tremulously rose up off his seat, craning his neck, his head moving like one of those bobble-head dolls as he peered over my shoulder. "A cop car just drove by. That's amazing. That's *fuckin'* amazing!" He then sat back down, more like he fell back down, scratching his chin and looking at me like I was some sort of evil omen.

Then he saw the recorder in my hand and his train of thought got knocked back onto its original track: "In '73, you didn't screw with anybody. And if you did, *hiccup* . . . if you did, your neighbor i'n't gonna call the cops, he's gonna shoot your dog, beat you half to death, but he i'n't gonna call the cops. And after it's over, *hiccup*, he i'n't gonna call the cops. It kept life very straight out here. That's the legacy of the Pranksters." He took a big, self-satisfied swig and sort of shook the bottle, indicating he needed more. Apparently that was it for the storytelling.

I thanked him kindly, turned off the recorder, and led Matthew inside, leaving Terry behind to watch for cops. The place looked like it hadn't changed in fifty years. Hell, it certainly hadn't been cleaned in fifty years. Plank floors, post-and-beam construction, big old wooden benches; thick tabletops; a long, dark bar with the clas-

sic mirrors and an old-time icebox behind it; a jukebox; faded black-
and-white photographs and license plates from all over cluttering
the walls; and on every out-of-the-way surface, dust. There was a
strong, bitter odor of stale beer and cigarettes emanating from the
place's decor. Chris, the bartender, was there with a wry smile, wip-
ing beer glasses and smiling from ear to ear.

I ordered three bottles of beer. Matthew insisted on paying for
Terry's, and while he brought Terry his beer, Chris began to talk. It
turns out he had almost bought Kesey's place a few years back, when
it was up for sale, but his wife didn't want it. The house, we learned,
was just a mile back the way we had come. Chris then launched
into a ghost story about the saloon. Apparently he was working by
himself not too long before when he heard snoring coming from the
bench by the window across from the bar. He went to look, but no
one was there. He says he hears the snoring every once in a while;
says it's the ghost of the former owner, who used to get drunk and
sleep it off on that same bench. I had no doubts at all that the spirit
world was alive and well at Apple Jack's. I wanted to have him tell
the story again, so I could record it, but I noticed the batteries were
low on the machine, and the beer was almost out of the bottle. We
also needed to get to San Francisco before dark.

We stood to go. At that very moment Terry came staggering inside with an anxious look on his face, as if he'd seen another cop.
Seeing us preparing to go, he invited us to his place, with the offer of
pig's feet and more stories. I humbly declined. Then, without as much
as a goodbye, he staggered back out the door, got into an old pickup
truck, and drove off. I turned to look at Chris with my eyes wide:
"He's driving!?" But Chris was inventorying and didn't respond.

We waited a few minutes to make sure Terry had a good head
start before we headed back the way we had come.

In *The Electric Kool-Aid Acid Test,* at the beginning of chapter five, "The Rusky-Dusky Neon Dust," there's a short poem that describes Kesey's log house to a tee:

A very Christmas card,
  Kesey's new place near La Honda
  A log house, a mountain creek, a little wooden bridge
  Fifteen miles from Palo Alto beyond
  Cahill Ridge where Route 84
  Cuts through a redwood forest gorge—
A redwood forest for a yard!
A very Christmas card

A mile down the road, we came upon a house on the other side of a short wooden bridge spanning a narrow mountain creek in the midst of a heavily forested gorge. I pulled over to the side of the road. We sat and stared. I believe we were both considering the same image: Merry Pranksters at play inside and outside, the Hell's Angels, too, beneath the giant redwoods, hi-fis blaring, war whoops aplenty, drums, India prints, naked people, the lime green bus Furthur, spelled with two *u*'s out in the yard, the ubiquitous smell of dope. The house, half in shadow and half in light, is a one-floor ranch. French doors span the length of the two sides of the house, which were visible from our vantage point. There was no sign of life.

"Are you going to go drive across the bridge and knock on the door?" Matthew asked.

I was asking myself that very same question. I didn't want to invade the stillness. Fortunately the answer presented itself. On our side of the bridge was a copse of redwoods, with an understory of big-leaf maples gathered at their bases, their slim, twisted trunks coated with moss like suits of grass. The trees had been silent witnesses and perhaps even active players in the shenanigans that went on during those acid-fueled days. I know that the Pranksters had painted some of the trees Day-Glo colors, and wouldn't it be wonderful to find remnants along the inside ridges of the bark?

KESEY LIVED A QUINTESSENTIALLY American youth. He began his life on his father's dairy farm in Colorado before moving to Oregon at age ten. It was there, in the great green vastness of the Northwest, hunting, fishing, and swimming in the broad rivers, that he developed his rugged individualism—the predominating theme throughout his works. And there could be no rugged individualism without trees. He knew that, and that's why he chose to live in the house over the little wooden bridge, in the redwood forest gorge.

"You know what? I don't think we need to knock on the door. There are plenty of big trees on this side of the bridge that were probably just as involved in the lives of those guys as the ones out behind the house," I said, hopping out of the car.

And there were plenty of seeds, too. Close to the wooden bridge were three redwoods, not as big as the ones behind his house, but close. And below them, like henchmen, were the most misshapen maples I'd ever seen. They were covered with a furry-looking light green moss, but best of all, their branches were leaden with fist-size clusters of seeds, all conveniently within arm's reach. When I happened to shake the tree, the clusters made a rattling sound.

We waded into the leaf-covered understory and began to dig

through the decaying leaves, searching down in the lush loam for the tiny sporelike seeds from the redwoods. There were millions and millions of them. Who knows how long both Matthew and I were at it, picking and packing and pulling morsels from branches and rooting around in the underbrush like robin redbreasts. All I remember is a car slowing down, doing a U-turn, and pulling up alongside me. There were two mountain matrons inside, smoking, squinting, ogling us. Locals. The electric window slowly came down, releasing a cloud of smoke.

"What're you boys doin'?" the woman on the passenger side called out. She had a grandmotherly face. Her complexion was craggy. She held a cigarette in her hand as if it were just another finger.

"Collecting seeds from the trees," I answered, holding up a baggy for her to see.

"Ooooh, that's what you're doin'. We thought you were looking for mushrooms. Okay, okay, that's all right. Hee, hee. hee." And just like that, off they went, giggling.

Matthew came over to me. "What did they want?"

"They wanted to know what we were doing. Someone must have called them from inside the house." And then it hit me: we had turned it around. Now the people inside the log house were wondering what the hell Matthew and I, the ninnies,* were up to. And to expatiate upon a more metaphysical theme, it was the perfect reverse of Krishnamurti's meditation "the observer is the observed." In our case, the observed was the observer.

---

* In *The Electric Kool-Aid Acid Test*, Tom Wolfe wrote, "And by and by, of course, the citizens of La Honda and others would start wondering . . . what are the ninnies doing?"

Loaded down with maple keys and teeny-tiny redwood seeds stuck to the moist underside of putrefying big-leaf maple leaves, we plopped back into the rental car and headed for San Fran, cruising through the dappled shadows of the towering redwoods, along the rusky-dusky, curvy-lurvy La Honda Road. I let Matthew drive while I daydreamed about Kesey's path.

A scholar/athlete (the most pampered darlings of our compulsory education system) from a middle-class family, Kesey won wrestling titles and college scholarships before volunteering to become a guinea pig for a CIA-sponsored psychedelic study. Held at a California veterans' hospital full of mental patients and amputated vets, the study was intended to study the effects of LSD on people. Administered by institutional men in white smocks, the acid Kesey dropped opened his eyes wide to "the falsity of the fabric of society" and to "that forbidden box in that other dimension,"* as he was quoted as saying on radio many moons ago.

From then on, Kesey became a defiant and intrepid explorer, seeking out the truth, whether in a mental hospital, on a psychedelic bus ride, on an acid trip, or at play among the Day-Glo-painted Sequoias in his beloved refuge in the woods.

The observed became the observer.

* From "Comes Spake the Cuckoo. Ken Kesey: The *Far Gone* Interview," conducted by Todd Brendan Fahey by phone September 13, 1992.

# John Muir

California laurel, a.k.a. California bay
(*Umbellularia californica*)
Deodar cedar (*Cedrus deodara*)
California horse chestnut, a.k.a. buckeye (*Aesculus californica*)
Canyon live oak (*Quercus chysolepis*)

CALIFORNIA BUCKEYE SEED POD

## San Francisco, California

I first visited San Francisco when I was seven years old. I still remember the free-falling feeling in the pit of my stomach as my father drove us down those stair-steep streets. I remember the sugar-white homes bent like canine teeth against the angled jawline of the urban hills, the trolley cars like giant toys running loose through the city. And I remember that golden sun pouring down on us like celestial honey. Those images all came flooding back to me as Matthew and I rolled down the off-ramp of Interstate 80 into the North Beach section of the city.

San Francisco is the epitome of what they were all referring to when they spoke of that "shining white city upon a hill" ("they" being Jesus Christ, John Winthrop, JFK, Ronald Reagan). It's definitely the Athens of the West. Some of the world's great artists and thinkers and political radicals have been drawn to its cultural ferment over the years. Unfortunately, the bohemians and beatniks, prodigal sons and daughters who once frolicked and agitated along its feisty streets, can't afford to live there anymore. In fact, San Francisco now has the lowest per capita population of young people among major cities in the United States. About the only insurrections being mounted there lately are by the few remaining families who simply want to improve the public schools and find ways to expand affordable housing. As a result, parts of San Francisco have become adult theme parks, with museums and attractions (e.g., The Beat Museum, Alcatraz Island National Park) featuring its most famous angels with dirty faces.

I discussed this state of affairs with Paul Yamazaki, the head book buyer at the famous City Lights Bookstore. I had come to San Francisco to meet with Paul, a well-respected personality in the bookselling world, to talk to him about my seed-collecting quest. It was my first opportunity to sit down with a bookseller and talk about *Seeds*, and I was dying to hear his take on the topic. We stood for a long time out on the sidewalk in front of the literary landmark, enjoying the last rays of the sun and tossing out cities that could, perhaps, one day replace the San Francisco of old as a Mecca for a new cultural insurgency: Pittsburgh, Cleveland, Baltimore, Detroit, Buffalo?

Before the sun fell behind the buildings to the west, we moved inside, climbing the rickety old stairs of the historic building to Paul's cluttered loft office. Upstairs in that constricted space, amid the overstuffed bookshelves and disordered desk, the conversation turned naturally to the history of City Lights, which is essentially the history of the Beat literary movement and of the indie presses.

City Lights Books was founded in 1953 by the Beat poets Lawrence Ferlinghetti and Peter Martin, and was the first paperback bookstore in America. Then, in 1955, Ferlinghetti launched the publishing end of things, issuing books by avant-garde authors such as Charles Bukowski, William Carlos Williams, Paul Bowles, André Breton, and most notably Allen Ginsberg. It was the publication of Ginsberg's groundbreaking poem "Howl" that really made City Lights shine bright. When "Howl" hit the streets, Ferlinghetti was immediately picked up by the police and charged with obscenity. He went to court to challenge the charges—and won. That court case established a new precedent for literary obscenity and ignited the literary world. From then on, banned books such as Henry Miller's *Tropic of Cancer* and D. H. Lawrence's *Lady Chatterley's Lover* could be sold in America with impunity. And ever since then, having your book banned has become the most prized literary honor of all.*

Paul was very excited about my project and was amazed that no one else had thought of doing it before. Sated with compliments and a long list of contacts, not the least of which was the famed Beat poet and Pulitzer Prize–winning writer Gary Snyder, we shook hands, and off I floated.

Paul had suggested that Matthew and I try our luck for lodging at the Green Tortoise, a hippy hostel just a block away from

---

* In 2001, both of my novels, *Life in the Rainbow* and *Goose Music*, were banned from the public high school library where I taught. Talk about proud!

the bookstore. Up a flight of wide wooden stairs, there's a reception area with classic pigeonhole mailboxes behind it. On the same floor is an enormous dining hall with a wide-screen television at one end and a cafeteria-size kitchen facility at the other. If you feel like cooking your own meal, you can. But best of all, the hostel was just fifty bucks a night. Our room was on the third floor, overlooking Broadway. Compact but commodious, it had a little sink, sixties-style wallpaper and carpeting, and a sturdy wooden bunk bed with drawers underneath full of extra blankets and pillows.

Matthew said he was heading back out to meet some friends, so I wandered the side streets of the North Shore and found it chock full of young people and live music. In all of my peregrinations to cities around the world, only in Nashville and Amsterdam had I found a live music scene as vital as this one. There was rock n' roll in one bar; across the street, blues; down the street, jazz; across from that, reggae; and around the corner, zydeco. A smorgasbord of sounds. My favorite was the blues joint right around the corner from the Green Tortoise, where a petite Japanese female lead guitarist scorched the place, biting into her Fender Telecaster like the Ice Man himself, Albert Collins.

I found a great little pizza parlor and, standing at the counter, inhaled a slice of thick-crust pizza with lots of sausage. Full of food and music, I headed back to my spot at the hostel on the lower bunk berth, and with the pillow under my head, shoes off, book in hand, and glasses on, I was out before finishing even one page.

## Martinez, California

The next morning we ate our fill of free breakfast and headed east. The John Muir National Historic Site in Martinez is a forty-five-minute drive from San Francisco. We crossed over the Bay Bridge, a double-decker suspension bridge that is like the Brooklyn Bridge times ten. Almost four miles long and five lanes wide each way, it seemed to be passing from one continent to another. Steinbeck's Oakland to the south and east was a compelling sight, bulging up out of the flatlands like a theatrical set, the green hills a pleated curtain behind it. But Route 80 takes a hard left away from Oakland and heads due north. Ten miles on, we exited onto Route 4, a beautiful four-lane divided highway with a well-manicured median that meanders up and around and through gently rolling hills and dales. The plump patterns and lush colors of the landscape reminded me of a Grant Wood painting. At the Martinez exit, we dropped quickly down the ramp, turned left under the overpass, and Muir's house was right there.

Of all the people on my list, John Muir was the one I felt most intimidated by. Creator of the National Parks Service and father of the Sierra Club, he literally hopped over his backyard fence and walked a thousand miles to the Gulf of Mexico just as the smoke was clearing from the Civil War. Fearless. Compassionate. Nature's most ardent admirer: "I used to envy the father of our race, dwelling as he did in contact with the new-made fields and plants of Eden; but I do so no more, because I have discovered that I also live in 'creation's dawn.' The morning stars still sing together, and the world, not yet half made, becomes more beautiful every day." *

As I swung the little fossil fuel burner into the parking lot, I could feel his hot beady eyes glowering down at me from the widow's peak windows atop his Victorian-era mansion. As a twenty-first-centurian, a galloping consumer of petrochemicals and polymer

* From *John of the Mountains*, University of Wisconsin Press, Madison, 1938.

products, a hot shower taker, a frequent flier, an occasional meat eater, and a card-carrying member of the Sierra Club, I am, vis-à-vis John Muir, guilty of profound hypocrisy. I may talk a good game about conservation and environmental stewardship, but I know full well that every day I lace on my shoes will be another day that I am adding my share to planetary perdition.

John Muir, who could have lived happily on a sack of stale bread-crumbs and a canteen of fresh spring water so long as he was outside between the mountains and molehills. John Muir, who wrote in his journal, "I only went out for a walk and finally concluded to stay out till sundown, for going out, I found was really going in." John Muir, the world's greatest environmental warrior, who fought against the age-old belief that nature's only purpose is to provide for stupid hu-man tricks. And I had the audacity to come to *his* house to collect seeds from *his* trees. Gulp.

I parked the car, collected my backpack and Ziploc bags, and diffidently walked toward the Visitor Center, shoulders noticeably stooped, two full strides behind happy-go-lucky Matthew.

I love the fact that National Park Rangers, whether located in the inner city or in our national forests, traditionally wear the stan-dard green uniform with, best of all, a circular-brimmed hat. I have to say, however, that I was a wee bit disappointed that neither of the two rangers inside the Visitor Center was wearing his hat.

I always go right for the postcards. If there were a major offered at the university in All Things Postcardy, I would hold a Ph.D. Bet-ter yet, if they could bioengineer a tree to produce postcards instead of seeds, that tree would be named after me, *Postcardia horanus*. On second thought, it sounds profane. Nonetheless, the postcards were cheap. In my opinion, most historic sites and museums charge way too much for postcards—oftentimes as much as a dollar a card. Not at the John Muir National Historic Site. Four for a buck. Now that's good Scotch thrift.

One of the hatless rangers led Matthew and me into a tiny theater, turned off the lights, and fired up a video, a twenty-minute bio of Muir. We learned about the Hetch Hetchy Valley of Yosemite and the dam that was built there. Muir fought savagely to prevent it, but in the end, the bill passed, clearing the way for the valley to be dammed. Muir died a year later. Many people, me included, believe that the fight to save Hetch Hetchy killed him.* But no dam could ever reduce the majesty Muir exulted. Yosemite, with its granite cliffs and spiraling domes and cathedral peaks, "the grandest of all the special temples of Nature," † would only grow in glory to become part of our national identity, thanks to him.

We walked out of the Exit door into the blasting rays of the sun. I moved as if in a dream, up the sloping driveway and toward the tall and grimacing mansion above. At the bottom of the hill, the house's angular countenance had a decidedly angry look, but the closer I got, the pleasanter it became, until the whole place looked like a great big smiling cartoon face. The widow's peak on top of the roof, in fact, reminded me of the hunter's hat worn by Elmer Fudd, and the two tall windows on the second floor with the thick trim articulations above looked like eyes. The jutting-out portico had a

---

* His hostility is palpable in the essay "In Defense of Hetch Hetchy," which he wrote during the battle to save the valley: "These temple-destroyers, devotees of ravaging commercialism, seem to have a perfect contempt for Nature, and, instead of lifting their eyes to the God of the mountains, lift them to the Almighty Dollar. Dam Hetch Hetchy! As well dam for water-tanks the people's cathedrals and churches, for no holier temple has ever been consecrated by the heart of man."

† From the official National Park Service/U.S. Department of the Interior Yosemite National Park map and guide.

definite fleshy nose quality to it, and the extended circular window casements that puffed out from the main part of the building on either side looked like cheeks.

The driveway resolved in a cul-de-sac directly in front of the mansion's front steps. In the middle of that island was a large, mature tree with a globular canopy. There were nuts all over the ground beneath it. I recognized the species from the tree's leaves, a California bay (I like to put the thick, thumb-sized leaves in my gumbo). The tree's golden nuts, about the size of acorns, look like giant dirty peanuts. I started to gather some; Matthew joined me. Then we both noticed at the same time tiny seedlings about two inches tall sticking straight up out of the soil. I didn't know at first what they were, whether they were from the bay tree or from the redwoods or cedars around the house. I also wasn't sure if I would get a citation for digging one up. Nevertheless, I threw caution to the wind and started spearing a little circle around one of the seedlings with my car's ignition key, like a golfer fixing a divot on the putting green. It was at this point that a ranger appeared from out of nowhere.

"Collecting mementos?"

"Hoh!" I gave a shout and popped up like a jack-in-the-box.

He looked down at what I was up to. He knew exactly what I was doing.

"Those are deodar cedars," he said, hunkering down on his haunches next to me and gingerly caressing the little seedling with his fingers. He stood up and pointed. "The parent tree is right over there." He was a short, middle-aged man, dark haired, with a clerk's complexion but a scientist's expression. He wasn't wearing his circular-brimmed hat, either. His eyes smiled.

"Did John Muir plant these trees?" I asked somewhat boldly, beginning to think I was not going to be issued a citation.

"Some of them. This bay tree here was [planted by Muir], and the cedars, too; the parents of the sapling you're digging up. But most of the other trees are second generation."

"Are there any other trees he planted that are still alive?" I asked humbly, even though I was rejoicing inside.

"Just the redwoods, of course, and the figs out by the adobe."

"The adobe?" I repeated, not understanding his reference.

"Out back, where he and his wife lived before moving into the main house here." Then he scratched his jaw and tilted his head. "You know, if you're going to dig up seedlings"—I felt a citation coming—"there are some older ones under the parent trees."

He took a few steps over to the other side of the driveway, got down on his haunches, and once again fondled some seedlings. Sure enough there were a half dozen tiny little cedars, four inches high, green needles as hard as toilet brush bristles, standing proudly in a row.

"Make sure you take some of the soil away with them; that'll help them grow." He stood and smiled at me. It was the purest smile I'd ever seen. "Enjoy yourselves," he said, and off he went.

With a big sigh of relief, I shouted to Matthew to come over and join me, and we hunkered down and attacked the ground around the seedlings again. Within ten minutes, we had six perfect little saplings well complemented with a hefty amount of native soil covering their skinny little roots. It was a bonanza. We placed two to a bag and gingerly arranged them at the bottom of my backpack. I felt a little contrite leaving behind a few divots, but that was minor compared to my days as a golf caddy. Besides, the ranger had insisted we take the soil away.

THE MINUTE I ENTERED the mansion, I felt palpable discomfort. The interior was completely devoid of charm. Tall ceilings, angular furniture, stuffy air, awful artwork, creaky floors, not enough light. I felt like I was walking around inside an empty train station. And as I strolled through the rooms, the discomfort never dimmed. The high ceilings were far too high, and the Victorian woodwork and paneling and wallpaper did not soften the square form of the interior space. I could tell that this house was used like a terminal, as a place in which Muir came and went but did not rest for too long.

Even Muir's famous "scribble den," his name for his office, didn't scratch my itch. This was the place where he had grudgingly written every single one of his elegiac books. I use the word *grudgingly* because Muir, admittedly, was a reluctant scribbler. Check that: he hated writing, and he hated books.* Unlike Thoreau, who took to the pen like a duck to water, Muir wrote only because he understood that the printed word was the only means by which he could catalyze his cause. No, Muir did not exceed Thoreau in poetry and philosophy; he exceeded him in work completed and in miles walked.

Leaving Matthew behind, I followed the stairs ever upward and came to the end of the tour at the widow's peak. There you can get a sense of Muir's ambivalence for his Martinez estate. From up above, he could stare down at the fruits of his labor: the long military rows of profitable citrus trees marching over hill and dale in colorful symmetry. Behind that, however, in his mind's eye, was an indelible vision of the wild, unpatterned majesty of Yosemite and of the capricious sublimity of the eastern deciduous forests and river

---

* "I have a low opinion of books; they are but piles of stones set up to show coming travelers where other minds have been, or at best signal smokes to call attention. . . . One day's exposure to mountains is better than cartloads of books."

valleys of his youth. They must have pulled constantly on his heart-strings.

Speaking of pulling strings, dangling above my head was a white cord connected to the original bell used to call Muir in from the fields for supper. I reached up and yanked it. The sound of that crisp note shot out like the report of a rifle, piercing the stifled air wafting up from below. It was not a folksy note, nor a beckoning note; it was a clarion call to action. That note, an unresolved F-sharp above a middle C, remains stuck in my head to this day.

Muir's estate is a mere semblance of its former glory. It originally spanned some twenty-five hundred acres, but today only about ten acres of the fruit plantation remain. The brochure handed out at the Visitor Center spoke at length about the original owner of the estate, Dr. John Strenzel, who was a fruit rancher and a horticultural pioneer. "He showed ninety-one varieties of seven fruits at one county fair."* Dr. Strenzel was Muir's father-in-law, and Muir helped him with the fruit ranch from 1882 to 1887. During those years Muir himself amassed a small fortune, but by 1887 his wife, Louie Wanda, had become concerned about his mental health and insisted he return to his true love: nature. He did, traveling up to Alaska to study glaciers, and then around the world to study plants and trees.

I HAD TO FIND THAT FIG TREE the ranger had mentioned, so we wandered down to the old adobe home. The adobe is a two-story structure built in 1849, and looks like something out of old Mexico. Muir and Louie lived there for eight years before moving into the

---

* From the brochure "John Muir: Fruit Rancher."

big house after Dr. Strenzel died in 1890. Our visitor's map indicated that the tree was somewhere around there, but every plaque we came across commemorated a different person, place, or thing. Matthew and I walked around and around. Finally, next to the north fence that separated the National Historic Site from a neighbor's backyard, was the plaque we sought. Standing directly behind it, more dead than alive, was the ancient fig tree, its branches bone white, the bole gnarled and scabrous.

There was no one else around. We looked at each other and then, without comment, dove into the leaves around the tree, pushing our noses right down close to the loamy bed. We pulled, picked, and swiped at the thick carpet of dead leaves as if looking for gold nuggets. Nothing. Then, suddenly, right up next to the tree's trunk, lay three chestnut-colored balls, nestled like curled-up mice.

My hands shook as I gingerly pulled one up from its nest. The golden brown nut was pristine, not a blemish or slice on it. The sunlight reflected off its glossy surface. I was a little confused, because the fig seeds looked exactly like chestnuts, but they had to be figs, because they were lying directly under the tree itself. Like raving robins, Matthew and I redoubled our efforts, flipping over huge handfuls of leaves looking for more nuts, until we had turned over every leaf in the bed. When we were done, we had located nearly a dozen more of the brown nuggets.

BACK AT THE VISITOR CENTER, when we glowingly showed the specimens to our ranger friend, he shook his head, pointed to a chart on the wall, and laughingly informed us that what we had found were California buckeye, not figs. We would have to come back in the fall for those.

"But they were right under the tree," I argued.

"Well, apparently the squirrels hid them there."

Matthew looked at me, and we both began to laugh. Fooled again by those wittle gway wascals.

## Back Home

THE CALIFORNIA TRIP was my first organized foray into the seed-gathering adventure, and it had ended with nature having had the last laugh. Yet I felt it had gone well. I had a plethora of inspiring seeds in hand, my enthusiastic nephew had added energy to the project, and I had met several sincere and true souls who had offered crucial assistance along the way. It was a great beginning.

When I returned home, I unpacked all of the seeds and lined them up in the middle of my living room. Some loot. With plenty of newspapers underneath to keep the mess in check, I set about the tedious task of sorting and labeling them before putting them into brown paper bags and covering them with cupfuls of bleached dry sand (the best way to store most seeds). For those seeds that had already germinated, I did my best to plant them in whatever vessels I could find (mostly milk cartons and plastic soda bottles cut in half), and put them in a sunny spot. I was out of space in the Florida room, so I began to fill up every available windowsill. I knew enough about propagating certain seeds to expect good results, and before too long I had a tiny forest advancing along every indoor sill in my house.

With the magic little saplings within sight all around me, I sat down at my computer and began typing up my thoughts. But as I wrote, I became aware of a growing anxiety. What would become of the trees? I knew that I had to get the saplings properly situated; they certainly couldn't go on as they were, living on a windowsill and a prayer. Spring was on the way, and I was preparing for a longer, more extensive seed-gathering tour through the South. So when I wasn't writing, I was following up on leads I had been given on names of biology professors and arborists who might be willing to help me raise these specimens. My expectation was that people would jump at the chance to be part of my historical project, but all of the professionals I contacted suggested the same thing: that I get a book on propagation and follow the directions or contract with a local nursery to do the job for me. That's not what I was looking for. What I sought was a partner, but none was available.

# Part Three

I like trees because they seem more resigned
to the way they have to live than other things do.

—WILLA CATHER, O PIONEERS!, 1913

# Pearl S. Buck

Bamboo (*Bambuseae*)
Silver maple (*Acer saccharinum*)
American sycamore (*Platanus occidentalis*)
Black walnut (*Juglans nigra*)
Lilac (*Syringa*)

BAMBOO SEEDS

## Perkasie, Pennsylvania

"Nothing must delay the story," Pearl S. Buck advised her audience when she accepted the Nobel Prize for Literature in 1938. Buck acquired this insight from her childhood and coming-of-age in China. She experienced firsthand how openly and directly the Chinese dealt with life's hard knocks, and this influenced not only her clear and simple writing style but also her life. During her lifetime, she wrote more than a hundred books, adopted seven children, and founded numerous schools and orphanages around the world. She did not dillydally.

I, on the other hand, was stuck in a real lollygag. What should have been a simple, direct, and easy fifteen-minute ride from my hotel in Quakertown to Green Hills Farm in the hilly Pennsylvania countryside south of Allentown and west of Philadelphia was, instead, a teeth-gnashing adventure of missed turns and misunderstood directions. At my wit's end, I finally managed to find my way to the sprawling estate in the town of Perkasie, Pearl S. Buck's home for thirty-three years. It was where she and her second husband, Richard Walsh, settled after her very last trip to China in 1934.

The meandering driveway was an impressive tree-lined affair, with stone pillars at the entrance, a massive green lawn to the east, and the regal eighteenth-century stone manor sparkling off in the near distance. Fifty meters in from the pillars was a tiny parking lot and a sign that read "Pearl S. Buck Gravesite." I parked.

It was a sparkling spring morning. The birds were performing for their mates. The air was crisp and smelled of ripe fruits and unfurled flowers. Enormous trees—pine, hemlock, ash, and oak—surrounded the grave site. A large rectangular slab of granite set lengthwise on the ground marked the spot under which Buck's remains lay. Her name was engraved in Chinese; I learned later that the Chinese characters spell the name Pearl Sydenstricker, not Pearl Buck. I also learned that Buck had designed her own gravestone, and this was a clear indication to me that she also knew right where she wanted to be buried. Looking around at the nearby trees, I felt confident that she had spent time in this corner of her property. (My guess was correct: when I asked the docent about this on my later tour, she nodded and said she was quite sure Buck had chosen that site.)

One of the most thrilling finds of my entire seed-gathering

career thus far I found right there at Buck's final resting place. Rising above her headstone was a large clump of bamboo shoots. The shoots were about eight feet high and consisted of about twenty-five stalks, or culms, as they are called. Scattered on the ground were hundreds of bamboo seeds; they looked like grass seed on steroids. Buck loved bamboo from her time in China and liked to plant it around her estate. So, ignoring the trees for now, I got busy gathering bamboo seeds. I was amazed at how many there were.

Bamboo, although technically grass, grows amazingly fast and can reach its full height in one season, but it has a short life expectancy, between five and seven years, so I was under no illusions that this clump had been around since before Buck's death in 1973. Bamboo normally reproduces via vegetative propagation; therefore, it was quite likely the clump around the gravestone had come from cuttings taken from the original parental plants. But what excited me were the seeds, suggesting that this clump of bamboo had recently flowered. Bamboo rarely flowers; and when it does, it is at exceedingly long intervals, in some cases in excess of a hundred years.

One theory about why this happens is that by having a flowering cycle that lasts longer than the lifespan of rodents (bamboo's natural predator), the grass can regulate animal populations by causing starvation during the period between flowering events. Bamboo is by far the world's most versatile and utile plant. Its renown in the culinary arts is almost as impressive as its renown in medicinal, ornamental, and musical arts. It is also becoming a major force worldwide in the green building industry, and the bamboo industry is expected to be worth $25 billion by 2012.*

---

* BooShoot founder Jackie Heinricher from GreenBiz.com, 9 July 2009, in an article titled "Growing the Future."

With a baggy full of bamboo seeds in my backpack, I felt absolutely buoyant as I angled back across the driveway and out onto the sweeping front lawn. The view of the house from there reminded me of the perspective from the woodland path at Monticello—hundreds of yards of scintillating green grass with big trees here and there, watched over by an august mansion at the terminus. The lawn to the east of the house ended in thick woods and drained down into a long, thin pond. All in all, it is a breathtaking place.

The first tree I came to was a soaring old silver maple. Because of the fullness of its canopy, I was confident that this specimen had lived a solitary existence without competition from other trees. Though it was still early in the growing season, there were plenty of fresh whirlybirds scattered on the ground, no doubt blown there by the still-urgent spring winds. I helped myself to what I found underfoot, but then I was drawn toward a more compelling sight: two large greenhouses jutting out perpendicularly from the main house.

A wheelbarrow out in front full of potting soil suggested someone was on duty today. I entered the first structure, but no one was around. Pink peonies in full bloom were the dominant species on display. In the second greenhouse were dozens of species in myriad colors, but I could find no one inside there, either. As I wandered back toward the front of the house, a monstrous sycamore arrested my attention. The colossus towered a hundred feet into the air and was close enough to the mansion to be a part of it; certainly its roots had long since embraced the house's stone foundation.

All over the lawn, countless seed balls awaited gathering. Many of the sycamore's little brown orbs, the size and shape of golf balls, were still intact; others, however, had lost their cohesiveness, burst open, and now lay in the grass like splattered animal hides. It took me no time at all to fill a baggy with the good ones.

I will admit that I didn't have a good attitude about it going in. I preferred to stay outside. I certainly didn't need to go in: I had everything my little heart desired, and more. And yet my inner cricket was chirping madly, vituperating about my not supporting the mission. So, with a heavy heart, I left the sweet-smelling air, the pullulating trees, the spectacular vault of blue sky, and entered the ersatz Pearl S. Buck International Gift Shop, where the guided tours begin.

I paid their eight-dollar admission fee and was told that the tour would begin in five minutes. The lovely woman behind the desk then pointed to a door, smiling from ear to ear and saying, in a mellifluous voice, "The tour will start in our new screening room. We just opened it yesterday. I hope you don't mind, but we will be training several new docents with your tour."

I looked over toward the new screening room and noticed a small pack of silver-headed docents, three women and one man, pacing back and forth in front of the double doors. When the tour began, docents outnumbered those of us taking the tour by four to three.

We were treated to a fifteen-minute video that highlighted Buck's illustrious career as a writer, human rights activist, and sponsor of orphans across the planet. The new screening room also had on display many of her awards, including the Nobel and Pulitzer Prizes, keys she'd been presented with to innumerable cities around the world, and silk gowns she'd worn in meeting presidents and foreign heads of state. Two large portraits of the great lady were mounted high on the wall, looking down on us all with demure inspiration. After a question-and-answer period, we were led out of the new screening room to the main house.

I won't bore you, my irreplaceable reader, with a recapitulation of the events of that tour. Suffice it to say that for two hours each docent in the pack provided background information on every eggcup, butter dish, cheese grater, relish dish, salad bowl, tureen, trivet, tea set, rice bowl, lampshade, porcelain vase, window treatment, chessboard, spice rack, nightstand, end table, coffee table, sideboard, bookcase, footstool, ottoman, chaise longue, bed knob, headboard, pillowcase, bedspread, Afghan, chest of drawers, doorknob, inkstand, towel rack, bath mat, toilet seat, washcloth, shower curtain, soap dish, faucet handle, mantelpiece, fire poker, bread warmer, dumbwaiter, Frigidaire, kitchen sink, and more.

It was a tragic case of overdocent.

At the two-hour mark, just prior to our entering Buck's office, we walked past an open doorway, and the Siren smells of the outside world beckoned me back outside into the open air underneath a giant black walnut tree. Walnuts were everywhere.

A half hour later, my swollen seed collection safely piled in the trunk of the car, but my physical and psychic energies utterly kaput, I opened the driver's-side window, dropped the driver's seat back to the reclining position, and took a much-deserved nap, dreaming, oddly, of drinking vessels—beakers, goblets, highball glasses, jiggers, magnums, shot glasses, tankards, tumblers, wineglasses, champagne flutes, snifters, beer mugs. . .

## Danby, Vermont

I hit the road again to meet up with a tree-loving man who had walked me around the reservoir in Boston many years ago pointing out tree species. His friends and I call him Krakow. We'd planned to gather seeds on the following day across the border in Vermont, at

Pearl Buck's latter-life redoubt, and then head south to North Bennington, to look for seeds at Shirley Jackson's homes. From there, we would head east to Jaffrey, New Hampshire, former stomping grounds of Willa Cather.

I arrived late, in the rain, and went straight to bed. The next morning I awoke to the smell of frying bacon and a loud racket going on down in the kitchen. Krakow, who not only gets up with the chickens but also sounds like an army of them, had already cooked and eaten breakfast, hoed his rows of garlic, mowed the lawn, cut the brush, and was now getting his sixth-grade daughter off to school. His wife, a nurse at the local prison, was already on the job. They are a salt-of-the-earth, workaday duo.

The rain had stopped, but the sky was overcast and grumpy, the air cool and brisk, with a bracing, wet breeze that had already rouged our cheeks. Holding four plastic bags jammed full of clothes and equipment, two in each hand, Krakow stood at the ready beside the back of the car, appropriately attired in his camouflage raincoat, leather boots, and fogged-up glasses. I opened the trunk and watched as he tossed his bags in and then pretentiously smacked his hands together. Although I couldn't exactly see his eyes, I could sense that he had a twinkle in them as he turned to face me while pulling the hood up over his cue ball head and tying the hood tight. In his fifties now, but no less spry and nimble than he was in his twenties, with a thick book in his hands, he reminded me of Felix the Cat's nerdy nephew, Professor Poindexter.

"You know how to get there?" I asked, rubbing my swollen belly from the country breakfast of bacon, eggs, and biscuits he'd served me.

"I think so," he clucked.

So off we sped.

**"THERE, SEE THAT?"** He kept pointing at an occasional flowering tree off in the woods, but I was driving and could get only a glimpse of them.

"Are you sure those aren't cherry trees?"

"No, no, those are the shadblow" (*Amelanchier canadensis*, a.k.a. juneberry, a.k.a. serviceberry, a.k.a. sugarplum, a.k.a. wild plum).

"Shadblow? What a name! Never heard of them."

"They're in bloom now." He had his all-prose-and-no-illustrations-or-photographs, out-of-print, six-inch-thick hardcover volume of Donald Culross Peattie's *A Natural History of Eastern and Central North American Trees* in his lap.* It was so Krakow, a man neither of this century nor of this New World, but from an era and a place long since past; hence, the Old World nickname.

I first met Krakow during college at a late-night party when I was twenty-one. Feeling claustrophobic and a bit overwhelmed by the gyrating masses, I escaped out into the comforting zone of a starry night and stood in someone's backyard leaning against a tree. Suddenly, I became aware of a person sitting above me in the branches smoking a joint, its glowing end reflecting off his glasses, giving him the effect of a red-eyed, grinless Cheshire cat. We began a conversation that lasted throughout not only most of the night but the rest of my college career and beyond. From that day forward, Krakow was for me proof positive that philosophers—real philosophers, not the pompous, self-serving, academic variety but the real ones, the enigmatic, inscruta-

---

* It was the 1964 second edition from Riverside Press.

ble rara avises whom Allan Bloom rued the loss of—still walk among us.* Like Socrates, Krakow is a man born to ask the thorny questions, to declare the inconvenient truth, and to forever remind us that man, though blessed, is the problem and not the answer.

Western Vermont is still wild country, dominated by sharp peaks, dark valleys, and thick forests. And though from Krakow's house Danby is no more than twenty miles as the crow flies, it took us a good hour to get there. At one point, we got lost and pulled into a general store to ask directions.

Entering Mach's General Store in the tiny hamlet of Pawlet is like going through a time warp. The place is a throwback to an era before electricity, when the aroma of fresh food and just-baked bread was the best part of shopping. The day we were there, locals sat around on wooden chairs—imagine, chairs in a grocery store—passing the time palavering about the weather and livestock. Krakow marched right in there and waved me over to a spot in the back of the place. There was a window framed right into the floor that looked down on a roiling cataract twenty feet below. It was mesmerizing. After an eye-full of river, I wandered through the place, taking note of all the locally made products, from wine to cheese to potato chips. And everyone, front to back, was as friendly as a beloved aunt or uncle.

When we returned to the car, replete with sandwiches, locally made soda pop, and fresh-baked cookies, Krakow began to squawk his chicken laugh.

---

* Allan Bloom, in *The Closing of the American Mind*, writes, "The real community of man, in the midst of all the self-contradictory simulacra of community, is the community of those who seek the truth, of the potential knowers, that is, in principle, of all men to the extent they desire to know. But in fact this includes only a few . . ."

"Boc boc boc . . . that old guy I was talking to, sitting next to the deli counter, did you smell him?"

"Smell him?"

"He reeked of cow manure. He was ripe. Imagine sitting around socializing and smelling like cow shit? Because he's proud of how he smells. That's the smell of the earth. That's the smell of his land and his life and his product. It represents him, and he represents it." He began to chuckle again. "Boc boc boc."

As we drove, I was amazed at how few signs there were. It didn't take us long to get lost again. Fifteen minutes later we stopped in front of another general store to ask directions. This time, however, we didn't need to go in: a young woman was sweeping the steps out in front of the place.

I asked, "Is this the town of Danby?"

"Well, this is actually Danby Four Corners," she said.

"I'm looking for the Pearl S. Buck house in Danby. Do you happen to know where that is?"

"Yes, that's down in Danby Center. Just follow this road, and when you come down the steep hill, her house is the big white one on the right, across from the town hall. You can't miss it."

We missed it. We pulled into the tiny hamlet of Danby with its dozen homes and parked right in front of the village crazy. He stood out on the porch of a large abandoned home listlessly talking to himself.

"My mother died last week. They want to put me up in a home. I ain't going, I told them . . ." I heard him repeating to himself as I got out of the car.

Krakow was already fifty paces down the road before I could retrieve my backpack from the car's trunk. When I got to him with my camera at the ready and my backpack stocked with baggies, he was shaking his head.

"This isn't it."

"But the plaque with Pearl S. Buck's name on it is right in front of this white house," I puffed, as I pulled up alongside of him and aimed my camera at the marker and the house.

"That's not white; it's beige. And it's a small house, not a big one. And look, no town hall across the street."

He had a point, but the marker next to the house still made me think he was mistaken. I was standing there scratching my head and looking at the little beige house when Krakow and the village crazy suddenly marched in front of me and around the bend at the intersection. Quite a pair, those two. I couldn't see them, but I could hear them.

"That's it. That one," the crazy man shouted, and came bounding past me.

I jogged around the corner after Krakow. A large, white, decrepit, and abandoned A-frame house, with second- and third-floor front porches, stared somberly down at me. There was an open window just below the peak of the roof and a person standing in the window holding a piece of paper. At ground level, Krakow, his arms pumping and his legs churning with great vigor, had already advanced into the backyard.

As I began to walk slowly toward the house, something odd happened. The closer I got, the farther back the person in the open window seemed to recede, and suddenly, as I stood directly below the second-floor porch looking up, the open window had turned into a closed window, and the person with the piece of paper had vanished from sight.

"Look at the waterfall!" I heard Krakow squawk from behind the house.

I had goose bumps all over. Everything felt strange and uneven and off balance. The house itself looked as if it were on a slant. The rain was coming down again now, and the sound of rushing water was all around. There was no one in sight. The entire town seemed abandoned. I stood there trying to get my bearings. I just couldn't assimilate it, having been, the day before, down in Perkasie, at the great manor house at Green Hills Farm with all pomp and circumstance surrounding the International Gift Shop and the Nobel Prize and Pulitzer Prize and all that stuff in the house.

Then Krakow came bouncing around the corner, his face all lit up like a small boy's, full of wonder and discovery. "She had a flower garden in the back here. And look, right next to you, lilacs."

I turned to my left and saw, within arm's reach, a large lilac bush, its winter-weary branch ends encrusted with seeds, standing guard over the small front of the forlorn property. Like a medic in combat, I dropped to one knee, pulled my backpack off, and got to work.

Sometime later, I went around the back of the house and found Krakow sitting on a large, square, moss-covered rock, looking down over the drop-off, his boyish exuberance transformed into somber contemplation. I stood next to him and looked down over the slope. To our right and pointed in a straight line toward us, a whitewater stream came flouncing down out of the surrounding hills, swirling and swaying back and forth against rock walls worn smooth by the grinding water. Directly below us, a waterfall dropping about six feet down spat white foam into a circular pool. From there, the roiling mix boiled up, oozed forth, and turned black before widening, then agitating off into the distance.

"Someone put this rock here for her to sit on," Krakow proclaimed loudly, over the thunderous torrent all around. "She sat right here, smoked her cigarettes, and let the sound of the water take her where she wanted to go. And I think the mountains, the way they rise right straight up out of the ground, reminded her of China."

The words stopped the rain and straightened the ground under my feet. He was right. That giant of a woman who never delayed a moment in fixing the broken world around her had come to this slanted place next to the roaring stream, in the middle of nowhere, to at last return to where she most belonged.

In 1949, Pearl S. Buck discovered that adoption agencies across Asia considered mixed-race children unadoptable. Outraged, she established Welcome House, the first international interracial adoption agency. In 1964, to provide support for Amerasian children who were not eligible for adoption, she also established the Pearl S. Buck Foundation, which provides sponsorship funding for children in many Asian nations. Pearl S. Buck's legacy reaches far beyond the pages of her many literary works. In my eyes, she should have won two Nobel Prizes, one as a writer and one as a humanitarian.

At the end of her life, Pearl S. Buck wrote, "People asked me, 'Are you going back to China?' I reply, 'I belong to China, as a child, as a young girl, as a woman, until I die.'" China had been closed to Westerners when she died in 1973; nevertheless, Buck went back— to her house in Danby, Vermont.

Alongside the cascading water, this is a little piece of China.

**Sugar maple** *(Acer saccharum)*
**White pine** *(Pinus strobus)*

SUGAR MAPLE
SEEDS

## North Bennington, Vermont

Route 7 south from Danby to North Bennington is as picturesque a stretch of highway as I've ever traveled on in America. Smooth and wide, with breathtaking scenery most of the way, it runs from the Canadian border clear down to the Long Island Sound. And on a late morning during the week there is virtually no traffic.

Krakow interrupted my reverie. "Hey, look over there. White cedars!" He pointed to a group of trees at the edge of a wetland to our right.

"White cedars? How'd you spot them?"

"Arthur had a lot of them growing on his land when I worked for him."

"The tree farmer you worked for?"

"That's him. White cedars live forever."

"Not anymore they don't. They're endangered," I informed him.

"They are?"

"Yeah, their wetland habitat has been decimated by suburban sprawl, and deer have pretty much destroyed what's left of them. You didn't know that?"

"How would I know that? I'm just a man of the earth. I plant my garden; I raise my kid, care for my fruit trees, can my vegetables, deliver the mail." (Krakow is a part-time rural route mail carrier.)

"Then how do you follow what's going on?"

"I read the local newspaper and watch television."

"Ever heard of Bill McKibben?"

"Nope."

"You don't have Internet?"

"I'm not paying fifty dollars a month so my kid can be distracted like that. We've got a library in town if we need information."

"Do you know about the changing chemistry of the oceans?"

"I'm not going to worry about all the details of our dying planet. My time's too precious. We're only here for an instant."

"But don't you care about your daughter's future on this planet?"

"What can I do about it other than be self-sufficient? Towns, cities, states, entire nations are in debt and living beyond their means. Meanwhile, a billion and a half Chinese are blindly following our lead and burning up mountains of coal so they can live like us. We're killing ourselves. I don't need to read about it to know we're doomed. Weather's changed completely from when I was a kid. Winters are warmer and spring comes much sooner. In a hundred years there won't be a winter, let alone food or water enough for us all. Maybe if we're lucky, an asteroid will come along and put us out of our misery, and then we can start all over again. Boc boc boc." He began squawking hysterically, as if he had just watched a small boy mistake a thistle for a dandelion.

I was stunned. All my anxiety through the years of trying to keep abreast of what was going on in the realm of politics, science, literature, education, music, and the environment, and here was the very person who had introduced me to the examined life, admitting that he did not concern himself with present-day issues.

We drove along in silence for a long time. He could see I was nonplussed, so he didn't interrupt my reflections. But then he said, "Look, I know that you're worried about the future for your daughters, and that you have to do something to help out. That's why you're writing this book."

NORTH BENNINGTON is an uber-quaint New England village, with the requisite red brick library, mansard-roofed train depot, and Greek-columned company store. The last, known today as Powers Market, is quite famous throughout the region. It is also where writer Shirley Jackson once did her grocery shopping, and where we stopped and ate our lunch.

Parking directly in front of the store, we sat and watched through the windshield the well-heeled citizenry enter and exit Powers Market. Sassy, confident women from the surrounding neighborhoods and some most likely on vacation from the high-fashion scene of Fifth Avenue, bounded into the place in their designer espadrilles and Polo jeans. Preppie-looking guys, too, casually clad in LLBean pullovers and khaki pants, sauntered along, pretentiously unshaven, looking like they were fresh from a GQ photo shoot. Krakow and I sat there giggling and eating and feeling downright outlandish, gorging on our salami-and-cheese subs.

Of all the many authors on my list, Shirley Jackson was the only one whose previous address I could not find no matter how many different word combinations I entered into my Google search. I confessed this to Krakow just as we were entering the John G. McCullough Free Library, directly across the road from Powers Market. He looked concerned. But there was no reason to be.

"Hi, I'm doing research on Shirley Jackson," I said, addressing the librarian on duty.

"Well, you've come to the right place. The terra cotta cat on top of the bookshelf behind you was a present from Miss Jackson to the library." I turned and looked. "And she lived right here in town for many years. The first house she lived in was the Greek Revival house around the corner, on Prospect Street. The house is the second on the left as you go up Prospect Hill. It looks very much the same as when the Hyman family lived there in the late 1940s and early 1950s. The family later moved to Main Street, two houses up from the post office, just over the railroad tracks to the left as you leave the library."

"That was easy." I smiled. She smiled.

Before we left, the librarian insisted that I take away two locally made CDs about Jackson, both of which featured reminiscences of her life in North Bennington as told by the people of the village who knew her back when. I learned from one of the CDs that every morning when she woke up, Shirley Jackson immediately typed up her dreams on a typewriter she kept next to her bed.

As we strolled around the corner to the Greek Revival house on Prospect, I told Krakow what little I knew about Shirley Jackson.

"She was born in San Francisco, but her family moved to Rochester, New York, where she grew up and went to school. You ever read 'The Lottery'?" I asked him, referring to Jackson's most famous work. He shook his head. "It's brilliant. It totally blew people away when it was first published in *The New Yorker* in 1948. It's so *Twilight Zone*. I won't ruin it for you. I have a copy in the car. You can read it later; it's only five pages long. But people freaked out, and a lot of stupid people thought it was a true story. Anyway, the thing I really love about her life is that she was persona non grata at the university. She was kicked out of the University of Rochester as an undergraduate; then she transferred to Syracuse University, where she eventually graduated. She and her future husband, Stanley Hyman, founded a campus humor magazine and later a literary magazine, and together they wrote scathing editorials and criticisms of the university's administration, until they were both booted out. Syracuse would not even recognize her literary contributions until she was on her deathbed in 1965—talk about a Confederacy of Dunces. I think they lived most of their married life here in North Bennington, from about 1940 until she died. The husband was a professor at Bennington College. Both of them were big smokers and drinkers, and she suffered from all sorts of physical and mental health issues, and likely died from an overdose of prescription drugs at age forty-eight."

In the time it took me to tell Jackson's story, we had arrived at her house. You can't miss it. Four giant Doric columns mark the domicile. We stood in the middle of the sidewalk, just off the driveway, taking it all in. There were three ancient maples at least a hundred years old in the small front yard. Krakow, without the slightest hesitation, trod right across to the biggest of the maples and began searching for seeds. I immediately called him back over, and just as I was about to deliver instructions on the protocol for seed gathering at lived-in houses, a car pulled into the driveway.

A woman got out of the car with a bag of groceries and didn't even look in our direction, though we were practically standing in her yard. As she headed toward the house, I jogged over to her. Smiling and fidgeting with my little digital camera looped around my wrist, I introduced myself and told her what we were up to.

She nodded agreeably. "Oh, sure. Go ahead, help yourselves. I wish my husband were home. He'd help collect the seeds, but he's out doing errands right now. He's a writer, too."

"This is a writer's house, I guess" was my weak comeback.

That was all there was to it, and she disappeared inside.

Gathering sugar maple seeds from an old tree is complicated when there is a Norway maple tree nearby. Norway maples are an invasive species, now banned in New Hampshire and Massachusetts. They will quickly dominate any area because of the great quantity of seeds they produce. That propagule pressure again. I would venture to guess that a Norway maple's seed output is five to one versus that of a sugar maple. Nevertheless, the seeds are easy to tell apart. Whereas sugar maple seeds turn sallow and feathery looking, with a long, pointy seed sac and elliptical dragonfly wing, Norway maple seeds are square at the snout and turn brownish red, with the wing end more circular in shape. It was a little bit of work and a lot of eyestrain to find the less numerous sugar maple seeds, but with persistence, we came away with enough to satisfy our need.

Content, we stood out on the sidewalk, looking back at the house and the yard and trying to visualize Shirley Jackson, author of horror classics, writing her off-center stories in that venue. It seemed to fit.

We then walked back to the car, opting for no particular reason to drive the few hundred yards or so to the next Shirley Jackson home. Like the Greek Revival house on Prospect Street, the second one, on Main Street near the post office, was large, eccentric, and prepossessing. An old rusty gate, a waist-high line of hedges, and a huge front porch greeted all who entered the yard, no doubt just as they greeted Jackson and her family when they lived there.

There is squiggly trim around the roofline, hand-blown window glass in every pane, and old-time wooden clapboard siding painted mauve. The color fit the bill for a house that once sheltered such an unusual author. In the back of the house was a huge barn, taller than the house but painted the same weird mauve color. It, too, had the squiggly roof trim and hand-blown windows.

On one side of the house were three ancient sugar maples, just like the ones at the Prospect Street house. However, when we rang the doorbell and spoke to the present owner, she insisted that her husband had planted all of the trees forty years before. I had to argue with her a bit, explaining that the trees we were looking at were far older than forty years, and after a little more insisting, she began to agree with me that, yes, those three trees had probably been there before they moved in, *but only those three.*

"They were bookish people," she said of Jackson and her husband. "They didn't get out much in the yard. They had over forty thousand volumes in this house when we bought it."

(I didn't tell the woman that I had found documents putting that figure at more than one hundred thousand.)

"They said that when he needed a book, Stanley [Hyman, Jackson's husband] would send a student over from the college with instructions where to find a certain book, on which shelf, in which room, and what color the book's jacket was. He knew where they all were." She paused, reflecting. "No, they didn't spend much time out in the yard. It was quite a mess when we moved in. I'd have my husband talk to you about the trees, but he isn't feeling well."

The woman looked like a character out of a Shirley Jackson novel. She was very tall, extremely light complexioned, and had an extreme air of sophistication—as if she had been a Shakespearean actress in her younger days, or an etiquette instructor at a girl's boarding school. She wore a wide-rimmed bonnet and a gardener's jumpsuit. She was clearly getting ready to work in her flower garden at the back of the house. In fact, a young woman had just arrived to assist her.

"Yes, yes, collect your seeds," she said. "Go ahead, I don't mind."

So we did. Because there were no Norway maples nearby, we had no problem finding what we needed. Then Krakow, being Krakow, walked around the back of the house and, even though the owner was there working on her rosebushes, he interrupted her, asking about the gargantuan butternut tree growing in the middle of the backyard.

He took a step toward it. "I've never seen one so big," he said, implying that it was probably old enough to have been alive when Shirley Jackson was living in the house.

"Oh, don't bother about that one," she said, holding her snippers in front of her like a delicate cocktail fork, but also as a sure warning sign to my unique friend not to advance any farther. "There just aren't any other trees like it in the area, so it doesn't get pollinated, and therefore it never puts forth seeds."

Krakow shielded his eyes from the sun and looked long and hard at the tree.

Once we were back in the car, he emitted a low growl, "Mmmmrrrrr," expressing his suspicions.

"I know what you're thinking," I said. "Maybe there aren't any other trees like it in the area and it doesn't get pollinated. Or maybe she just didn't want us plodding around in her flower garden."

One thing I knew for sure: had it been his book we were in town researching, we would have camped out in the car until nightfall and then slipped onto the property for some guerrilla seed stealing. But I wanted to get on the road. I turned around and dug the copy of Shirley Jackson's short stories out of a pile of stuff in the backseat and handed it to him.

"Here, read 'The Lottery.' It's the last story in the collection. In fact, why don't you read it out loud to me."

Then I did a U-turn in the middle of Main Street and headed west for New Hampshire.

## Willa Cather

**White pine** (*Pinus strobus*)
**Spruce** (*Picea*)

WHITE SPRUCE CONE

### Jaffrey, New Hampshire

Even though Krakow's nickname suggests he's Polish, he's not. He's Bohemian. As were both of his parents, long deceased. I was able to meet them before they died, and whenever I recall them I hear a baroque suite played in a minor key in my head. They had thick accents, homespun talents, and Old World sensibilities—much like the Bohemian families featured in Willa Cather's magnum opus *My Ántonia*.

Krakow himself is a male version of the book's main character, the indomitable Ántonia, who embodies not only the bold pioneer spirit but also the harsh and unyielding frontier landscape itself. In fact, as I rode along next to him in the car, I couldn't help but feel a little bit like Jim Burden, the book's narrator. Burden, a city-slicker lawyer who grew up on the plains, becomes nostalgic for his days on his grandparents' Nebraska farm, and thus pens the memories of his childhood home and his beloved friend Ántonia.

As a boy, Krakow grew up in Puerto Rico. The beautiful descriptions he used to recount of the lush land of his youth still waft through my thoughts like the intoxicating odor of a sizzling steak. He spent his childhood diving into turquoise lagoons and drinking bubblegum-flavored soda pop and climbing tall coconut trees with his barefoot, brown-skinned, Spanish-speaking friends. Later he went to college, first at Paul Smith's, in the Adirondacks, where he got a two-year degree in hotel and restaurant management, then to Boston College, where he worked full time in the morning as a cook in a dormitory kitchen and, in the afternoon and evening, studied full time in pursuit of a degree in business management. After he graduated college, his plan was to get a job at a hotel in San Juan, but he ended up working for a land baron, as he called him, a recluse who owned ten thousand acres along the Adirondack Mountains, mostly pine and hemlock forest. He married his hometown sweetheart and moved to Manhattan, where he worked for more than twenty years managing a famous restaurant on Central Park South. When his daughter was born, he quit city life and moved back upstate, taking a job at a well-known resort near Lake George, from which he had recently been canned. But his life is rather mundane in comparison with his father's.

Born just after World War I in Czechoslovakia, Krakow's father lived and worked as a young man in Germany as a jack-of-all-trades. When the Second World War came, Krakow's father escaped to America to avoid inscription into the German army. In America he met a Bohemian woman, married her, and had three children with her. But they divorced, and he married her sister, Krakow's mother, with whom he had five more children. After all of the children had grown up and left the nest, Krakow's mother, an eminently practical woman, put her family care skills to remunerative use by providing room and board to developmentally disabled adults who were wards of the state. The first time I met Krakow's mother, in fact, she was serving up Thanksgiving dinner to her merry band of boarders, three young dames. They smiled beatifically while mashing and spooning platefuls of homemade chicken potpie, hot out of the oven, into their toothless maws.*

So it was that fate had brought us, some thirty years later, to the Jack Daniels Motor Lodge in Peterborough, New Hampshire, sitting on top of our respective queen-size beds that Saturday morning while I read aloud for him the unforgettable story of Peter and Pavel and the wolves from My Ántonia.

After the story and some breakfast, we headed out to find the Shattuck Inn in Jaffrey Center, where Willa Cather wrote My Ántonia and where she is buried.†

---

* That sublime table scene was frozen in still life into my brain, and years later, when my wife and I were in dire need of extra income, I remembered Krakow's mother, promptly inquired about a local program, and just like that, for the next five years, we were family care providers for a wonderfully varied cast of developmentally disabled adults who lived with us in our home in Oswego. Krakow's mother must have been a human dynamo to care for three people at the same time, because my wife and I tried and failed miserably to care for two adults at once. We lasted about a month before throwing in the towel and retreating to one single charge.

† I won't ruin one of the greatest stories in literary history by telling what happens, but I will say that as a result of Peter and Pavel's actions, even their mothers couldn't look at them anymore, which is why they moved from Bohemia to the Great Plains.

THE SHATTUCK INN, an Adirondack-style lodge, was an abandoned building. It stood at the apex of a hill overlooking fairways and greens. Nary a tree within a hundred yards of it. We parked in the large dirt driveway and climbed up onto the long front porch. Looking in the windows, we couldn't figure out if they were fixing the place up or getting ready to tear it down. It didn't look that old and in such disrepair to need to be torn down, so I figured they were fixing the place up. I had my Google printout in hand and began reading aloud how Willa Cather used to live up on the third floor at the back of the place with her lover, Edith Lewis, where they had majestic views of Mount Monadnock from three corner windows.

We trudged around to the back, but because of the rain, we couldn't see the mountain off in the distance; just the woods, fairways, and greens. We returned to the front and looked around like lighthouse beams, searching for trees. Krakow became interested in two large but odd-shaped spruces down in front of the parking area. We marched over to them.

"These aren't Norway spruces," he averred. "These are something else. And notice how they line up. There used to be a dozen of them." He made a motion with his cocked arm, indicating that the spaces between them were evidence that there had once been a row of spruces.

"Well, they're definitely old," I said.

Over the next few minutes, we managed to find a half-dozen pinecones, but the likelihood of their containing viable seeds was slim to none.

Another fifty yards back down the road, away from the inn and toward the caddy shack, we spotted an old locust tree, but after closer examination we failed to find even one seedpod. We slowly wandered around toward the front of the inn and stood in the same spot as before, searching and searching, and soon we became aware of a triangular patch of woods to the north, in the opposite direction of the spruces, where the road forked about a hundred fifty yards down the road. It was full of towering white pines.

"You know, when you initially arrive at a site, you think there's nothing there, but after spending a little time looking around, trees begin to appear," Krakow said.

"You noticed that, too?" I smiled.

The white pines were impressive. All well over a hundred feet tall and straight as telephone posts but three times taller. I took a snapshot through a line of pines, with the inn in the background.

"You can see why the early settlers cut all the white pines down and sold them to shipbuilders to use as masts," Krakow squawked.

We scoured the land for pinecones, but it just wasn't in the cards. Krakow came over to me at one point with a tiny white pine seedling pinched between his thumb and forefinger.

"This is what's available," he said.

We gleaned the ground for the tiniest saplings we could find and put them in a baggy next to my backpack, their little bristles sticking out of the open bag. Suddenly, a dog appeared, wagging its tail and sniffing around us excitedly. Then another arrived, a bigger one, but it kept its distance. A few moments later a woman's voice broke the silence.

"May I help you?"

Krakow must have spotted her before she spoke, and he was advancing toward her. I quickly put the baggy with the seedlings into my backpack, lifted it onto my back, turned and walked toward the woman.

" . . . private property." I heard her saying to Krakow in a scolding tone as I drew near. She was a short, older woman and her face was completely enclosed by the hood of an army-green raincoat.

Then her tall, professorial husband arrived on the scene in a matching raincoat, his Scandinavian complexion contrasting egregiously with the dark green jacket. He was practically marching.

"Can I ask you gentlemen what you're doing?" His tone was authoritative.

"We're doing research on Willa Cather and we noticed the old trees here," I sputtered, stepping over a little stone wall as one of the dogs sniffed at my heels. I hopped down onto the dirt road and stood next to Krakow, who was facing them directly, his hands on his hips.

The mere mention of Willa Cather's name changed the dynamic completely.

"Oh, Willa Cather!" the woman tittered and tilted her head back.

"She lived at the inn, you know," the husband said didactically. "Of course, the inn's not there anymore."

"What do you mean?" I didn't follow.

"What's there now is the annex. The original Shattuck Inn was torn down." The dogs were moseying on ahead of us, anticipating our eventual direction, so we all started to follow them back toward the annex.

"Did you notice the big dirt parking lot?" the man asked.

"That's where we parked," I replied.

"Well, that's where it stood," he informed me.

"Ahh, so that's why those two big spruces are planted there," Krakow piped up loudly. He asked if they remembered more spruces being there, and they didn't recall, but they hadn't lived there long enough to remember.

Within a few minutes, we were standing in front of the annex making small talk. The woman revealed to us that the main reason the couple had moved to Jaffrey in their retirement was because of her fondness for Willa Cather's works. Then she began to tell us some of the history of the author's life in Jaffrey.

"She first came to Jaffrey in 1917 and said it was her favorite place to write. The first year she was here, she actually lived in a tent on a friend's farm not too far from the inn. She wrote most of *My Ántonia* inside that tent, if you can imagine. But from then on, whenever she returned to Jaffrey, and she only came here in the summer, she would stay at the Shattuck Inn. Before she died in 1947, she asked to be buried in the Old Burying Ground behind the Meetinghouse. Her companion of many years, Edith Lewis, helped make the arrangements. Have you visited her grave site yet?" the woman asked.

"No, not yet," I answered.

"Well, it's right up that road to the left," She pointed it out to us. Squinting, I could just barely see it. "If you go up that road, you'll come right into Jaffrey Center and the old Meetinghouse. The graveyard is there behind it. She's buried near the edge of the cemetery, right in the corner under the trees," the woman directed.

A car appeared on the road, moving ever so slowly, before it finally pulled into the driveway and parked next to our car.

"Oh, there they are." The couple waved. "Well, nice meeting you. We're meeting our friends for a walk," the woman said happily.

A couple, also in matching rain gear and also with two dogs, disembarked ever so slowly from their car. Krakow and I scampered across the rain-slick slope and down to our vehicle, trying, unsuccessfully, to avoid being sniffed at by two more canine noses.

THE GUY AT THE GAS STATION was right: only old buildings and old people, even dead people, can be found in Jaffrey Center. It looked like something make-believe, like a movie set created specifically for filming Colonial American scenes. The old wooden Meetinghouse, with its toylike white spire, stood at the corner of a perfect square, around which stood a handful of white, wooden, museum-piece houses.

Krakow wasn't interested in architecture; he had already broached the graveyard. I quickly gathered my backpack and camera and scurried over to the cemetery, entering the stone-studded grounds through a stockyard-like gate. By the time I entered, he'd found Cather's headstone. It was at the very far left corner, right at the angle of an old stone wall and under a group of enormous white pines and ancient sugar maples.

Directly beside Cather's headstone was a small square slab marking the resting place of her longtime companion, Edith Lewis.

"On a clear day I'll bet there's a view of the mountain," Krakow said, motioning toward the north. "She definitely chose this very spot before she died."

"You know, I made a vow not to collect seeds at grave sites, but I have a feeling this place is different. I read that she and Edith Lewis, the summer before My Ántonia came out, would go into the woods near the Shattuck Inn, sit on rocks, and read the manuscript. Well, look at all the rocks there." I pointed at the stone wall. "I have a hunch that the two of them came right here, sat on the wall, and read."

We stepped over the stone wall and, as before, proceeded to gather what tiny white pine saplings we could find. We could not, however, find even one maple seed, though we looked and looked.

Just before we left the spot, the sun broke through the clouds. The dazzle of sudden sunlight made the trees sparkle and broke loose, in my memory, a passage from *My Ántonia* about hollyhocks and Bohemians. I had a copy of the book in my backpack and started leafing through the pages.

"Here it is, in the last chapter." I read: "'Through July,' Ántonia said, 'the house was buried in them [hollyhocks]; the Bohemians, I remembered, always planted hollyhocks.'"

"She wrote that? Wow." Krakow beamed. "My mother always had hollyhocks around the house," he added wistfully. "And my Uncle Earl. My sisters, too, have them. I have them!" It was obvious that this fact had never before occurred to him. "Does she say anything about pussy willows?"

"I don't think so."

"I know in the Old Country they used pussy willow branches instead of palm fronds for Palm Sunday because they couldn't grow palms in that climate. My mother always had lots and lots of pussy willows around the house. She'd take meticulous care of them, too."

I found another passage and began reading again: "... As we walked through the apple orchard, grown up in tall bluegrass, Ántonia kept stopping to tell me about one tree and another. 'I love them as if they were people,' she said, rubbing her hand over the bark. 'We planted every one, and used to carry water for them, too ...'"

I stopped reading suddenly and looked at him with a smile. "You're *my* Ántonia!"

His face was lit up like a Christmas tree, as we sat together, quietly, in the presence of great stones and words and trees, cherishing this friend-drenched moment.

## Back Home

MY WIFE HAD BEEN GOING ALONG with this whole thing without as much as a tongue click, but one day she hit the breaking point as she watched me watering one of the ubiquitous saplings on the windowsill in our bedroom.

"Are you ever actually going to plant your little friends outdoors?"

"Soon as I find someone to help me out," I responded, sounding as if such an event were imminent.

She looked at me as if I had trees growing out of my ears. "You know, sometimes they find reclusive people dead in their homes surrounded by five-year-old newspapers they couldn't throw away and the desiccated bodies of their pet cats. I can picture you dead on the floor with tree roots entwined around your decomposing cadaver and branches growing out of your skull's eye sockets." And at that, she chuckled and strode out of the room.

Her comment brought to mind another vision: me as Mickey

the Magician in *Fantasia*, trying to keep it all in synch. Anyway, that episode put a fire under my butt to find someone who would be willing to help me grow my small forest of seeds and saplings.

However, not before I had to leave once again on another seed-gathering expedition.

# Part four

The forests are disappearing, the rivers are running dry, the game is exterminated, the climate is spoiled, and the earth becomes poorer and uglier every day . . . When I plant a little birch tree and then see it budding into young green and swaying in the wind, my heart swells with pride . . .

—ANTON CHEKHOV, UNCLE VANYA

# Flannery O'Connor, Carson McCullers, Ancient Creek Indians, and F. Scott and Zelda Fitzgerald

**Magnolia, a.k.a. cucumber tree** (*Magnolia acuminata*)
**Pecan** (*Carya illinoensis*)
**Hackberry** (*Celtis occidentalis*)

HACKBERRY

MY EDITOR PUT ME IN TOUCH with an old friend of his from Atlanta, Wallace. Over the course of a few months, via e-mails and phone conversations, he and I hashed out a plan to visit the homes of some of the South's most famous writers. It would be a fast and furious trip, just three days all told. He would be my tour guide.

On a Friday morning in mid-May, I was sitting out in front of my hotel near the Atlanta airport reading a copy of William Bartram's

*Travels and Other Writings,*\* with my luggage at the ready, when Wallace pulled up. He hopped out of the car and bounded over to me, offering his hand. Verging on gray and an inch taller than I am at five eleven, he is a square-shouldered, straight-backed, rosy-cheeked, wide-eyed Southern gentleman with an avuncular mien. One look into his eyes and I knew he was as boyishly enthused about our pending adventure as I was.

It took me no time to get to know Wallace, for he wears his heart and soul on his sleeve. Born and raised in Montgomery, Alabama, Wallace is a maniacally caring individual, possessed of that rarest of human qualities: humility. Wallace embodies the quintessence of Southern gentility. He is never vulgar; he is loquacious, enthusiastic, amiable to a fault; and when he speaks, he always speaks in full and complete sentences (a real joy in this sound-bite day and age), crossing his *t*'s and dotting his *i*'s, so to speak, sounding a lot like a radio announcer for a classical music station.

## Milledgeville, Georgia

With Wallace at the wheel and me kneeling, instead of sitting, in the backseat (back trouble), we headed south for Milledgeville, Georgia, home of Flannery O'Connor and her famous abode, Andalusia. The hour-and-a-half drive along two-lane country roads was a concen-

---

\* "Artist, writer, botanist, gardener, naturalist, pioneering ethnographer, and intrepid wilderness explorer, William Bartram was the first American to devote his life to the study and appreciation of the environment. The most important nature writer before Thoreau and a nature artist who rivals John James Audubon, Bartram traveled through the southern American forests and swamps in the 1770s." From the back jacket of *Travels and Other Writings* by William Bartram; Thomas P. Slaughter, editor; The Library of America, New York, 1996.

trated lesson in natural history. Even at sixty miles an hour, Wallace was able to point out just about every species of tree and flowering plant that appeared in the windshield, particularly mimosas and the two types of vultures that forever flew into our ken. I had a case of wryneck within a few minutes. Then, out of the blue, he turned his head back toward me, lowered his voice, and began to speak in a reverential tone before turning back again to face the road:

"You know, I've been thinking about the work you're doing here, giving back life in the form of trees since so many gave theirs to give us the writers' words on the printed page. We must never underestimate the magnitude of our forests and trees. They have given us warming, shelter, the very air we breathe, and the ability to read the thoughts and ideas of very gifted individuals, and yet we take these magnificent gifts of nature for granted. I will be very interested to hear what you have to say in this book. The stately old trees of our past are like the lost cathedrals of Europe after World War Two. Much is lost and too few are nurturing their return. "

As I processed Wallace's epiphanous, deep, measured statement, I managed to squeak out a paltry "Uh-huh."

A CATHOLIC IN A PROTESTANT LAND, O'Connor penned tales that borrowed on her upbringing and won over critics. She produced two novels and thirty-two short stories. Unfortunately, no one knows what more she could have produced, as she suffered horribly from lupus and died young, at age thirty-nine. As a child, she taught a chicken to walk backward; a film was made of it and was shown all over the country, bringing her fame at an early age.* I

---

* Of the experience of appearing in the film *Little Mary O'Connor,* O'Connor

maintain that it was that backward-walking chicken that provides the reader with a key to her themes.

Flannery O'Connor's short story "A Good Man Is Hard to Find" is to the Southern Gothic genre what Lou Reed's "Walk on the Wild Side" is to rock 'n' roll. In it, a family driving to Florida on vacation turns off the paved highway and onto a bumpy dirt road to investigate an old plantation the grandmother visited in her youth. The grandmother's cat suddenly jumps out of its basket, upsetting the driver and causing him to lose control of the car, which rolls into a ditch. Soon afterward, three misfits happen upon the scene and stop to help. But they don't help; they cold-bloodedly murder the family. The dialogue is full of ticklish Southern expressions, such as "Don't see no sun but don't see no cloud neither" and "I pre-chate that, lady" and "Seen a man burnt alive oncet." This maca-bre little story resonates through so many famous Southern writers' works, from Truman Capote's In Cold Blood to James Dickey's Deliv-erance. There is something so god-awful twisted about O'Connor's stories that defy any tortured intellectual commentary and make them truly astonishing.

The sun was high and the air-conditioning was cranking as we turned off the paved highway and onto the dirt road leading into Andalusia. But luck was not on our side. Wallace jammed on the brakes just a couple of feet from the closed iron gate. No Trespassing signs were posted every which way. I slowly got out while he made a phone call. I peered over a barbed-wire fence at a large hayfield that ran off into the woods a thousand yards away. There were trees out

said, "When I was six I had a chicken that walked backward and was in the Pathé News. I was in it too with the chicken. I was just there to assist the chicken but it was the high point in my life. Everything since has been anti-climax."

there, hardwoods mostly, but they were completely out of context. I needed to see the house where O'Connor had lived, the land on which she'd walked, and especially those chicken coops! Wallace's phone call produced no results. Ever the optimist, he assured me we'd be back.

I knew going into this game that not all my visits would bear fruit. It wasn't that I was crossing names off a list in ink, so I hoped I could get back here later in the year and find what I had come for, because Flannery O'Connor is one of the all-time best. I always loved the way she ended that story, after the Misfit shot the grandmother: "'She would of been a good woman,' The Misfit said, 'if it had been somebody there to shoot her every minute of her life.'"

## Columbus, Georgia

We headed for Columbus, Georgia, and the home of Carson Mc-Cullers. As we motored along the state road, Wallace edified me with a history of Columbus, describing its prominence before the Civil War as a river port that supplied the international markets with cotton, and how it was the last stop on the Federal Road before the western wilderness began. He talked about nearby Fort Benning, home to the U.S Army Infantry, the parachuting school, and its one hundred thousand military personnel and family population.

Unlike Andalusia, McCullers's home was as accessible as a park bench. A classic bungalow-style structure, impeccably maintained and located in an upper-middle-class neighborhood close to downtown Columbus, the Smith-McCullers House has a large bronze plaque out front explaining its place in literary history. There was no information about tours or hours of operation, however. Wallace,

forever on the move, jumped out of the car and raced up to the front
door, his long Bermuda shorts held high and cinched tight with
a thick leather belt. He cavalierly rang the doorbell. No one answered, so he proceeded to investigate the grounds, walking around
to the back of the house with his neighborly gait.

It was hot and the sun was blasting down on the backs of our
necks. I scanned the area for trees. There were three towering oaks,
one across the street, one behind the house, and one to the north,
but all three stood a distance from the house. However, standing
like a two-story, pyramidal Christmas tree alongside the house was
a magnificent magnolia. (What a knockout!) And splattered all
over the ground were its spent flowers, like unhidden Easter eggs
waiting to be snatched up. (What I didn't know at the time was that
the seeds inside the husks had long since dissolved.)

Magnolias are prehistoric-looking trees. Their leaves, fat and
hearty as shoe leather, seem to bulge with extra dark green chlo-
rophyll. And as I collected the dried cones, also called cucumbers
because of their size and conical shape, I began to think about the
abiding remnant I had recently become aware of. It was growing
ever more obvious to me that during each visit to collect seeds at
the homes of these national treasures, I was receiving a subtle but
clear message communicated by the authors from the beyond. For
example, it was no simple case of bad luck that we had been prohib-
ited from entering Flannery O'Connor's Andalusia. The locked gate
and the No Trespassing signs emphatically signaled that O'Connor
does not suffer nosey over-readers gladly. Her stories shouldn't be
read for hidden allegories or abstruse allusions, with esoteric mo-
tifs like some kind of literary lagniappe. And for that matter, neither should the fiction of Carson McCullers. But McCullers, unlike
O'Connor, would never discourage her readers from taking away

anything their hearts desired, so it was no surprise that her majestic magnolia would be standing there to greet us without obstruction.

Life itself is McCullers's message, case in point being "The Jockey," as perfect a short story as has ever been written (along with Gogol's "The Overcoat"). It is a tale right out of commedia dell'arte, depicting the interaction between an overwrought jockey and those invidious characters who make their living off the business of horse racing. The picture she paints is so vivid and so realistic that it takes your breath away. To my mind, Carson McCullers is hands down the best damn short story writer America has ever produced.

Wallace came scampering from around the house with a frightened look on his face: "Don't go back there. I peered in one of the windows and I saw someone sleeping on a bed." I could tell he felt bad. "Weird how they have the marker out front but no other information."

"It is a bit askew," I agreed, borrowing a line from *Seinfeld*.

Wallace kept on talking. "You know, Bartram was the first person to send magnolia seeds back to England, and from then on they became kind of the prized specimen of the New World, a symbol of beauty and bounty."

We stood together on the front lawn looking up at the beautiful tree, shielding our eyes from the blazing sun overhead. I had him take a picture of me beside the magnolia, before I put a half dozen of the dried-out husks in a Ziploc bag and carried them back to the car.

## Tallassee, Alabama

We headed west again, talking all the way. In that conversation I discovered that Wallace and I share the same fantasy: to be transported back in time to America prior to 1492. For us, the vision of this land of our birth prior to industrialization is the most thrilling of all possible prospects. And within that vision, the most inspiring of all is the uncut forests. Both of us would trade all that we own to walk in that world for just one day.

Wallace has a theory.

Two miles south of the city of Tallassee, Alabama, and along the Tallapoosa River, directly below the dramatic Tallassee Falls, rendered silent now by the hydroelectric dams built on top of them, we stood next to a large field. Wallace pointed to the tree line at the eastern end of the cultivated land, about a mile away, and told me that beyond the trees lay an unusual oxbow—where a river meanders in a U shape around a point of land—of the Tallassee River. (He later showed me an aerial photograph of it. It looked like a Pinocchio nose with a dollop of cream on the end of it, jutting straight out above the squiggly lips and below the straight forehead of the north-to-south-flowing river.) In most cases a flood creates an oxbow, but rivers' circuitous routes usually straighten over a short period of geological time. This one hadn't.

According to Wallace: "This oxbow has been here for well over two hundred years. While I am not a geologist, I find it interesting that despite the dynamics of this river prior to the dams being built, the oxbow was never severed. Looking at satellite maps and historical maps, the course of this river and this oxbow in particular has not changed in all that time. Prior to the three dams being built, the estimated ten-mile stretch that approached this oxbow was one of the most spectacular displays of falls and rapids in the eastern U.S. And yet, this dramatic bend in the river still carries no name, to my knowledge, despite the history associated with it. Bartram spent a lot of time in the Indian village on the banks of this river bend. He gives detailed accounts of the magnificent size of this village named Tuckabatchee. This was the site of the largest Creek Indian village ever recorded by white men. The Native Americans inhabited this area for quite some time. Despite the strong currents that were created by the long, straight falls that approached this oxbow, it appears that the river never bisected the bend, shortening the course. I believe that the ancient Creeks somehow manipulated the land in order to maintain their village here."

I felt like I was listening to a brilliant historian in a Ken Burns documentary. "So how would you investigate a theory like that?"

"I don't know," he said breathily, looking at me with his arms crossed. "I don't know. But look back there and what do you see?"

I turned and looked across the state highway at three large trees. "Oaks."

"Exactly. Look at the trees over there. Not long ago, there were many magnificent oaks that had to be well over a hundred years old. This site is historic, but forgotten by most Alabamians. Some of those trees right over there may be the only witnesses to the once-great Creek village that stood here for millennia. I believe the Creeks manipulated the flora as well." His eyes were alive.

I got out the Bartram book and Wallace stood next to me and helped me find the passage about the area. Looking out toward the fields and trees, I read aloud. The town was named Coolome, and there was a large village on the very spot where we stood. He writes about the size of the houses and the quality of the water, but he waxes poetic about the trees: "Venerable spreading oaks . . . their enormous limbs loaded with *Tillandsia usneadscites* [Spanish moss] waving in the winds . . ." Wallace then directed me a few pages back in the book, to a section in the narrative where Bartram and company have camped for a week at a large village just a few days' travel from Coolome. With him pointing to the passage, I began to read aloud again.* According to Bartram, the Creeks who lived at that village knew nothing about the original inhabitants who had significantly manipulated the land.I did not gather acorns under the trees there. Those were for Wallace to collect.

We drove up the south-facing cuesta, a hill or ridge with a steep face on one side and a gentle slope on the other. From near the oxbow, where we stood reading Bartram, to the city of Tallassee is about two miles. Tallassee is located along a series of rocky cataracts that have been virtually obliterated by the hydroelectric dams. What a travesty. The erstwhile rocky falls were once a true natural wonder, but they have been dwarfed and rendered feckless. Fortunately, I could still see and hear the falls as they once looked and sounded through Wallace's magical mind's eye: the rocky shelves . . . water spitting and hissing violently . . . the air all around alive with ionized and iridescent particles . . . the trees along the river's edge lush and vast . . . the cascading waters roaring, echoing, singing.

---

* "One day the chief trader of Apalachucla obliged me with his company on a walk of about a mile and a half down the river, to view the ruins and site of the ancient Apalachucla: it had been situated on a peninsula formed by a doubling of the river, and indeed appears to have been a very famous capital by the artificial mounds or terraces, and a very populous settlement, from its extent and expansive old fields, stretching beyond the scope of the sight along the low grounds of the river. We viewed the mounds or terraces, on which formerly stood their town house or rotunda and square or areopagus, and a little behind these, on a level height or natural step, above the low grounds, is a vast artificial terrace or four square mound, now seven or eight feet higher than the common surface of the ground; in front of one square or side of this mound adjoins a very extensive oblong square yard or artificial level plain, sunk a little below the common surface, and surrounded with a bank or narrow terrace, formed with the earth thrown out of this yard at the time of its formation: the Creeks or present inhabitants have a tradition that this was the work of the ancients, many ages prior to their arrival and possessing this country."

"This is it, the end of the Appalachians, where the world's oldest mountains drain down into one last withering gasp before giving way to the flatlands and eventually the alluvial planes of the Gulf of Mexico," he said, without looking at me, as he waved his hand wistfully across the northern horizon, painting this sublime, geological ending.

As we cut through the downtown of Tallassee, back toward the highway and Montgomery, he admitted to me in a quiet, resigned voice, "Sometimes I think about moving here and opening a little bookstore with an upstairs office, and maybe writing a book, but . . ."

He stopped there. I didn't pursue it.

## Montgomery, Alabama

Next was Montgomery, capital city of Alabama and Wallace's hometown. I could feel him growing more and more tense as we drew nearer to the city of his birth. As we drove, I spied orchard after orchard of pecan trees running in rows on either side of the highway as far as the eye could see. Many of the orchard plantations looked well maintained, but others appeared old and abandoned. Wallace told me about the pecan orchards of his youth, playing in them and eating the nuts raw. Pecans are the only native nut tree cultivated in groves for its produce, like apples. Prior to the tree's domestication, the method for harvesting wild pecans was to go out in the forest and cut the tree down.

We exited the highway and proceeded through the upscale neighborhood of Cloverdale, directly to the F. Scott and Zelda Fitzgerald Museum on Felder Avenue. Francis Scott Key Fitzgerald, from St. Paul, Minnesota, met Zelda Sayre, a native of Montgomery, Alabama, while he was stationed at the nearby army base; I believe it was at a dance at a local country club. The couple married after he was discharged a year later. They lived for a year in the Felder Avenue house upon their return to America in 1931, after many tumultuous years in postwar Europe and shortly after Zelda's first breakdown. Fittingly, Fitzgerald wrote *Tender Is the Night* while living in the house. The story of Dick and Nicole Diver turns a mirror on the Fitzgeralds—his transcendent gifts, her festering madness, and the debauched and despoiled postwar society around them. It is my favorite Fitzgerald novel. Fitzgerald died at forty-four, his literary ambitions, combined with his delicate genius, proving far too magnificent for any mortal to support. Fortunately, we have his stories.

The Felder Avenue house is a classic aristocratic affair and reminded me of the kind of opulent mansions you find in posh sections of cities such as Buffalo and Pittsburgh, what with its brown clapboard siding, numerous chimney spires sticking out of a bold triangular roof, wide trim around the nine-over-nine windows, second-story verandas built under the eaves, and the solid red brickwork foundation, front stoop, and walkway all the way to the street. We didn't go inside. In fact, the museum was closed by the time we got there. To our surprise, the house is only part museum; the other part of the house is rental apartments. One of the tenants was just leaving as we pulled up. Gregarious Wallace greeted the young man as we stepped out of our vehicle.

While he schmoozed, I went right to work. My eyes were drawn immediately to one of the largest hackberry trees I'd ever seen. It was right along the driveway, its branches laden with dark green berries. Hackberry trees have the most distinctive, wart-ridden bark of any tree; they remind me of a witch's complexion: gray and full of corky warts and deep wrinkles. The leaves are interesting because they look like elm leaves, but the jagged teeth along the edges are ever so much finer and sharper than an elm's. They are shaped like Cleopatra eyes, oblong and tapering.

The wood of hackberries has never been used commercially because it's extremely soft and has a propensity to rot when exposed to the elements. What was unusual about the Scott and Zelda tree was that it was where it was: hackberries usually grow around streams and in river bottoms, preferring to have their feet wet. I concluded that the tree was older than the house itself, which had been built in 1901, and must have been there when Cloverdale was nothing more than a swampy meadow irrigated by rivulets. I picked up berries to my heart's content, mostly those that had fallen in the driveway.

Wallace soon joined me, and together we wandered around to the back of the house, where we both gawked in unison at a singular sight: the largest pecan tree either of us had ever seen. For me, that's not saying much—being from the North, I had seen precious few pecan trees—but Wallace grew up in the heart of pecan country. This monster soared a hundred feet into the air, with a massive canopy almost as broad as the tree was tall, and it appeared as healthy and vigorous as a doted-on nursery shrub one tenth its size. The trunk was never-ending, the first branches appearing a good sixty feet up. The tree was one of the most spectacular I had yet seen, similar in size and shape to the great tulip trees at Monticello and Mount Vernon I would later encounter. I recall reading about how Thomas Jefferson grew pecans at Monticello and sent some over to George Washington, who made a grove of them, calling them "Illinois nuts." (Some of those same trees were still alive as recently as twenty-five years ago.) *

* Donald Culross Peattie, *A Natural History of North American Trees*, New York: Houghton Mifflin, 2007, pp. 182–83.

I envisioned Fitzgerald taking a break from writing *Tender Is the Night*, walking over to the back window, and because of the tree's propinquity, following the soaring bole up, up, up with his eyes, from base to canopy, and lingering there in the spangled green cloud of foliage, with the silken azure vault peeking through from the beyond, until eventually, ineluctably, the swell of divine afflatus flooded his senses, compelling him back to his desk to write and write and write the story of his tragic downward spiral, though pining to be forever "loitering among the fallow rose bushes and the beds of damp sweet indistinguishable ferns."\*

Wallace bent his head up, a huge grin on his face. "Never knew pecans could grow this big. Never. Amazing."

I searched and searched the yard, in among the pachysandra, under the lilacs, around the tool shed, and beside the back steps, finding just a couple of frost-burned nuts that probably weren't viable. I would have gone on searching until dark had Wallace not pointed to the menacing sky above. No sooner did I look up than a bolt of lightning cleaved the air, followed by a nearly simultaneous explosion. As we ran for cover, the sky opened up. It wasn't a subtle sign at all. We jumped into the car and, before the next zap of lightning shook the welkin, Wallace had exited the grounds. I was satisfied with my hackberry seeds and the two pecans I'd collected.

IN THE MORNING, with a heavy heart, Wallace took me into downtown Montgomery. It was a Sunday, so all was quiet as we drove up the wide boulevard toward the State Capitol. There was very little traffic moving along the streets. While visiting the cozy

---

\* From *Tender is the Night*, New York: Scribners, 1934, page 201.

cottage-like Capital Bookstore (where Wallace once worked and Harper Lee's family were customers), we learned about a tree that had been taken from a Civil War battlefield and planted on the State Capitol grounds. We weren't told which one exactly, just a battlefield at which the South had been victorious. Finding that tree was now our goal.

The Capitol is as impressive an edifice as one can find in America, with its classical cupola, soaring Ionic columns, and innumerable granite steps where Jefferson Davis was inaugurated president of the Confederacy in 1861. Wallace informed me that the order to fire on Fort Sumter had come from this building. Spread out on all four sides of the sprawling structure was an odd mix of gigantic hardwood specimens: oaks, maples, and sycamores.

Wallace was uncharacteristically reticent as we climbed the steps of the Capitol looking for the battlefield trees. He led me to a huge oak that he believed was the one I was looking for, and then went back to the car. There were two enormous oaks on the grounds that had been recovered from the battlefields. I could find no acorns under either one, but I didn't pursue it, because the trees had a very odd aura about them: it was almost as if they had been neutered or domesticated and were no longer wild organisms capable of reproducing. Standing under their massive branches, I felt uncomfortable.

Back in the car, we drove one block and then, without comment, Wallace did a U-turn and parked in front of an adorable red brick church. I marveled at its white Rialto Bridge–style staircase entrance. Then I read the plaque: "The Dexter Avenue King Memorial Baptist Church and Parsonage." This was where Dr. Martin Luther King, Jr., had been pastor. A tour bus was idling nearby. I leaped out of the car and took pictures of the church.

Unfortunately, there were no trees in sight, nothing. Not even a shrub. In fact, the closest trees were the neutered giants up on the Capitol grounds staring down at us hollowly. It was an amazing juxtaposition: one of the birthplaces of the civil rights movement under the shadow of one of the starting points of the Confederacy. Then it hit me—Wallace's ambivalence: What history. What majesty. What bigotry.

As we pulled away from the church and headed east out of the city, a huge plume of black smoke appeared to our left and to the right of the Capitol. It leaped higher and grew darker with each passing second, like a hideous monster growing as it consumed all in its path. We drove to the crest of a hill and stopped at a red light. From there, looking back over our shoulders, we could make out the outline of an old antebellum home alive with bright flames, likely fueled by its own inflammable drapery. I could smell the smoke. In the distance, sirens wailed. A police cruiser raced through the intersection, its red flashers spinning wildly.

Ashes began to rain down on the car. Wallace turned on the windshield wipers and pulled away from the intersection. He drove slowly along the deserted streets, through the smoky, noonday ashes, putting precious distance between the conflagration and us. In the rearview mirror, I could see a fire burning in Montgomery.

Pecan (*Carya illinoensis*)
American chestnut (*Castanea dentata*)

PECAN TREE SEEDS

## Monroeville, Alabama

As Wallace drove us to the Deep South hamlet of Monroeville, Alabama, home of Truman Capote and Harper Lee, he told me about his youthful days working in a bookstore an hour away and how members of the Lee family were regular customers there. He told me how he had written ahead to see if we could meet Harper Lee, but Miss Lee's sister, Alice, had said that her time would be taken up entertaining a group of actors and old friends who would be in town that very same weekend for the annual Monroeville production of *To Kill a Mockingbird*.

Wallace knows everyone. His good friend from college and a

fellow bookseller Nathan Carter still lives in Monroeville and is Capote's first cousin once removed (his father and Capote being first cousins). Wallace arranged for us to stay with Nathan at his house, the very same farmhouse where Capote used to stay whenever he came home for a visit.

But a funny thing happened along the way. Stopping for gas a half hour from town, I had to get some pain relievers for my aching back. I could see the lineup of medications on the shelf behind the clerk, and spying the dark green Advil envelope, I indicated that that was the brand I desired. Back in the car, I took three pills because I was pretty uncomfortable. As we were pulling into Monroeville, I started feeling very strange: my eyes wouldn't stay open and everything seemed to sag and fade in and out. I sent my hand into my pocket in search of the remaining pill. Sure enough: Advil *PM*. I had taken sleeping meds instead of pain relievers. What a *moron*.

The next four or five hours are pretty much a blur. I remember meeting Nathan and his golden retriever, Moses. Nathan was the spitting image of Danny Kaye as he looked in *White Christmas*. It was uncanny, and I had to force myself not to say anything even though I was obsessing over it. I also remember sitting out on the front porch of his home in a rocking chair listening to other voices, other ruminations. I remember driving into Monroeville and visiting the courthouse that is the setting for the 1962 movie of *To Kill a Mockingbird*. It is now a museum, and also where the town's annual play is performed. Inside, I recall foggy images of a large crowd of people waiting to get an autograph from Mary Badham, the actress, now in her fifties, who played Scout in the movie. I could barely see her, through the thick veil of somnolence, sitting up at the defendant's table shaking hands and signing publicity photos of herself at age twelve.

I remember climbing the creaking, clattering stairs up to the top floor, where the museum dedicated to Truman Capote and Harper Lee is located. There were lots of photographs. Huge black-and-white photographs. The one that I remember most is an aerial view of the street and the two houses where Lee and Capote lived side by side, with a little red arrow pointing out the oak tree that was the inspiration for the tree where Boo Radley placed his gifts to the kids.

Sleepy, droopy, wobbly, I tried to keep up appearances, but it was no good; I couldn't shake it. As the three of us sat in the plush chairs at the local bookstore talking to the lovely owner, I was incapable at that point of keeping my eyes open, let alone carrying on a conversation. So I came clean and announced to all in attendance what I had done. By then I was talking in slow motion, slurring some of my words, my mouth dry as a cotton ball, one eye open and the other closed. Great peals of laughter startled me. I do remember people from the store being called over to rubberneck.

Next thing I knew, we were at a little roadside eatery. Wallace was buying me something to eat because I had taken those sleeping pills on an empty stomach. The three of us sat eating hamburgers in an empty lot on top of an old stone foundation. Nathan sat next to me, describing the locale.

"This drive-in is where Nell's childhood home once stood, and where we are sitting is what remains of Truman's aunt's home and the house he grew up in." He pointed at a bronze plaque turned perpendicular to us out on the roadside. I got up, staggered over to it, and read it, the words coming in and out of focus. But sure enough: Capote's childhood home.

Feeling a little more aware of my surroundings with some sugary ice tea in me, I was able to fish around the empty lot and find a few pecans from a very old tree that had probably been alive when

Capote was scampering about in his Buster Browns. Where Harper Lee's home used to be, there was nothing but the drive-in and the parking lot. Then Nathan pointed at the schoolyard, fifty yards away and across a side street.

"That's where the oak tree from the book used to be," he said matter-of-factly. "I don't remember when they took it down. Ten years ago maybe. It had some disease, I think. Maybe you can find something there."

I stumbled across the street. A cyclone fence enclosed the entire perimeter of the schoolyard. There wasn't even a stump remaining. The gate was locked, and to get access to the school grounds I would have had to scale the fence. Not in my condition. But there was nothing at all to gather anyway. I could see a middle-aged oak at the back end of the playground, but it didn't inspire me to climb over. For the first time on my adventure, I felt very disappointed.

We drove to Nathan's farmhouse, which was a few miles outside of town, and all three of us sat on the front porch and rocked. Well, they rocked and I drifted in and out of sleep. Wallace and Nathan must have chatted for hours. Southerners have that capacity; Northerners don't, drugged or otherwise.

After dinner, Nathan led me back to a little cabin a hundred yards behind the main house, and I slept the sleep of the drugged. The next morning I was up early, and as I made my way back toward the main house for some much-needed coffee, something caught my eye: two large American chestnut trees, bushy and fat as apple trees, sitting in and among a small pecan grove. American chestnuts! I rubbed my sleepy eyes, thinking that maybe I was mistaking them for beeches or elms. The grove, surrounded by barbed wire to keep goats out, had no more than ten trees in it. I had to walk up to the main house to get inside through a gate.

They were chestnuts all right, American chestnuts. American chestnut leaves are a radical affair, long and narrow as a little girl's shoe, with a thick waxy cuticle, dark army green in color, with needles on the edges like fine fish teeth. The golden brown, needle-spiked pods were everywhere underfoot. I remember reading somewhere how to find the seed pods of American chestnuts with the viable nuts inside: you step on them. A nut pod with a hard center is an indication of a viable seed inside. Sure enough, after a half hour of this foot-stomping ballet, I had found two fertilized seeds. Viable seeds can be in the minority if there is a lack of pollinating trees in the area. The majority of chestnut seeds one finds look like tiny deflated brown triangles with little white tails attached; fertilized seeds are fat as squash balls, somewhat triangular in shape, with hoarfrost on the underside that glows an iridescent blue. I couldn't believe my luck.

Nathan and Wallace were sitting on the porch where I had left them the night before, smiling broadly. As I approached, I held up one of the chestnuts between thumb and forefinger and cock-a-doodle-dooed, "American chestnuts!"

"Oh, right, the chestnuts," Nathan said, frowning at himself. "I forgot about them. You know there are two more behind the house," he added.

I didn't even stop for the proffered coffee before I was out behind the house looking for more. Within an hour I had found three more viable chestnuts from two different trees. I was beside myself, marveling at my good fortune. Then I began to wonder about the chestnut trees themselves. Who had planted them? How old were they? Did Capote ever interact with them or talk about them? How about Harper Lee? Did she ever come to the property and walk in the chestnut grove? Nathan didn't have any answers to those questions.

He told me only that his mother and aunt did harvest the chestnuts and pecans in the fall, often baking cakes and pies with them.

That's when he introduced me to "The Fruitcake Lady." He brought me into the house, put a DVD on, and there was Edna Marie Rudisill, Truman Capote's ninety-year-old aunt, who had helped raise him. The DVD was of *The Tonight Show with Jay Leno* and Rudisill was responding to viewers' questions. The story goes that she wrote a book called *Fruitcake*, which had helped her, along with her being Capote's aunt, land an invitation as a guest on the show. Her performance that night was a tour de force, and earned her a regular appearance, in a segment called "Ask the Fruitcake Lady" (which you can find on the Web). Hysterical stuff. What a character. After seeing that, I concluded that Capote's greatest gift was to have grown up among larger-than-life female role models, Harper Lee being one of them.

I felt sadness as we said goodbye to Nathan and Monroeville, because I hadn't gotten the chance to meet and talk with Harper Lee; nor was I able to find any seeds directly associated with her.

"Wallace, do you think we can come back in the fall and talk to Miss Lee then?"

"I don't see why not."

"Thank you, kind sir."

"Okay, now I'm going to tell you a little story about Alabama armadillos," Wallace said with his sweet drawl, smiling at the road in front of him.

## Muhammad Ali

**Northern catalpa** (*Catalpa speciosa*)

NORTHERN
CATALPA

## Louisville, Kentucky

Louisville, Kentucky, is home to three American classics: the Louisville Slugger, the Kentucky Derby, and Muhammad Ali. It's a hybrid city, part genteel South and part hurly-burly North, chock-full of art galleries, theaters, and a potpourri of eateries from gumbo shops to five-star restaurants. To the north, separating Louisville from the industrial works of Indiana, is the churning cream-and-coffee-colored Ohio River, where you can still take a ride on a riverboat with a paddle wheel in the stern.

William Clark grew up outside the city, and it is where he and fellow explorer Meriwether Lewis concluded their famous expedition through the Louisiana Territory in 1806. Clark's grandson Meriwether Lewis Clark, Jr., founded Churchill Downs and the Kentucky Derby.

I was in Louisville along with thousands of other English, history, math, language, and physics teachers to read and score the Advanced Placement exams for the College Board. Imagine a vast convention center filled with thousands of tables, chairs, and teachers reading and grading student essays in total silence eight hours a day, seven days a week. A veritable hotbed of tranquility. (There's a whole lot of self-medicating that goes on after hours when the scoring is done for the day.)

The day I arrived, once I'd checked into my hotel room, my first visit was to the Louisville Slugger Museum, just three blocks away. It's hard to miss: a six-story bat leans up against the façade of the bat factory's original brick building. (It looks like wood, but it's actually steel.*) And they still make bats at the factory. The museum itself has some of the greatest Louisville Sluggers ever used by the likes of Babe Ruth, Mickey Mantle, Ted Williams, and Rod Carew.

The bats are made from either northern white ash or maple, and are harvested primarily from forests in northern Pennsylvania and southern New York State. Of those Major Leaguers using Louisville Sluggers, 52 percent use ash and 48 percent use maple; some players use both. On average, a Major Leaguer will go through about a hundred bats each season (when broken, maple shatters, while ash splinters), and Louisville Slugger makes approximately a half million bats a year. However, the Slugger folks assure everyone that

* For a picture of the bat and the museum, go to www.sluggermuseum.org.

more trees are planted than are cut down each year. This piece of information made me feel a little better.

The best part of the tour is the batting cages. One buck will buy you ten balls and/or ten swings, thrown at forty miles per hour by a pitching machine. It's the most fun a dollar will buy you these days. I paid two bucks for twenty balls, acquitting myself quite well—not whiffing once, even though I hadn't hit a live ball since my days teaching on the U.S. Army base in downtown Seoul, South Korea, ten years before.*

IN 2005, the Muhammad Ali Center opened in downtown Louisville. It's a massive structure that leans out over Interstate 65 and looks out at the Ohio River into which teenaged Cassius Clay is reputed to have thrown his 1960 Olympic Gold Medal.† The museum is an odd rhombus shape, with a two-story broad mosaic wainscoting that wraps around all four sides of the structure. A montage of iconic Ali boxing images subtly blend in with the colors, squares, and lines, creating a cool effect: the farther away you are from it, the clearer the pictures become.

But inside the multilevel, multi-venue, multimedia, multiculti museum, you can't see the real Ali for the fanfare and fee (adults:

---

* In Seoul, batting cages and driving ranges are common sights along busy streets, on rooftops, and even at department stores.
† After he won the light heavyweight boxing gold medal at the 1960 Olympics in Rome, a Soviet news reporter asked a young Cassius Clay what it felt like to be denied service at a restaurant because of his race back in the United States. He responded: "Russian, we got qualified men working on that problem. America is the greatest country in the world." No sooner was he back in Louisville than he was called a "Nigger" while eating in a diner. Later that day he reportedly threw his gold medal into the Ohio River.

nine dollars). There's even a bit of an Oz effect when you stand in the vast entrance hall. As you proceed through the immaculate stages of Ali's life, from childhood to boxer, from political activist to religious acolyte, from goodwill ambassador to humanitarian, with ten-foot-tall photographs of The Greatest everywhere you turn, you start to look for the Wizard behind the curtain. Compared with Monticello and Mount Vernon, even Graceland, none comes even close to the degree of apotheosis on display here. I'm an Ali fan, with an autograph signed by the Greatest, but this place was way too much. Why must our museums trim away the rough edges of our heroes (often the most interesting parts), and recast them as deities rather than as the down-to-earth, hardworking folks they really are?

I soon got out of there and over to Ali's childhood home on the west side of the city. At least there I was sure to find the real Muhammad I sought. On the way I stopped for a beer at a pub in the middle of Fourth Street Live!, an indoor/outdoor restaurant/ retail district in the heart of historic Louisville, two blocks long and covered by a triangular glass roof. It was filled with lots of young people and excitement; a stage in the middle of the road featured a live band. I sat at the bar with my back to the stage and pulled out my MapQuest printout. I couldn't decide whether to walk the four miles or just take a cab. I had all day, and it looked like a pretty straight shot. I asked the bartender his advice, having to shout over a drum solo.

"Cab'll cost you ten bucks. Take the bus, man. It goes right by there, and you can use the bus pass for three hours whether you're going or coming back. But I'd get there before dark; that's a pretty rough section of town."

I took his advice and rode the bus. He was right about one thing: it was a pretty rough section. But he was wrong about another: the bus didn't go right by the house. I still had to walk almost a mile from where I got off, but it was well worth the effort, because of what I found waiting for me. Grand Avenue, on the west side of Louisville, is a wonderful little street, populated with double-shotgun-style houses, front porches, and well-maintained yards. Ali's childhood home was exactly halfway down, on the right. There was only one house on that side of the road with a big tree out front. Guess whose it was?

Perfectly proportioned, with a healthy head of green, a straight trunk, and muscular branches, it stood out proudly in the middle of a stretch of treeless lawns. As I got closer and closer, my heart suddenly skipped a beat when I realized what species it was: a catalpa. Catalpas have the largest leaves of any tree in North America— about the size of a standard sheet of paper and shaped exactly like a heart. The tree looked to be about seventy-five years old, more broad than tall, with hundreds of engine-oil-brown bean pods dangling from its branches like chocolate Christmas ornaments.

I stood out on the sidewalk and just stared up at it for the longest time before I thought to remove my camera and take pictures. I snapped away from all sorts of angles until I had used up my batteries. Then I tucked the camera back inside my backpack and looked toward the house. The tiny house that Muhammad Ali grew up in appeared uninhabited. There were no signs of life at all: no bikes, no open windows, no shoes left out on the porch, no cat, nothing. But the house next door, twenty feet away, looked alive, with a cat in the window and mail sticking out of the mailbox. I marched up and knocked. A teenage boy answered right away. I told him that I was interested in gathering seeds from the catalpa tree, and he shook his head.

"That's not our tree. Ask them."

"You mean someone lives there?"

"Yeah, they live there."

That was that. I was more than a little hesitant, to tell you the truth; the house seemed all closed up. But what I discovered once I knocked was the complete and total opposite of what I had expected. A little girl answered right away. She flung the door open as if she had been expecting Santa Claus and looked up at me with the most adorable eyes. Her caramel-colored face was all smiles and dimples, and her frizzy hair, pulled up high on her head, bobbed back and forth as she moved excitedly. I was tongue-tied. I had expected an agoraphobic old lady, sneering, suspicious, contemptuous—not an angel. Before I was able to form words and speak, her mother appeared. The woman was a ravishing beauty herself, also wearing a bright smile and great big soft eyes.

I finally got the mouth working. "I'm writing a book about famous people's trees, and I know that Muhammad Ali grew up in this very house."

"Yes, that's right, he did," she said, nodding.

"Would you mind if I take some seeds from your tree? I won't hurt it, I promise."

"Sure, why not," she said, shrugging.

Then the three of us stood there looking at one another. I had to say something, so I told her my name, and where I lived, and how much I admired her catalpa tree. She just nodded her head and smiled. The smile communicated to me that I didn't need to explain myself because someone knocking on her door and wanting nothing more than to take pictures and seeds from her tree was explanation enough.

What a magical moment that was as I turned from the closed front door, fully sanctioned, staring up at Muhammad Ali's childhood catalpa tree. I hopped off that top stoop and rushed to my task.

Two varieties of catalpa, also known as catawba or Indian bean tree, are native to North America: northern and southern. It's hard to tell the difference between northern and southern catalpas; however, the northern has slightly longer and more pointed leaves. The bean pods, too, give a clue: northern pods are thicker than southern pods. I was sure the species I was collecting was a northern catalpa, because the pods were quite thick.

I was having a hard time finding pods with the cottony little seeds still inside. Most of the pods that were hanging on the branches had opened up already and dropped their contents, which had either melted down into the soil or been carried away by the wind. There was, however, one long seedpod dangling from a branch about ten feet up that was closed up and no doubt held what I was after. I took a running start and jumped, trying to knock it down. I wasn't even close. I tried several times, and was so intent on my mission that I didn't even consider the possibility that people in the surrounding houses might have been watching me. I finally just took off my belt and hit the pod with it, like a piñata. It was full of seeds.

WALKING BACK TO THE BUS STOP, I was overflowing with certainty that what I was doing had merit. These visits to the homes of great personages to interact with the trees that had watched over them way back when were real, 100 percent all natural, without any artificial ingredients. The northern catalpa tree on Grant Avenue was the *real* Muhammad Ali Museum. Forget the ridiculous $60 million cathedral with the super-ginormous escalators and the multimedia wizardry. No amount of money or architectural prestidigitation could ever represent a man like Muhammad Ali; only the heart-shaped leaves of the catalpa tree growing in the front yard of his childhood home could come close.

Muhammad Ali once said, "The man who has no imagination has no wings."

The lives and deeds of our heroes cannot be replicated by institutions. Only the joys and creativity of our own imaginations can do that.

MY BACK MUCH IMPROVED, and with me percolating with positivity after finding that adorable catalpa tree out in front of Ali's childhood house, I dove right back into my seed-and-sapling storage dilemma. I had a whole new list of names and numbers to call for help in my planting project, and I did just that. Unfortunately, they yielded nothing.

Undaunted, I set off on the ultimate pilgrimage: to gather seeds from the trees of our great nature writers Thoreau, Emerson, Carson . . . and a few surprises.

# Part five

Except during the nine months before he draws his first breath, no man manages his affairs as well as a tree does.

—GEORGE BERNARD SHAW,
"MAXIMS FOR REVOLUTIONISTS"

**Red oak** *(Quercus rubra)*
**White pine** *(Pinus strobus)*
**Eastern redcedar** *(Juniperus virginiana)*
**Apple** *(Malus domestica)*

APPLE SEEDS

## Walden Pond

Just because America has no church-sanctified saints or holy land doesn't mean it doesn't have them. We do. Walden Pond is as sacred a place as there is on this planet, and its most famous inhabitant, Henry David Thoreau, is as saintly a prophet as has ever walked the earth. The crystal clear waters of Walden Pond possess no less curative powers than the babbling spring at the grotto of Lourdes, and Thoreau's love for and consanguinity with the creatures of the kingdom and with mankind are no less beatified than St. Francis of Assisi's.

To visit Walden Pond is to make a pilgrimage. I last visited Walden Pond in late summer. I was alone. It was mid-morning. The sun was round and golden bright, just above the trees, and the air was warm and sweet as privet flowers. Overhead, the sky was a vault of pure azure with a smattering of hawks circling lazily. And all around was the staccato hammering of woodpeckers hard at work.

The trees at Walden Pond are a handsome bunch, tall and straight, green and lush, hale and hearty. The dominant two species are red oaks and white pines—the meat and potatoes of New England forests.* Red oak is the species most commonly used to make furniture: desks and chairs, cabinets and tables. White pine, in floorboards and wall studs, supports many of us and our homes with its sturdy, straight-grained wood.

I entered the park from the southwest, turning off Route 126 from Framingham and parking directly across from the main entrance, next to the nature center. Amazingly, the small wooden building and the half dozen parking lots behind it blend in quite unobtrusively with the natural surroundings. The nature center is ostensibly a classroom, where educational tours commence and where lectures are conducted, but there is also a tasteful gift shop and bookstore inside. I went in looking to buy some postcards and a map of Walden Pond. It took me less than five minutes to find what I was looking for: postcards of the famous daguerreotype portrait of Thoreau done by Benjamin D. Maxham in 1856, as well as a fresh

---

* For a comprehensive description of New England's forests, go to the U.S. Geological Survey, www.nwrc.usgs.gov/sandt/Nrtheast.pdf.

copy of *Walden Pond; or My Life in the Woods*. On the postcard, Thoreau is dressed in a dark jacket and a bowtie, with his great big blue eyes beaming mystically. Those eyes, along with his muscular nose, uncombed hair, and steeply sloped shoulders, reminded me of one of his famous lines from *Walden Pond*: "It is an interesting question how far men would retain their relative rank if they were divested of their clothes."

I would gladly have sauntered naked into Walden Pond if I could have done it without getting arrested. Instead, with the postcards and a copy of *Walden Pond* "enlightening" my load, I marched across Route 126 and down to the main beach. The paved walking path leading to the water was steeper than I expected, like the aisle in a movie theater. Arriving at the sandy strip beside the seasonal bath-house, I noticed that the building was closed, yet there was a gaggle of folks out in the water splashing around, murmuring in a foreign tongue, and floating on their backs. I was so damned relieved to find no ersatz museum, no long lines, no entrance fees, and no soda machines, that I stood for a while and metaphorically floated with them.

I counted five more swimmers out in the middle of the pond cranking out laps, their arms and legs churning with reckless abandon, fore and aft, bound for the distant shore. Walden Pond is a half mile long and a quarter mile wide, so these were serious swimmers. And along all four shorelines, fishermen sat in their boats, facing toward the water, rods in hand. In sum, this was a living museum, a sacred place, but still in use, not just stuck in amber.

Thirsting for the nearby essence of Walden Woods, I skirted the thin little beach until I came upon a trail leading into the thick of the woods, on the south side of the pond. No sooner had I entered than the wind picked up and it literally began raining acorns. It was as if the oaks had been lying in wait for me, and as soon as I was in position, they let fly their wooden missiles. Prior to my pilgrimage to Walden Pond, I was plagued by self-doubt, inhibited by insecurity, and wracked with guilt about whether what I was doing was not in some way presumptuous, callow, or exploitative. (The certainty I felt after visiting Muhammad Ali's house hadn't stuck.)

Before visiting Walden Pond, I learned that in 1938 a hurricane had raged through the area and toppled all of the old-growth trees. There was not one single tree remaining from Thoreau's time, so my plan was simply to find the oldest trees I could, especially those closest to his cabin, and to collect what seeds I could find. Sitting there with acorns falling like pennies from heaven, I decided that all of the seeds from all of the trees were collectible; no tree was more important than any other. With that thought in mind, I vaulted back to my feet and gathered acorns.

"It would be some advantage to live a primitive and frontier life, though in the midst of an outward civilization," Thoreau wrote in the first chapter of *Walden Pond*. Walden Pond, then, could be considered America's first suburb and Henry David Thoreau its first suburbanite. That cake-and-eat-it-too fantasy does make sense as you stroll around Walden Pond. Boston is just eighteen miles away, but in the midst of the woods, on the eastern side of the pond, atop the knoll called Emerson's Cliff, there is enough altitude that you can look across Walden Pond and see nothing but the lollipop treetops undulating off into the distance, suggesting an indivisible, never-ending forest. At Walden Pond, Thoreau lived just beyond the pale, and that was his point.

I walked on out into the open, and I sat, as Thoreau must have done many times, beside the Haywood Meadow, now more a swamp than a meadow, in quiet meditation. I pulled out my copy of *Walden Pond* and began reading the chapter entitled "Solitude." To read a work of art where it was conceived and created is the best of all possible conditions. For example, after perusing the line "Shall I not have intelligence with the earth? Am I not partly leaves and vegetable mould myself?" how could I not shout out, "Yeah, baby!" My outburst was punctuated by the sound of an acorn plunking into the sleepy swamp waters in front of me. The sound at first startled me, but when it happened again, it made me giggle. The echoing bass note *ploonk* of a meaty acorn falling into still water is one of nature's comic punch lines.

I had not come across one human being the entire time I was in the woods behind Walden Pond, a round hour at least. It's a testament to the folks at the Massachusetts Department of Conservation and Recreation, who have somehow managed to preserve enough of the environs around the pond so that visitors coming to experience Thoreau's Walden can do so with a degree of authenticity. It's the trees that keep the show going, year after year. The trees show no signs of foreign diseases, nor do they appear overly pampered, or Disneyfied in any way. And beneath their bold stems, human feet have not trampled to a pulp the vital understory that is their future. The only signs of the present day, save the nearby MBTA train tracks and the ever-roiling Route 2, are the well-worn hiking trails that meander every which way. No, unfortunately, you can't get lost at Walden Pond.

Laden down with a half dozen baggies full of acorns, smiling, and replete, I hit the main hiking path called the Healthy Heart Trail, which circles the entirety of the pond. The trail is wide and graded, hemmed in on either side by a four-foot-high wire fence. As I walked along the water's edge, I came upon a veteran, a fishing pole in his weathered hands and a baseball cap on his head that proudly proclaimed his Korean War unit affiliation.

"Catch anything?" I asked.

"Yeah, nice ones. Look at 'em." Without hesitation, he put his pole down, opened his cooler, and pulled out a glistening, rose-glowing rainbow trout packed in Saran wrap; it was about a foot long. He'd caught two of them.

"My wife prepares and cooks 'em for me. I just catch 'em and eat 'em."

"The great thing about trout is you don't even have to scale them. Just gut them and throw them in the fry pan," I offered.

"She usually bakes 'em."

"Oh, well, that'll work, too,"

He looked me up and down; then he gazed at the baggies in my grasp and asked straight out: "What're you doin' with the acorns?"

So I told him. He just smiled and nodded his head. We stood looking at one another for a long moment without uttering a word, yet in that ineffable silence we exchanged a thousand tidings. Since there was no possibility of a swap (you can't really trade trout for acorns), we got back to it.

"Well, keep up the good work," I exhorted.

"You, too," he replied. And with an arcing wave of his hand that resolved in the grabbing up of his fishing pole, we parted ways.

My chance to get naked came shortly after my communion with the vet. The Healthy Heart Trail, as I said, is lined on both sides by a waist-high wire fence, so the saunterer is obliged to stay on the trail at all times. However, at regular intervals, the fence on the pond side opens up to granite steps down to the water's edge, inviting swimmers. The boulder stairs reminded me of photographs I had seen years before of the sacred city of Varanasi, where stairs, or *ghats*, as the Hindus call them, provide pilgrims easy access to the sacred waters of the Ganges. What with the sun high in the sky, the heat of the day, and my brisk walking, I was primed for a dunk.

There was no one around, so I stripped off my clothes, hung them on the fence, and dove in. The temperature was sublime. Like a sated crocodile, with only my eyes and the top of my head above water, I looked up at the trees and the bright blue sky. In the soothing aqua, I began to compare Thoreau's America and my America. Thoreau's America had one twelfth the population of today, with nary an automobile, interstate highway, shopping mall, nuclear plant, Brangelina, or Dr. Phil. Thoreau "went to the woods . . . to live deliberately, to front only the essential facts of life." But floating there naked out in the middle of Walden Pond, looking up at the trees that surrounded me, I realized that America, its present predicaments notwithstanding, still had the trees and the woods enough for those inspired few who wished to live deliberately. And as I climbed out of the water, shivering from the breeze against my skin, I found myself confronting a downside of spontaneity: no towel.

I brushed off the beads of water as best I could, dressed, and continued along the path. A hundred yards from the dipping point, near where Thoreau once cultivated a bean field, I came upon an American chestnut tree. I would later learn from one of the park's rangers that, indeed, there were once many native American chestnut trees at Walden Pond, but none ever lived long enough to enter the gametophyte (reproductive) stage and thus bear fruit.

Anyway, I didn't know any of this at the time, and with my heart pumping, reenergized from my baptism in the Walden waters, I began riffling through the underbrush, digging, raking, and kicking with my hands and feet under the man-tall tree. Of course, there was nothing, but I was madly determined to find something. I was going at it pretty well for about ten minutes before reality set in: there were no chestnuts. Of course, the few passersby thought I was insane, and I was, to a certain extent.

Not far from there, I came to the area where Thoreau's cabin once stood. There is no replica of the cabin extant, thankfully (there is a replica alongside the parking area). What is there now is a huge pile of rock or, more poetically, an embowered cairn of stones, deposited over the years by pilgrims who have come to pay tribute to the great prophet. John Muir and Walt Whitman visited the site back in the late 1800s and they, too, deposited stones on the shrine. I couldn't resist, and I placed one of my acorns atop the highest rock. I stood back and admired my brown little nipple, wondering how long it would remain there before the wind, rain, or a squirrel carried it off.

Not far away, in various postures of disinterest, sat a class of high school students pretending to listen to a male teacher standing in their midst lecturing them on transcendentalism. He was tall, dark-haired, and mustachioed, with a pale complexion. The sight of it gave me the willies, having been a boring and ignored teacher myself. The students' body language ran the gamut of boredom from weariness to monotony to gloom. I wasn't sure with whom I empathized more: the harried teacher or the hapless students. One thing I knew for sure: you can't teach Thoreau, even at Walden Pond; the best you can do is walk in his shoes.

Trying my best to ignore the tableau, I began gathering acorns in and around the area. There were some tall white oaks up the slope that looked old, so I made my way up there, gathering as I went. Then, as I stopped to place a full baggy of acorns in my pack, I looked back down at the class to discover that every eye, save the teacher's, was on me. And as I slung my backpack across my shoulders, one of the students reached down and picked up an acorn lying next to his sneaker. He held it reverently in the palm of his hand, examining it. Another student did the same thing. And then another.

Thoreau wrote: "I have great faith in a seed . . . Convince me that you have a seed there, and I am prepared to expect wonders."*

Me, too.

## Concord, Massachusetts

Where Thoreau lived by Walden Pond is a mile due north as the crow flies from Ralph Waldo Emerson's home and the cozy hamlet of Concord. Concord is to quaint New England villages what a fashion model is to a photo shoot, i.e., possibly too perfect. It's got a voluptuous village green fronted by a pearly white Congregational church; a plethora of Ye Olde Shoppes and signs above the doors to prove it; and historic clapboard homes painted in Colonial colors, glistening with glass held in place by a million mullions, and ultra-glossy paneled front doors. In sum, Emerson is rolling over in his grave. From the opening paragraph of his 1836 masterpiece "Nature":

> Our age is retrospective. It builds the sepulchers of the fathers . . . Why should not we have a poetry and philosophy of insight and not of tradition, and a religion by revelation to us, and not the history of theirs? . . . [W]hy should we grope among the dry bones of the past, or put the living generation into masquerade out of its faded wardrobe? . . . Let us demand our own works and laws and worship.

* From Thoreau's last manuscript, *Faith in Seed*.

I drove into the candy-coated maw of Concord after two miles of twisty-turny roads from the blessed shores of Walden Pond. Sitting in traffic, just past the center of the village, I noticed an interesting historic marker involving a tree, so I pulled over and parked in front of the village green, hopped out, and jogged over to investigate the plaque.

The sign claimed that on that spot in 1635, under an ancient oak known as Jethro's Tree, a major named Simon Willard and some of his henchmen bought from the Indians a six-mile-square area of land "ordered by the general court for the plantation of Concord September 12, 1635." The word *ordered* put my nose out of joint and conjured up an image of some white-wigged grandee with a painful-looking underbite signing "the order" with a big bold stroke of his quill.

Putting my nose back in place and averting my eyes, I decided to walk through the village to the Concord Visitor Center, where I aimed to inquire about this so-called Jethro's Tree. The attendant on duty had no answers to my questions: "Why was it called Jethro?" "When did the tree die?" "Is the present black oak standing in its stead related to the celebrated tree?" She was, however, able to tell me where Emerson's house was. I walked back through the village, past Ye Olde Bric-a-Brac Shoppe, past my parked truck, all the way to Emerson's house. It took me seven minutes.

A handwritten message on a piece of paper taped to the doorframe above the doorbell instructed me to ring and wait. A few moments later, a woman answered the door. She gave me the once-over, and then let me in. I felt as if I were entering a nunnery, mostly because the matron who admitted me looked like Sister Marie-Rose from the parish church of my childhood neighborhood. A tour was under way, and I was instructed to join it in the dining room. The slanted floors creaked obstreperously as I followed the droning voice to the back of the house.

It sure is humbling to visit the homes of our nineteenth-century heroes, as it provides us with a welcome perspective on our present-day creature comforts. Emerson was not a rich man; he was not a poor man. Esteemed by all during his day as America's greatest philosopher, he cobbled together a living as a minister, speaker, and educator. By today's standards, he would be considered a celebrity, yet the way he lived would have sent cold chills down the spines of most of us. *Creaking*, *drafty*, *sagging*, *smelly*, and *dingy* are just a few of the adjectives that come to mind when I remember the interior of Emerson's home.

From the outside, Bush, as Emerson referred to the residence (a reference to the former owner), is quite impressive: broad, square, with three tall chimneys tickling the sky, plenty of yard on three of the four sides, and everything well cared for. But inside, the Emerson family-owned museum is crammed full of faded paintings, dusty volumes, worm-eaten furniture, sallow window treatments, and fraying carpets—in sum, a firetrap. Worst of all, it's located at the confluence of the heavily traveled Cambridge Turnpike and Lexington Road. Every few minutes, the whole house shook as another semi rumbled by.

The docent wore a frozen smile as she delivered her monologue, and I began to kick myself for having decided to take the tour. I should have been outside on the front lawn, where swollen acorns and pregnant pinecones beckoned to me to pluck them up. I made a vow right then and there that I had just taken my final museum tour. For eight dollars, I did learn one thing: that a young Henry David Thoreau had a key to the house and came and went as he pleased. I wondered if the weary prospect of having to stay another uncomfortable night in Emerson's dreary house had inspired young Thoreau to move out to Walden Pond.

I slipped away from the group, closing the door behind me. It took me no time to collect acorns from an oak just a few yards from Emerson's study. The tree was tall, massive, and old; no doubt it was there in the 1880s, when Emerson was alive and kicking. Then I did an about-face, walked ten yards along the property line, and promptly came upon a white pine directly across from Emerson's bedroom. There were pinecones all over the ground. I greedily harvested those gummy green cones, which were oozing pine tar, getting a bit gummed up in the process.

But then I stood there contemplating Emerson and his love of nature and trees. I thought of him traveling out to Yosemite in 1871, an old man then, and meeting the young John Muir in the Sierra Mountains. I remember a passage from Muir's journal where he told of how he talked Emerson into camping out under the big trees of the Mariposa Grove and how, when he described to Emerson what it would all look like at night, under the stars, around the light of the campfire, Emerson smiled like a little boy.*

I continued around the grounds, somewhat surprised to find that many of the shrubs and trees were not well cared for. I suspect

* The complete quote from Muir's journal reads as follows: "He came again and again, and I saw him every day while he remained in the valley, and on leaving I was invited to accompany him as far as the Mariposa Grove of Big Trees. I said, 'I'll go, Mr. Emerson, if you will promise to camp with me in the Grove. I'll build a glorious campfire, and the great brown boles of the giant Sequoias will be most impressively lighted up, and the night will be glorious.' At this he became enthusiastic like a boy, his sweet perennial smile became still deeper and sweeter, and he said, 'Yes, yes, we will camp out, camp out.'" William Frederic Badè, *The Life and Letters of John Muir*, Vol. 1, Ch. VIII, Houghton Mifflin, Boston & New York, 1924 (F866.M8.B3V.1 & V.2). Online text: Chapter VIII, "Yosemite, Emerson, and the Sequoias."

what is considered Emerson's property today is much reduced from what it was back when he was alive. I could tell that there had been gardens, both of the flower and vegetable variety, but none are maintained today, besides a few flowering shrubs. On the east side of the house stood ancient cedars full of clusters of viable seeds. I plucked seeds off this tree as if picking berries.

Across the bustling Cambridge Turnpike, catty-corner to and a mere stone's throw from Emerson's house, stands the Concord Museum. A brochure I picked up at the Concord Visitor Center indicated that Emerson had an apple orchard on this land. I was curious and strolled across the pike to yet another laminated historical museum. The Concord Museum is American history preserved not in amber but in Waterford crystal.

John Chapman, a.k.a. Johnny Appleseed, planted apple trees all over the Midwest during the early part of the nineteenth century, but he was born, coincidentally, not too far from Concord, in Leominster, Massachusetts. Recently, I had found out that one of Johnny Appleseed's original trees is still alive today,* so I was on

---

* The tree, located on a farm in Nova, Ohio, recently blew down. However, one of its shoots remains. Chapman planted the tree around 1830. Not much is known about his life prior to his planting trees, but the most likely scenario is that he started out from Pittsburgh in two lashed-together canoes full of apples and headed west down the Ohio River about the time of the Whiskey Rebellion of 1794. In *The Botany of Desire*, author Michael Pollan theorizes that many plants use humans to improve their condition the same way humans use plants to improve theirs, and he offers the apple tree and the mythic character of Johnny Appleseed as proof. He highlights Chapman's life, describing how, in the latter part of the eighteenth century, Chapman sallied into the western frontier, mostly Ohio, and would plant groves of apple trees from seed, then move on. But the story of Johnny Appleseed that most Americans know is the Disney version of an eccentric young man, sans shoes and with a pot on his head, keeping the settlers well stocked with edible, vitamin C–rich apples. Nuh-un. Pollan sets the record straight once and for all: apple trees planted

the lookout for elderly apple trees that might have been planted by Emerson himself.

There was a very old apple tree right outside the front door of the Concord Museum (there were two others on the small area of lawn) that made me wonder if the tree wasn't from Emerson's original orchard. The trunk looked more like an oak's than an apple's, and the branches had been cropped with care. Best of all, dangling tantalizingly at arm's length was a heaping helping of ripe red fruit. I picked one and bit into it. Marvelous and juicy. It was a variety I had never tasted before, another sign that it might have been an original.

I ENTERED THE MUSEUM. The hermetically sealed building stank of sweetmeats. Chewing cavalierly on Emerson's apple, my footfalls echoing deafeningly against the non-porous walls and glistening crystal, I approached the ticket counter. Every bite of the apple sounded like an explosion.

Canny eyes, well protected behind wire-rimmed glasses, scrutinized my footstep, bite, and swallow. (I think it's appropriate to point out at this point that I was wearing a T-shirt that read "Afraid of Clowns.")

I chewed one more time, swallowed, and then asked, "Excuse me, but do you know anything about the apple tree out front?"

My voice had a percussive quality to it, and it rumbled forth, ricocheting up to the rafters before bouncing down the hall to-

---

from seed ain't the eatin' kind; them apples was for drankin'. In other words: Johnny Appleseed was America's first bootlegger, only without the boots. He planted apples for making hard cider, sour mash, hooch.

ward the back of the museum " . . . [like] the shot heard round the world." * "No!" the white-haired ticket lady said.

I turned and exited back out into the open spaces and fresh air. As I came abreast of Emerson's old apple tree, I couldn't resist picking a few more. They were as sweet and wholesome as his words were a hundred and fifty years ago and still are now.

* *By the rude bridge that arched the flood,*
  *Their flag to April's breeze unfurled;*
  *Here once the embattled farmers stood,*
  *And fired the shot heard 'round the world.*
From the opening stanza of Ralph Waldo Emerson's "Concord Hymn" (1837), which describes the first shots of the American Revolution, fired at Concord's Old North Bridge on April 19, 1775.

## Robert Frost

Red maple *(Acer rubra)*
Apple *(Malus domestica)*
European pear *(Pyrus communis)*
Sweet cherry *(Prunus avium)*
Red oak *(Quercus rubra)*
Eastern redcedar *(Juniperus virginiana)*
White pine *(Pinus strobus)*

WHITE PINE CONE

## Derry, New Hampshire

Writers come in two varieties: them what wanders and them what
stays put. I was under the distinct impression that Robert Frost was
of the latter variety, but upon further investigation, I came to find
out that he was of the former. A veritable moving target throughout

his life, Frost lived in the most varied of places. Born in San Francisco, he lived for a time in Lawrence, Cambridge, and Amherst, Massachusetts; London, England; Glasgow, Scotland; Ann Arbor, Michigan; Derry, Franconia, Plymouth, and Hanover, New Hampshire; Middlebury, Vermont; and Miami, Florida.

Another aspect that didn't fit my preconceived notion of America's most celebrated pastoral poet is how beleaguered he was by death, depression, and mental illness. His father died when young Robert was eleven, leaving the family penniless. Four years later, his mother passed away from cancer. Of Frost's six children, only two outlived him: two died in infancy, another died while giving birth, and Frost's second son, Carol, committed suicide at age thirty-eight. On top of that, both Frost and his mother suffered from depression. But perhaps worst of all, Frost had to commit his younger sister, Jeanie, and eventually his own daughter Irma to mental institutions. Even his wife died before him, of heart failure, in 1938.

In 1942, Henry Holt published a collection of Frost's poems, which went on to win him a record fourth Pulitzer Prize. It was called, A *Witness Tree*. The first poem of that collection, called "Beech," * alludes to the book's title:

Where my imaginary line
Bends square in woods, an iron spine
And pile of real rocks have been founded.
And off this corner in the wild,
Where these are driven in and piled,
One tree, by being deeply wounded,
Has been impressed as Witness Tree

* Reprinted by permission of the publisher, Henry Holt.

And made commit to memory
My proof of being not unbounded.
Thus truth's established and borne out,
Though circumstanced with dark and doubt—
Though by a world of doubt surrounded.

I was excited when I came across that title, because it matched
up perfectly with the purpose of my seed gathering. However after
reading the poem and the line about the "Witness Tree," it left me
feeling gloomy and downright "bounded." It was not at all what I
had expected; nor did it match my objective. In fact, after reading
it, I became aware for the first time in my life that I wholeheartedly
disagreed with a poem. And wouldn't you know it, not once in my
umpteen torturous years of compulsory education had I ever been
taught to disagree with a poem. Well, here is my rebuttal:

### Reach
Set out upon the open road
With plastic bags and maps my mode
To gather nuts and berries and cones
At the homes of the vaunted literati
Removed with love from branches bent or shaken
Or from mossy earth or weedy grasses taken
Off that proverbial pie in the sky,
The apple of my eye—A Witness Tree
That holds cellulosic memory
Solid proof of things unbounded
By wooden truths ne'er borne out,
Without denial or doubt—
By a world of squirrels surrounded.

Frost's home in Derry couldn't be a more mundane structure. A basic A-frame with an A-frame barn twice the size of the house behind it, both painted an artless white. Unfortunately, State Route 28 now fronts the farmhouse, and the traffic whizzes by in the sixty-plus-miles-per-hour range. It was late September and close to dusk when I pulled into the driveway. No one was around. The place was closed. The sky to the west was on fire: thick cumulus clouds floated overhead, glowing sailor's delight red, with wistful blue around the edges.

On the highway and just thirty feet from the house was a neat little plaque next to a small tree commemorating the spot where once stood the famous maple tree that was the subject of Frost's beloved poem "Tree at My Window." The tree was cut down in 2007. Another maple, now about seven feet tall, was its replacement.* Directly behind the house, I found one old maple, tired and shabby looking, and several fruit trees. I searched the ground for maple keys but could find none. However, there were plenty of apples and pears on the ground and in the trees. The apples were ripe. I ate one and kept the core.

The true pleasure of the Frost Derry farm is to be found farther behind the house, where a lush meadow undulates for several hundred meters, surrounded by a thick and purposeful New England woods. I followed a wending path that led me along the perimeter of the ample meadow. Only one tree broke the plane of the grassy lea, and that was an odd little cherry tree full of bores or some such infestation that had caused the branches to grow gnarly and full of

* Wood from the maple tree cut down in 2007 is for sale from Charles Dent, 75 Bypass 28, Derry, N.H. 03038; the proceeds will be used to maintain the farm.

warts. It did not seem particularly old to me, but it was arresting in its singularity and deformation. I harvested what cherry seeds I found under the branches and then proceeded on. The sun was sinking fast, the tops of the trees from the bordering woods casting grotesque shadows. It made me feel anxious, so I hastened my gait.

The path through the meadow eventually led me into the woods at the far end of the field. Old trees soared skyward: hardwoods, pines, even hemlocks. Chickadees cheeped occasionally. The temperature was a good five degrees cooler under the trees. I walked for a while until the path forked and then I found myself staring at two roads diverged in a wood, and I . . . I took neither and just stood. I couldn't be sure the path I was on was the inspiration behind the famous poem "The Road Not Taken." In any case, the association was close enough. At the fork was an ancient oak tree with plenty of acorns all around it, enough to fill an entire baggy. I hadn't been planning to visit the Derry farmhouse anyway; this was all a great find.

Looking up from my task after ten minutes of focused work, I realized that the sun had fully set. "And knowing how way leads on to way, I doubted if I should ever come back . . . and that has made all the difference."

## Franconia Notch, New Hampshire

A little over a hundred miles from Derry is Franconia Notch, where Frost lived, on and off, for twenty years. There is a glittering generality that can be made about the homes and retreats of great artists in the midst of their working careers: they're drop-dead gorgeous. The Frost Place, in Franconia, is built on the side of a hill with a charming front porch that looks east toward the Presidential Range of the White Mountains. The view from there is like a picture window looking out on heaven, with the pine-dark forests carpeting the muscular curves of the soaring peaks all the way up to their collars and below their granite faces and bald pates. Frost and his family lived in the house year round after his years in Derry, from 1915 to 1920; afterward, the family summered there for an additional twenty years. Since 1977, the Frost Place has awarded a residency (with a cash stipend) to an emerging American poet, who gets to live and write in the house during the summer months. Lucky bastard.

It was early on a Sunday morning a few days after my visit to the Derry farmhouse when I arrived. It was about 8:30 A.M. The crows were raising Cain, but no one else, not even the poet-in-residence, was around. I had the place to myself. An interpretive walking path skirts the dark woods back behind the house. I took it.

The woods are not a sweet and inviting place; rather they look like a primeval forest, with a mossy bog in the background anxious for an opportunity to advance into the light of day from the shadowy depths of the inner woods, and in the foreground, naked tree trunks lie one on top of another like the bones of ancient creatures. Every hundred feet or so, a large wooden plaque offers the visitor a renowned Frost poem, written in big bold black stencils. I meandered along this coarsely maintained trail, which describes a circle, stepping over little stumps and avoiding puddles for several hundred meters before ending up back at the house fifteen minutes later. No tree stood out along the trail. Pines, maples, poplars, and birches are the dominant species. I was struck by how all of the poems offered to the visitor spoke of trees or seeds: "Putting in the Seed," "The Sound of the Trees," "Tree at My Window." Trees were more than poetic inspiration for Frost; they were family.

Back at the house, I peered in the windows. Everything looked so tiny and antique—the furniture, the lamps, the pictures, the staircase, even the floors—and simple to the extreme. I tried to guess the R value of the walls and ceiling. How could they stand the winters there? On the front porch are comfortable wicker chairs, so I sat, took out my notebook, and began to write a poem. The scene in front of me, filled with serrated mountaintops and voluminous trees, virtually placed the pen in my hand, held it, and moved it across the page for me. The result was the following little ditty, in contemplation of a burr stuck to the laces of my shoes:

## Burr
Spiny, sticky attaché
Velcro's feral cousin
Ragtime thistle stowaway
Canine's unlicensed bo'sun
Make your way by filch and cadge
Hop on saps to spread your seed
Worn on breast like Sheriff's badge
Perfidious, Pernicious weed
Alons, au revoir, bon voyage!
Won't find work as a corsage

On the left margin of the scene in front of me, a fecund cedar burst with seed clusters. To my right, a great mast of a white pine soared skyward a hundred plus feet in the air, its limp-wristed branches full of long, delicate needles swaying about in the wind like a choreographer's gesticulating arms. The giant was certainly old enough to have witnessed the Frost family as they moved about through their morning mazes. Best of all, underneath the tree lay a hundred sap-soaked, multicolor cones practically flapping about on the lawn like freshly landed rainbow trout.

I sat for a spell longer and then gathered handfuls of them.

LIKE EDISON TO THE LIGHT BULB, Einstein to $E = mc^2$, or Madame Curie to the isotope, Frost is synonymous with what he's brought to the grateful world. Robert Frost is not so much a man as he is poetry itself.

White pine *(Pinus strobus)*
Horse chestnut *(Aesculus hippocastanum)*
Sugar maple *(Acer saccharum)*
American chestnut *(Castanea dentata)*
Red oak *(Quercus rubra)*
Tulip poplar, a.k.a. tulip tree *(Liriodendron tulipifera)*

HORSE CHESTNUT POD and SEED

## Pittsfield, Massachusetts

Arrowhead Farm in Pittsfield is where Herman Melville lived from 1850 to 1863, and where he wrote *Moby Dick*. Surrounded by the hills and forests of western Massachusetts, Arrowhead is normally a long way from the briny deep; not so much today. The rain was coming down so hard that the windshield wipers on the car couldn't keep up as they jerked and gasped from side to side.

Joining me on my seed voyage for the first time was my musical wife, Mary. Sitting beside me as we zoomed along at fifty-five miles per hour, she caught a glimpse through the starboard-side window of a tiny white whale on a small sign. I slowed, turned aft, and maneuvered the car into the narrow driveway, drifted slowly around obstacles of pooled water, until finally coming to rest in the small visitor's parking lot behind a building. Through the aqueous humor of the windshield I could just make out the blurry forms of a house surrounded by trees. I had brought no rain gear—no impermeable parka, no umbrella, no galoshes. Mary and our family dog, a black border collie/golden retriever mix, were watching me to see what would happen next. It wasn't fit for man, woman, or beast outside.

Then, as the sky completely opened up, blistering the roof of the car with a deafening roar, I fell into a strange reverie: Terra firma gave way to bounding main. I felt like the small vessel in which I sat was being lashed about by lambent waves. And way down deep, below the pounding of the enraged waters, I imagined a man's voice, exhorting, plaintive, maniacal.

"Pull, will ye? Pull, can't ye? Pull, won't ye? Why in the name of gudgeons and ginger-cakes don't ye pull?—pull and break something! Pull, and start your eyes out! Here!"*

"Here!"

"What?" I was snapped out of my interlude by something fully obstructing my field of vision: an object, dark and limp, held in a firm white fist.

"I brought a rain jacket. You can use it; I'll just stay in the car," my wife said.

Then, as if by magic, the deluge ebbed. A few moments later it

* From *Moby-Dick*, chapter 48, "The First Lowering."

stopped altogether. I opened the car door and let the dog out. She stretched, sniffed, peed, and then raced off toward the house, disappearing around it in a splash of galloping paws. We followed her.

We had to navigate around pools of standing water as we made our way across the back lawn toward the honey-brown home. The place was all shut up like a morning glory, but the trees were open for business. Three giant white pines, all in a row and equidistant, stood to leeward of the house like the towering masts of a great schooner sunk in an earthly grave. Oddly, a branch almost as thick as the trunk itself on one of the pines jutted out perpendicular a few feet off the ground before turning skyward, like a boom mast.

We stood before it, transfixed, wondering if Melville had planted and then manipulated the tree to this effect. Beside the pines, we came upon an ancient Chinese chestnut and a very old maple out in front of the house. Everywhere we looked, under water and on dry ground, were countless pinecones and chestnuts and maple keys. I gathered to my heart's desire.

Bent over and focused on the ground and on gathering seeds, I felt the dog sniffing around me, freaked out by the fact that I was on my hands and knees. I suddenly stopped and looked around at where I was and what I was doing: Herman Melville's house! The trees above, giants themselves now, had no doubt witnessed this remarkable literary giant when they were mere saplings. It began to rain again. I couldn't have cared less.

Melville is to the ocean what Thoreau is to the land. Born in 1819, he was just two years younger than Thoreau, and even though they lived in the same state and not too far apart, the two never met. Melville, like Thoreau, could not earn a living from his writing. *Moby Dick* did not even sell the initial three thousand copies printed, earning him only a total net income of about five hundred

dollars. To avoid the poorhouse, Melville had to work. Besides pulling duty as a cabin boy on a whaling ship, he worked as a farmer,
a customs inspector, a teacher, and a lecturer—all the while scribbling, scribbling, scribbling through bouts of alcoholism, mental illness, and depression.

There is no fathoming the depth of Melville's love for high sea
adventure, as there is no measuring the distance of his metaphors.
All of his stories are told with a boy's heart but with a man's brain.
Melville was not an expert seaman, and unlike Twain, he never cap-
tained a ship. In fact, he was only at sea for a couple of years during
his early twenties, yet he has no equal in the realm of the seafaring
novel, proving that a ripe imagination is all that is needed to fill
the sails of one's genius. Had he set out on horseback for Alaska
or Costa Rica, or been born a century later and ventured forth
by car, train, or bus, the result would have been exactly the same:
". . . having little or no money in my purse, and nothing particular
to interest me on shore, I thought I would sail about a little and see
the watery part of the world . . ."* How many singular lives have
begun this way? Where we go and what we do in our inspired youth
is of little importance; what is important is that we go in our youth
*inspired*.

"Look!" Mary was standing over me holding something in her
hands.

I was kneeling down and couldn't see it from my angle. "What
is it?" I stood up.

It was a fat American chestnut. "Where'd you get that?"

"Over there." The tree, like many of the American chestnut
trees alive today, looked more like a misshapen fruit tree or an

* From the opening line of *Moby-Dick*, chapter 1, "Looming."

exotic shrub than a sturdy hardwood. Its half-dozen thigh-thick branches, covered by deeply grooved bark, shot directly out of the ground without the aid of a central bole.

But perhaps the most distinctive feature of the American chestnut is the seed's outer covering. The spiny burrs are the most spiteful little spiculae that ever pricked. Chestnut seed coats, rosebushes, and hawthorns have always made me scratch my head about evolution. I understand that adaptation through natural selection has provided us all with the means to defend ourselves; however, there can be such a thing as too much protection. We had no gloves, no pliers, nothing whatsoever to protect our tender fingertips from the prick of those dastardly quills. The ground under our feet was too wet and too soft, so we couldn't simply step on them as I had done to good effect at Truman Capote's cousin's house. So, one by one, we had to pry them open to look inside. It got pretty ugly.

My wife is a Midwesterner through and through. Her response to pain and inconvenience is to laugh out loud, and the worse it gets, the louder she barks. She let go some hearty ho ho hos, let me tell you. As for me, I tend to take it all personally.

Much worse for the wear, we found what we were after—a dozen or so viable little chestnuts—and unloaded them into the trunk of the car with the other baggies of pinecones, maple keys, Chinese chestnuts, and an odd nut I didn't recognize. All in all, it was quite a haul. We had resigned ourselves to being rained on, and though drenched through and through and with fingertips athrob, we went over to look in the windows of the "museum."

Reading the sign next to the entrance made me laugh out loud: "Open Memorial Day to Columbus Day." It was the weekend after Columbus Day. Looking in the windows, I found that the digs reminded me of Emerson's home, only darker and dingier, but there's only so much you can see peeking through a window. I was secretly relieved about not having to announce myself to another guide or curator.

The rain let up a little, so we decided to take a walk back behind the house. A wide trail had been mowed through the tall grass of a hayfield. (I learned later that the unplowed field was part of the original Arrowhead Farm.) The field sloped upward toward the west and was bordered on two sides by a thick forest that continued on up the side of a high hill. We strolled toward the woods, the rain now no more than a mist. The trees on the edge of the forest were young, but I was curious to see if there were any ancients in there that might have had contact with the great man. The dog bounded ahead of us off the trail to our left, boinging up and down in the tall grass like a rabbit. We stopped and watched her; it was always a show. That's when I glanced back and noticed that the long dark line of hills looming off to the east in front of the Melville home about a mile away looked like a tidal wave careening toward us—a mountainous wave. I wondered if Melville had likened the same image to a wave.

"You said that Melville only went to sea for three years?" my wife asked, as if reading my thoughts.

"About that, yeah. He'd graduated from college and wanted an adventure, so he signed up to work on a whaling ship. When they landed on some South Sea island like a year later, he deserted and went native. Ran around naked with cannibals. I think he was with them for like a month before he saw another ship out in the lagoon and decided he'd had his fill of primitive life and signed on to that one, which took him to Hawaii. He lived there for about a year before he eventually sailed back to Boston. Start to finish, I think the whole adventure was three years and change. But he was the first one to go to that part of the world—before Twain, before Gauguin, Robert Louis Stevenson, and all the others."

"It's amazing that it was just three years but was enough to last him a lifetime."

We started walking again.

"I was thinking the same thing. Somewhere along the line we've missed the point, you know? It's about the adventure, not about the skill. Kids are going off to college thinking they have to learn how to become an expert at something. That's not it at all. Thoreau—or Whitman, I'm not sure which one—wrote that the thrill is in the not knowing." (It was Whitman. I was thinking of his words from *Specimen Days in America*: "You must not know too much or be too precise or scientific about birds and trees and flowers and watercraft; a certain free-margin, and even vagueness—ignorance, credulity— helps your enjoyment of these things.".)\*

We were approaching the woods. The dog was already fully invested in them. We walked where Melville may have stretched his legs and cogitated about his white whale. It was a poignant moment for me to think of the wild-eyed genius, his thoughts at sea but his feet solidly on New England ground, strolling among the immaculate trees: the trees from whose buoyant flesh those magnificent ships were crafted; the trees whose soaring lengths provided the towering masts that held the engine sails; the trees who offered quiet comfort and constant companionship throughout his tempestuous life.

But not these trees. All the trees within our ken were young,

---

\* Walt Whitman, *Specimen Days in America*, London, Walter Scott, 1887, pages 282–283.

and nary a one had ever lent root or limb to him.* We turned
around and exited the way we had entered.

The dog came charging after us, tongue dangling out of her
mouth, and, uncharacteristically, she lost her footing and crashed
headlong into the back of my wife's legs.

"Oww! Nikki! Ha ha ha! That really hurt," Mary said, rubbing
her leg and laughing. The dog just stood there looking at us, wagging her tail.

The rain was falling again, coming down hard. At the car, the
three of us stood like creatures from the black lagoon, woefully wet
and dreadfully drenched.

"Heaven have mercy on us all—Presbyterians and Pagans
alike—for we are all somehow dreadfully cracked about the head,
and sadly need mending." †

---

* As Alan Weisman points out in *The World Without Us*, farm fields left alone,
and unpolluted by chemical fertilizers, turn back into forest in a few decades,
as is happening throughout northern New England.
† From *Moby-Dick*, chapter 17, "The Ramadan."

**Red oak** *(Quercus rubra)*
**Tulip poplar, a.k.a. tulip tree** *(Liriodendron tulipifera)*

TULIP POPLAR

## Saratoga Springs, New York

Yaddo, which rhymes with shadow, has hosted some of America's
most celebrated writers, composers, and artists since the turn of
the last century. Several of the writers from whose trees I was able
to gather seeds were once fellows there—Truman Capote, Carson
McCullers, Eudora Welty—but it was the list of writers whose
homes I wasn't able to find or get to—Katherine Anne Porter, Jean
Stafford, James Baldwin, Langston Hughes, John Cheever, Sylvia

Plath, Saul Bellow, Alice Walker, Wallace Stegner, William Carlos Williams, Mario Puzo—that compelled me to visit the retreat. Not that quantity matters, but Yaddo offered a ten-to-one payoff that I just couldn't resist.

Under a moody sky, driving through the resort city of Saratoga Springs, New York, my wife and I motored past the State College, past the National Museum of Dance, past the National Museum of Racing, past the Performing Arts Center, past the Saratoga Springs Spa State Park, and past the Saratoga Race Track, until we came at last to the redoubtable entrance gate of Yaddo, one of America's premier artists' retreats. We drove up the august driveway, turned right where a huge sign threatened anyone who wasn't authorized to turn right with prosecution, and trundled cautiously along the winding drive. We passed in front of the mansion itself, lugubrious with its gray stone pillars, porticos, and towers, all shrouded in dark shadows by scores of soaring white pines along its front and sides. We continued past it for a hundred yards before turning into a parking area near a smaller building. I had a two o'clock appointment with the Yaddo publicist, and she'd warned me about the renovation work being done. Boy, she wasn't kidding: the place was littered with pickup trucks, Dumpsters, and piles of lumber.

It wasn't the sights that didn't live up to my expectations; it was the sounds. Interstate 87, also known as the Northway, borders the Yaddo property. Built in 1961, the Northway not only connects New York City to Montreal but also completely corrupts Yaddo with noise pollution 24/7, as tractor trailers and automobiles roar by at seventy miles per hour along the property's eastern perimeter. What a racket.

"Better take the leash just in case," I suggested as I stepped out of the car and watched the dog take off after a squirrel.

"What?" Mary shouted, unable to hear my mutterings over the cacophony of zooming cars and trucks in the near distance.

"Better take the leash!" I cupped my hands and yelled over the hood of the car.

The absurdity of it all hit us at the same moment, eliciting frowns on both our faces. I shook my head, turned, and walked, as instructed, toward the side of the building where the stairs to the publicist's office lay.

If the noise outside wasn't enough to drive you to distraction, the drilling, sawing, and hammering inside the building was. At one point during our conversation, I was told that everything possible was being done to keep the noise from the construction site down to a minimum so as not to bother the artists, but the publicist had to say this twice, because I couldn't hear her over the drilling, sawing, and hammering. It was all I could do to keep from bursting out laughing. After about fifteen minutes, at my urging, we carried the Yaddo history lesson away from the dust and clamor and out onto the beleaguered grounds of the famed estate.

The chapter on art patronage throughout the ages, especially as told by the artists' themselves, has not always been a cheery one, from Benvenuto Cellini's autobiography, which documents his abusive and demoralizing relationship with the Vatican, to Vincent Van Gogh's abject letters to his tight-fisted and inconsistent brother, Theo, and his uncle Cent. As I listened to the publicist's grandiloquent description of the late industrialist turned philanthropist Spencer Trask, and his indomitable wife, Katrina, and their fabulous riches and ill-fated losses, along with their desire to help the artists, it struck me just how naïve it all sounded. Poverty and privation, not money and comfort, are the artist's most complementary patrons.

These were the thoughts whizzing through my head as we walked down the stairs and back out toward the parking lot. Mary stood there, a contrite look on her face, with the dog next to her on the leash. Apparently, there'd been a little incident. Right after I left them to go inside, they had headed off toward the buildings behind the offices, where the artists reside and work. Our dog, Nikki, is a border collie/golden retriever mix. She's as smart as, and infinitely more obedient than, most adolescents and just as mindful of traffic and trouble, so we don't need to leash her unless absolutely essential. Near one of the studios, the dog had run after a rabbit, which prompted a frock-coated painter to come charging out of one of the cottages wielding a paintbrush. When she saw my wife, she settled down. Mary, who is as friendly and gregarious as a Salvation Army bell ringer, quickly resolved the situation by showing the painter how obedient and friendly the dog is; she also told her who she was and what she was doing there. They parted ways all smiles, but with the dog on her leash.

After I explained this little mishap, the publicist launched into a horrific tale of a pit bull that had run amok on the estate grounds a few years back, mauling a visitor before it was caught and drowned by some anonymous man in the rose garden fountain. The person who got mauled sued the foundation, winning the case and costing Yaddo two hundred thousand. This, we were told, was why a dog off leash at Yaddo is taboo, and why the artist was so uptight.

As she told us this story, we strolled slowly along the driveway toward the mansion, and by the time the story was finished, we were standing directly in front of the stone edifice, our eyes drawn upward toward its crowning tower. Taking just a moment to catch her breath, the publicist then filled us in on the historical background of the estate, starting with the original owner of the land, Jacobus

Barhyte, a Revolutionary War veteran who was a dear friend of Edgar Allan Poe. The story goes that Poe wrote his immortal poem "The Raven" while visiting the property on which Yaddo now sits. After being apprised of this tidbit, my mind went to work editing the history as the publicist had told it, so that by the time she was done, I had convinced myself that the great gray stone mansion was the actual model for Poe's "The Fall of the House of Usher"—even though it hadn't been built at the time of the story's writing. I have an active imagination.

And as we came around to the back of the estate, where the sweeping lawn rolls down into the roaring throat of the Northway—easily seen through the thin wall of leafless trees—I realized that my seed gathering at Yaddo was to be a supervised affair. The publicist was bent on accompanying us the entire time.

The back lawn was the place where the whole cast of writers who had stayed at Yaddo would have at some point during their stay strolled along and ogled the lovely trees at the edges of the slope. I spied two soaring hardwoods halfway down the sweeping expanse: a red oak and a tulip poplar. Both were at least a hundred years old, and on the well-manicured lawn, under their massive horizontal branches, I quickly found five pristine acorns and one small tulip cone full of samaras. (A samara is also called a key, a whirlybird, a helicopter, a whirligig, or a polynose. I really appreciate the fact that I have a choice of terms to use for seeds.)

That was the extent of it. I put them in the same baggy and slid it into my back pocket like a thief.

Back at the car a half hour later, with a handful of seeds in my pocket, we bid our host adieu, offered a heaping helping of thank-yous, slipped into the soothing quiet zone of our automobile, and rocketed out of there as if the woods were on fire.

Before we had even exited the property, Mary turned to me with a sarcastic smirk: "So, are you going to apply for a residency?"

"I don't think so," I said, frowning.

"Why not?"

"I'm not Yaddo material."

"What do you mean you're not Yaddo material? You're an award-winning novelist."

"Come on, look at me! My nose is all smooshed in and broken; I've got scar tissue around my eyebrows, and I don't know if I ever told you this, but growing up, a heck of a lot of my friends and relatives used the plural pronoun 'yous.'"

"So what? Didn't you tell me Mario Puzo was a resident?"

"Yeah, and so was Sylvia 'I-want-to-kill-myself-and-crawl-abjectly-back-into-the-womb' Plath." (The actual quote from Plath's journal reads, "I want to kill myself, to escape from responsibility, to crawl back abjectly into the womb.")

"I didn't know that."

"You know where she wrote that, don't you? No, the only application I'd ever submit is for a job as groundskeeper. Besides, that place gives me the creeps," I protested.

"What, you don't like the sound of flowing traffic?"

"Nah, don't."

"You mean, *yaddon't.*"

"Exactly!"

Tulip poplar, a.k.a. tulip tree *(Liriodendron tulipifera)*
Northern catalpa *(Catalpa speciosa)*
Black cherry *(Prunus serotina)*

BLACK CHERRY

## Springdale, Pennsylvania

I went to grad school at the University of Pittsburgh for two years, and I'm embarrassed to say that I was not aware how close I was to Rachel Carson's hometown. Heck, I used to work as an admissions clerk in Pitt's Cathedral of Learning and ride the 1930s-style elevator all the way up to the top floor to enjoy the view during my breaks—I probably could have seen Springdale from up there.*

---

* The Cathedral of Learning, at 42 stories and 535 feet, is the tallest education building in the Western Hemisphere. Worldwide, it is topped only by a

God only knows what the world would be like without Carson's masterpiece *Silent Spring*, which points out the proverbial eight-hundred-pound gorilla in the room: "Chemicals are the sinister and little-recognized partners of radiation in changing the very nature of the world—the very nature of life."*

With my youngest daughter, Evelyn, in tow and Mary at home with a full-time job, I shuffled off to Buffalo to pick up my eldest daughter, Katherine. From there, the three of us were bound for Pittsburgh and Rachel Carson's childhood home.

Jared Diamond postulates that the lateral orientation of our nation accommodates the movement of genes and genius in flora and fauna.† America's uniqueness lies not only in its geography and people but also in its infinite points of interest, and the highways, parkways, and thruways that crisscross this land connect the dots, forming fantastic patterns and possibilities. Just in the elongated state of Pennsylvania (*sylvan* meaning "of or characteristic of the woods or forest"), with regard to its former residents, the juxtapo-

---

university building in Moscow and two in Tokyo. It was begun in 1926 and dedicated in 1937. The Cathedral's first floor is called the Commons Room, a fifteenth-century English perpendicular Gothic-style hall with arched ceilings reaching over fifty feet high. The room was financed by Andrew Mellon.

\* The *New York Times* quoted Miss Carson's position in her obituary: "The sprays, dusts and aerosols are now applied almost universally to farms, gardens, forests and homes—non-selective chemicals that have the power to kill every insect, the good and the bad, to still the song of birds and the leaping of fish in the streams—to coat the leaves with a deadly film and to linger on in soil—all this, though the intended target may be only a few weeds or insects . . . Can anyone believe it is possible to lay down such a barrage of poisons on the surface of the earth without making it unfit for all life? They should not be called 'insecticides' but 'biocides.'"

† *Guns, Germs, and Steel* by Jared Diamond. However, he goes on to postulate in his sequel, *Collapsed*, that the default position of human civilization is self-destruction.

sitions run from Ben Franklin to W. C. Fields, Andy Warhol to Arnold Palmer, Ethel Waters to John Updike. And straight down, from the birthplace of Lucille Ball, the determined and beloved woman who made television history, is the birthplace of the fearless heroine who silenced the spray guns full of DDT.

Springdale is a gritty, rawboned mill town eighteen miles northeast of Pittsburgh, nestled on the banks of the westward-flowing Allegheny River. Small no-nonsense brick houses dot the slopes that look down on the active waters. One main artery runs north to south along the river, and the rest of the streets run straight up the slopes like the tines of a comb.

Springdale has pawnshops, dollar stores, bars, auto body shops, churches, and elementary schools. But what dumbfounded me was the sight of two imposing smokestacks rising high above the town at its southern end like goalposts. Where, pray tell, were the signs with the environmental slogans "This Is a Pesticide-Free Zone"? Or "Reduce, Reuse, Recycle"? Or "Protect Our Environment"? As a matter of fact, signs for Rachel Carson's home, a National Historic Landmark, were hard to find. In fact, if I didn't know any better, I'd be inclined to think, by the lack of celebratory signage, that the people of Springdale are not the least bit proud of their hometown heroine.

Keeping one eye on the driving and the other peeled for signs to her house, I finally found my way to the quaint Carson farmhouse up the hill, just a few blocks off the main drag and less than a half mile from the center of town. The classic eighteenth-century structure was closed for business; it was Easter Sunday. Fortunately for me, trees are always open for business.

I found a massive tulip tree standing between the driveway and the house as I hopped out of the van. The white farmhouse had a gorgeous front porch that looked out over the river a half mile below. On the south side of the Allegheny, a twin ridge rose up like a reflection, with its perfectly straight top looking more like a great green levee. In its day, before the mills and smokestacks, the little farmhouse must have felt like paradise to young Rachel. It's still pretty beautiful today. All around, the birds were chirping and squirrels were chasing one another in the branches above. The neighbors on both sides of the place were out raking leaves. There were kids playing and shouting in the street. My progeny were both asleep in the backseat. All was right with the world.

I REMEMBER VIVIDLY as a little boy being outside on a summer's day playing in the street. Suddenly one of the kids from around the corner would shout out, "Here it comes!" And from around the bend a monster would appear in the form of a tanker truck. It was preceded by a weird cacophony: a combination drone from its engine, whirs from the spray machine, and hissing from the pressurized fogger as it hit the swaying leaves and branches of the trees. I remember that my mother, God bless her, would come running out of the house and scream at my sister and me to get inside behind closed doors. But I also remember how some of the neighbor kids, whose parents weren't around or didn't think the way mine did, would stand there with their eyes closed and their fists clenched with big smiles of anticipation on their faces as a great billowing cloud of DDT white-outted them from sight.

It took Rachel Carson, a marine biologist from this tiny town in Pennsylvania, to point out that the manufacturers of DDT were poisoning the world with increasingly deadlier doses. With each new batch, Darwin's principle of the survival of the fittest kicked in and the next generation of insects grew resistant and even more numerous.* By the time Carson came along, this silent chemical holocaust was on the verge of not only exterminating our national emblem, the bald eagle, but also silencing our spring. The chemical industry felt threatened enough to try to fight back. Monsanto, for example, responded immediately to *Silent Spring* with an article, published in October of 1962, a month after the book came out, entitled "The Desolate Year," which warned of worldwide famine as a result of overregulation of pesticides.†

My only disappointment about the house being closed was the fact that I couldn't ask questions specific to the vegetation on the grounds. I circumnavigated the house and peered in the windows, hoping that someone might be there. No luck. Undeterred, I found plenty of big old trees on the little half-acre lot just waiting for me. I could collect what looked good and ask questions by phone later. So, starting with the big tulip tree next to my car, I began to fill up my baggies with seeds.

There is a narrow little pathway etched into the half-acre property that serpentines around the yard and disappears up the ridge behind the house. I followed it along, noticing that most of the trees around me were young and some recently planted. Eventually the path led me up a steep ridge, which broke out from the trees onto the south lawn of a modern school building. The patch of grass between the trees and the school was about ten yards wide. I couldn't help but imagine kids playing on that lawn during the day, oblivious to the historic home below them. There was no trail

* Carson describes the phenomenon as a "flareback," where sprayed populations of insects, once inured to the poison, actually come back in numbers greater than before.
† Information available at www1.umn.edu/ships/pesticides/library/monsanto 1962.pdf.

marker, but I could tell by the worn-down grass which way to walk. The path took me along the school grounds for about twenty yards before it dipped back down into a small lot of woods—one square acre full of old-growth trees. This was all that was left of Carson's childhood woods.

It made me sad to think that this is all that our exalted nation could preserve of such a meritorious life's work. The trees themselves were surprisingly misshapen and in ill health. No doubt the mission statement was to leave the little wood in its original state. The well-worn path did a cursive loop through the wood. It certainly wasn't the typical interpretive nature walk with the requisite plaques, tree markers, and benches, but what it lacked in industry it made up for in diversity. There were all kinds of hardwoods and conifers: northern catalpa, black cherry, maple, oak, locust, and hemlock. It was hard to say which trees had been alive during Carson's time. I assumed all of them had and chose the biggest ones. I found cherry seeds that had actually sprouted, and plenty of maples and enough catalpa pods to populate a small forest. In a half hour, my work was complete.

Back at the van, I found that the girls had woken up. They were looking at me through the tinted windows as if I had grown another head. I could tell they were thinking "Where are we now? This can't be the place." I opened the doors to let the fresh air in and unburden myself of my bags of seeds.

I hustled Katherine out of the vehicle to take a picture of me standing on Rachel Carson's front porch.

"You've got something green in between your teeth, loser," she scoffed. (In our family, *loser* is a term of endearment.)

"I know. It's my tribute to Rachel Carson," I responded. "Just take the picture, loser."

Looking at her, all of nineteen years old and laughing at me, I wanted to say something meaningful about where we were and to whom we were paying homage on this sunny Easter Sunday. She lowered the camera, indicating that she had snapped the photo.

Trying hard to think of something to say, I turned my back to her and wandered a few paces toward the front door, where two copper plaques, brown from oxidation, had been screwed into the siding. I turned to her and gesticulated. "Come closer." I wanted to be sure that the information from the plaques would be in the photo. She frowned in annoyance and shuffled closer, with her head pitched to the side. I studied her as she walked toward me.

She had dropped out of college at the end of her third semester, completely disillusioned by her experience in higher education. And this was a student who, as a freshman, had been the principal bassist in the university's symphony orchestra, and who, effervescing with extreme enthusiasm, spearheaded environmental-improvement initiatives on campus. But what she discovered was that the only higher aspect to her education was the cost of tuition, room, and board, and the size of the piles of irrelevancy she had to surmount. Smarter than the average bear, she dropped out and found a job working in a school for the profoundly disabled as a one-on-one aide with a blind, deaf ten-year-old girl with Down syndrome, thus discovering for herself her own version of a higher education.

"All right, go ahead and flash your gang sign," she said as she held up the camera.

"The green on my teeth is my gang sign."

She snapped it. "Should I take another one?"

"Nah, that's enough."

We walked back toward the van in silence. But before we got

there, I stopped, because I finally had something to say to her: "I'm sure you know all about Rachel Carson, right?"

"Al Gore dedicated *The Inconvenient Truth* to her."

"But do you know what she did?"

"She stopped them from using DDT because it was killing all the eagles and poisoning the drinking water and us."

"Right, but more important, she's proof that one person can make a difference."

She looked at me with a patronizing smirk. "Okay, I suppose now you're going to tell me that I can make a difference?"

"You already are."

She laughed, and then looked at me challengingly: "And what about the guy who invented DDT? Doesn't he get some credit for, like, helping stop the spread of malaria and saving millions of lives?"

I went to open my mouth to say something witty about the difficulty of balancing good intentions with harmful side effects. About making the world a better place. But my kid already knew all about that, as Rachel Carson knew.

# Back Home

THINGS WERE PRETTY BLEAK as far as my saplings and seeds were concerned. The latter, stored in row upon row of boxes in my basement, were starting to look a little bit like the Norwegian "Doomsday" Seed Vault.* In fact, I wrote to them to see if I could store some of my seeds, albeit temporarily, under their Upper-*Upper* Norwegian permafrost. Unfortunately, that's not how it works.

As for the saplings: my wife, who had long since lost her confidence in my underwhelming class of over-watered "weedlings," as she wistfully called them, had rescued all but a few of my favorites

---

* Also called the Svalbard Global Seed Vault, the seed bank is located on the Upper Norwegian island of Spitsbergen far above the Arctic Circle. Plant seeds from tens of thousands of varieties of species are kept in an underground cave. The idea is to keep extra copies of seeds in gene banks in case of a large-scale global disaster. Storage of seeds in the seed vault is free of charge. Norway and the Global Crop Diversity Trust (GCDT) will pay operational costs. The Bill & Melinda Gates Foundation, United Kingdom, Norway, Australia, Switzerland, and Sweden fund the GCDT. Other funding has also been received from many other sources including Brazil, Colombia, Ethiopia, and India.

by putting them outside (it was springtime), where they sat in their lowly makeshift pots next to her glorious flower bed, looking like true losers alongside her colorful and redolent azaleas, begonias, irises, marigolds, daffodils, peonies, petunias, and roses. There was one good thing about the new arrangement: I was relieved of the onus of watering.

With a slightly new outlook on things, I departed for another expedition down South to take away seeds from some of my all-time favorite writers' homes. And best of all, I'd be joined by old friends and family.

## Part Six

You ever notice that trees do everything to git
attention we do, except walk?

—ALICE WALKER, *THE COLOR PURPLE*

Tulip poplar, a.k.a. tulip tree *(Liriodendron tulipifera)*
Sugar maple *(Acer saccharum)*
Eastern redbud, a.k.a. Judas tree *(Cercis canadensis)*

TULIP POPLAR

## Mount Vernon

With its Ionic columns, horizontal posture, riparian geography, and botanical splendors, Mount Vernon indubitably befits a man of mythic proportions, so it is no wonder that George Washington was proud of his home and of his ability to gainfully manage his estate. (In the colonial period, many of the great estates throughout Virginia were chronically in arrears.) During his lifetime, he hosted multitudes of admirers, and he did not turn away the pilgrims who came to pay him homage. Unfortunately, there was a downside to his hospitality: relic takers. People of all stripes pilfered anything that wasn't nailed down, inside the house and out. Even today, the staff of Mount Vernon is on high alert for would-be thieves. Alas, today I might be one myself, even though I will ask before I take.

As we pulled into the parking lot (yes, I still had the two losers with me), I noticed a large complex of Quonset hut greenhouses at the bottom of a slope. Once we were out of the truck, I led the girls to the greenhouses. A constant flow of green-shirted workers bounded around the buildings, bent to their tasks. I figured I had better not mess around, so with backpack securely in place and my Ziploc bags out of sight, I led my daughters straight over to the first door. I didn't knock (you don't knock at farms or nurseries); I just opened the flimsy glass door and walked in, signaling to the girls that I'd be back in a flash. They knew better, however.

A gray-haired, grandmotherly-looking woman was hard at work potting plants at a large worktable. She wore an official Mount Vernon green shirt with matching apron. I went up to her, introduced myself, and described my quest. She was very pleasant. She smiled, nodded, blinked a couple of times, and then began to tell me that she was a volunteer. But before she could finish her explanation, another woman, younger, with darker hair and not so pleasant, came rushing over. She stopped abruptly as she drew abreast of us, arrested by my unofficial garb. She looked me up and down; then she asked if I needed help. I repeated my spiel. She didn't smile. She didn't nod. She didn't even blink. Her response was accusatory:

"You do realize, of course, that we grow and sell legacy trees ourselves."

"No, I didn't know th—"

"What's going on here?" A tall, athletic, fiftyish, smiling, bald man came charging out of a nearby office, dusting the crumbs from his green shirt; he was still chewing on a sandwich.

Once again I explained myself.

He scratched his nose, looked at his watch, and then swallowed what was left in his mouth.

"Yes, hmmm, well, there are only nine original trees left on the estate dating back to Washington's time." He said this in a way to suggest that my idea, though valid, would yield little if anything of interest to me. I wasn't dissuaded.

"Only nine? What about all those huge oaks I saw coming in on the Memorial Highway?" I jerked my thumb back over my shoulder.

His eyes got big and bright; it was as if I'd said the magic word. "Interesting you should mention that! We haven't done a complete survey of the surrounding forest yet, but we're planning to. There are over three hundred acres here as a kind of buffer zone against urban pressure, but we don't fully know what's out there."

"Really?"

"We've had a group of paleobotanists come and do preliminary surveys, and the results do indicate that there are probably speci-mens dating back over two hundred years. Have you ever partici-pated in a forest survey?"

"Not a forest survey, no, but I have surveyed the trees in my own neighborhood." (That was slightly more than a half-truth.) I got the feeling he took me for some sort of journalist or ignorant researcher, because he launched right into an explanation.

"They conduct what's called a point-center quarter sampling by setting up four quadrats [an ecological term signifying a square or rectangular plot of land marked off for the study of plants and animals] placed around a central axis point. The closest tree to the center point in each quadrat is measured for diameter at breast height and the species of tree is recorded. They work from the center out with very exact measurements, taking into account . . ."

At that point my eyes sort of glazed over. When he was finished with the explanation, I disingenuously asked again, "So, only nine original trees remaining, huh?"

"We had twelve up until last year, but we lost three, unfortunately. The tulip poplars on the bowling green are doing great, and so is the cypress up there, but we have some problems with the others, specifically verticillium wilt, but—" He suddenly looked at his watch; then, with a shrug, he offered me his hand. "Hey, time to go. Enjoy your visit."

"Thank you, I will," I said enthusiastically.

Bounding out the same door through which I'd entered, I ran smack-dab into the unhappy faces of my girls.

"What took you so long?" Evelyn groused

"I'm really sorry. I got my ear talked off."

That quieted them for a moment.

A few strides past the entrance gate, we entered the Ford Orientation Center to buy admission tickets. I paid the fifteen-dollar-a-piece entrance fee, and we dutifully followed the crowd through the glistening marble hallway. We almost had to shield our eyes against the sheen bouncing off George Washington's glossy white statue. All he needed, I concluded, was a fountain of water spouting out of the top of his head or his penis and he could have stood in the entranceway of any garish Las Vegas restaurant. What is it about America that must laminate its history and its heroes?

The high ceilings, marbleized floor and walls, and cranked-up air-conditioning created the effect of a sterile mausoleum, and we enthusiastically exited the building with a gasp, our lungs drinking in the elixir of salubrious Potomac River air. The iconic house was to our left, but the path led us to the right as it circuitously looped around to the magnificent front side. Before we had walked twenty yards, the meandering line of people came to an abrupt stop. We overheard someone say it was a two-hour wait to tour the house itself. Forget that.

Mount Vernon's curators have strategically placed corrals of sheep at various locations around the grounds as props or, from my cynical perspective, to remind us of how we should behave. There was a corral just to our right, so we wandered over to it. We leaned on the split-rail fence, looking at the sheep. They seemed delighted to see us and came right over. Katherine spontaneously launched into a spiel on animal husbandry, explaining that some sheep have horns that will grow in complete circles, eventually growing right back into their skulls. They have to be slaughtered, she informed us, because the syndrome is hereditary. Her story really set the mood. I stood scratching one of the wooly mammal's necks, wondering if its horns were growing into its brain. We did an about-face and headed over to the bowling green, where we found two towering tulip trees, one on either side of the lawn, each soaring more than a hundred and forty feet into the air.

They were monsters, the biggest hardwoods I'd ever laid my eyes on. Tulip trees are the tallest of North America's hardwoods, with some specimens reaching two hundred feet in height. In most eastern forests, they stand head and shoulders above the rest of the trees. That these two specimens had attained such stellar heights described for me a time even before Mount Vernon was built, when the area was a forest of hardwoods since, without competition, Tulip trees will extend their bowers perpendicular to the ground rather than skyward, and their trunks will grow in girth like middle-aged linebackers. Incorrectly categorized as a poplar because of its soft, waterproof wood, the tulip was once highly prized for its insulating capacities and floatability. It was said that Daniel Boone carved a sixty-foot canoe out of a tulip tree, "and into it he piled his family and his gear and sailed away down the Ohio River into Spanish territory away from ingrate Kentucky."* I was certain that these two counted among the nine remaining trees that the horticulturist had mentioned.

Searching the area underneath them, I couldn't believe my eyes. Nothing; not a single tulip seed! Tulip tree seeds are the most prolific seeds in the kingdom, even more so than maple keys. The groundskeepers must literally vacuum them up off the grass; there was no other explanation. But as luck would have it, at the base of one of the giant trees was a very large green shrub fully in bloom with an accommodating canopy. I was able to stoop down, walk inside, and be hidden from view. At this point, the girls pretended that they didn't know me and wandered off down the green lawn, leaving me to my illicit work.

It was as dark as an unlit basement in there. I got down on my haunches and sifted through the wood chip mulch. In the dark, the tulip seeds were the exact same color as the mulch. I had to pick up fistfuls of mulch and blindly winnow the seeds from the chips. After about twenty minutes, I had found perhaps two dozen of the little flesh-colored, toothpick-size seeds. Whoever is in charge of denying tree seeds to visitors at Mount Vernon does a damn good job.

Satisfied with my meager haul, I went in search of the girls. I found them in Washington's herb garden smelling the parsley, sage, rosemary, and garlic. All around the herb garden were the most

* From *A Natural History of North American Trees* by Donald Culross Peattie.

intriguing apple trees I'd ever seen. They were manipulated in such a way as to be growing like fences, their branches stretched laterally for several yards in both directions along a wire. The beautiful white-pink flowers gave off a delicious aroma. There was a staff member nearby watering them, and I took the opportunity to ask him about the trees. He told me that the foundation had started them; they weren't originals. That was enough information for me. We left in search of Washington's tomb.

On the way, I looked around for the cypress mentioned back at the greenhouses, but I couldn't find it. I did notice a huge white oak tree on the steep slope between the vegetable garden and the Potomac River. I hopped over the embankment and slid down an unused path, quickly searching through the undergrowth for acorns. Nothing. I was waxing agitated. I abandoned the acorn search and caught up with the girls.

Reading about Mount Vernon before this trip, I found the estate described as having fallen into complete disrepair by the middle of the nineteenth century.[*] In 1858, a group of women calling themselves the Mount Vernon Ladies' Association bought the place and began restoring it. To this day, the MVLA has owned and maintained the estate as a living memorial.

During the Civil War, Mount Vernon was the only neutral ground in the entire United States.[†] To make sure all was fair, the MVLA even kept one woman from the North and one from the South on the property at all times. Another fact that few realize is that slavery has forever dogged the legacy of Mount Vernon. Most

---

[*] *Sarah Johnson's Mount Vernon* by Scott E. Casper, Hill and Wang, New York, 2008.
[†] Ibid.

people think that Washington freed his slaves before he died. Some of them he did, bestowing land on them as well, but many of the slaves who lived and worked at Mount Vernon were not his to free; they belonged to his wife, Martha's, first husband, so they remained "dower slaves," which in turn created great hostility between them and the owners through the years.*

From the same book, I also learned about West Ford, born a slave at Mount Vernon but later freed. He worked for more than forty years on the estate as a carpenter and eventually as manager. He was a trusted friend and employee of the Washington family, but his greatest contribution to Washington's legacy was his stories. He was a master storyteller (think Uncle Remus), and the tales he told about his friendship with the father of our country became legend, apocryphal though many of the stories were. For decades after Washington's death, people came to Mount Vernon not only to see the president's sarcophagus but also to hear West Ford tell his stories. Following Ford's death, Edmund Parker, a former slave and an equally gifted raconteur, carried on the tradition of standing guard out in front of Washington's Tomb and delighting visitors with his storytelling.

After reading all this, I was extremely disappointed to find a June Cleaver look-alike greeting visitors beside the tomb, which is carved into the side of an embankment, with an iron gate in front of the sarcophaguses of George and Martha. West Ford and Edmund Parker's replacement stood in front of the gate smiling bright but saying absolutely nothing. I asked her if she knew about West Ford or Edmund Parker; she didn't. That's when it hit me like a brick. Something's missing at Mount Vernon: black people.

* Ibid.

Since about 1920, few African Americans have worked there.*
Today only white folks dressed in knickers and tricorn hats hoe
the rows and greet the people. Perhaps it's too painful a past to cel-
ebrate, or maybe Attorney General Eric Holder was right when he
said that when it comes to race, America is a country of cowards.
But the fact remains that African Americans operated and cared
for Mount Vernon for most of its history, something that should
not be kept locked inside the tomb, so to speak. I concluded that
the present-day "Mount Vernon Tour Program" is like listening to
the story of "Br'er Rabbit" as narrated not by Uncle Remus but Mis-
ter Rogers. Oh sure, they offer "Slave Life Tours" to visiting school
groups, making it a point to remind the kids that Mount Vernon
owes much to the un-free labor that toiled there. And there is a
Slave Memorial close to Washington's Tomb, which we wandered
over to, but it's not enough of the truth, not nearly enough.

"Come on, let's get out of here," I told the girls, who stood looking down at the Slave Memorial marker. Both girls had big fat question marks on their faces. The whole scene just didn't coalesce.

We walked briskly back toward the exit. Once there, we were
horrified to find that in order to exit the grounds, we were obliged to
go through the Donald W. Reynolds Museum and Education Center, a.k.a. the gift shop. The crowd was thick as briars in there. Many
people were snagged out in front of a small theater, waiting to see
the next showing of *George Washington: First in War, First in Peace,
First in the Hearts of His Countrymen.*

And, evidently, "first in pain"! As we squeezed through the

* "By 1920 almost everyone . . . working there was white . . . Sarah Johnson's
Mount Vernon was being obliterated, a nineteenth-century place erased by
Jim Crow and historic preservation." From the introduction to Casper's *Sarah
Johnson's Mount Vernon.*

crowd, we found ourselves face-to-face with a multimedia presenta-
tion the likes of which the world should never see: *The Agony and
the Ecstasy of George Washington's Teeth*. Poor Evelyn, who, like her
father, is a bit of a hypochondriac, has yet to fully recover from what
she saw that day. She stood watching with eyes wide as saucers as
the video explained how impacted wisdom teeth led to many a pre-
mature death among the colonial population, and how our hapless
first president's rotten choppers caused him no end of pain during
his lifetime. In fact, Washington's dentures are on display in a glass
booth. The dentures are extraordinary, not because they are made
of wood (they're not; they're from hippopotamus ivory) but because
the lower denture has a hole in it, allowing it to be anchored tightly
to the one remaining tooth in the presidential mouth (eventually
causing even that tooth to loosen and fall out). Apparently they
have no qualms about putting the father of our country's woeful
dental history on display for the entire world to see, yet any mention
of slavery is taboo.

Back inside the car, Evelyn was massaging her jaw. She had recently been to the dentist about her impacted wisdom teeth.

"Dad, what's the next step for getting my wisdom teeth removed?"

"I wouldn't worry about it too much," I counseled. But I knew
she would . . . for the rest of the trip.

## Monticello

Outside the Smith Education Center, which happily looked more
like an art gallery than a visitor center, we paid the steep admission price of twenty dollars each—with no discounts for students,
teens, or educators. We held our noses as we walked past the idling

shuttle busses parked outside, but then joyfully promenaded onto the Saunders-Monticello Trail, which led up the hill to the back of Monticello.

Gorgeous redbud trees in full bloom greeted us as we emerged from the trail's canopy. The redbud was called the Judas tree in the Old World, because of the belief that Judas Iscariot hanged himself from the branch of one, turning its formerly white flowers red. It is well documented that both Jefferson and Washington loved to dig up these trees from the surrounding woods and plant them on their grounds so they could enjoy their flowers in the spring. They produce seedpods, and I wandered up to look for some. I could find nothing. Over their shoulders, at the far end of the plateau hilltop, Jefferson's iconic red-white-and-black neoclassical home bulged up from the ground, its round dome and Ionic columns a wondrous sight in that semi-alpine setting. Jefferson chose himself quite a spot up there. Monticello sits 850 feet above sea level, with a picturesque view of the Atlantic Coastal Plain that draws the eye eastward out across the blue verdure below. Whereas Mount Vernon describes a man of mythic proportions, Monticello describes a man of harmonic proportions.

A few yards from the end of the trail, we came upon Jefferson's graveyard and tombstone. It's a tiny cemetery, rectangular in shape, about forty yards by ten yards, surrounded by a no-nonsense cast-iron fence with spikes on top. Just beyond the locked gate is the third president's imposing bone-gray gravestone, towering ten feet in the air. And beyond that, packed cheek-by-jowl in the puny cemetery, is a crush of smaller granite headstones marking the remains of his descendants.

Evelyn: "Dad, didn't Jefferson have children with his slaves?"

Me: "Yes, he and Sally Hemings had children together."

Evelyn: "Then shouldn't those people get to be buried here, too?" *

Me: "I don't see why not. But according to our visitor's guide, the African American graveyard is back down at the bottom of the hill, next to the parking lot."

We stood holding on to the bars of the iron fence, staring at the gravestones, saying nothing but feeling sad that the revised history of our old heroes could never be etched into the stone.

We wandered up toward the house via the vegetable garden. Everything here was much more understated than at Mount Vernon. The garden was ample but without all the ornamentation. The bowling green was long but not so majestic and sweeping. The house was beautiful but not palatial and ostentatious. Most noticeable to my daughters was the crowd: it was significantly reduced from the crush of humanity we had experienced at Mount Vernon. The girls didn't want to take the house tour, and I didn't insist. They just wanted to see the slave quarters, which surprise, surprise, don't exist at Monticello either. The closest we could get to vestiges of the estate's slave past were the kitchen and cook's and servant's quarters, located in the cavelike structure called the South Dependency, the wing of the house built at ground level that housed the aforementioned and gave them tunnel access to the basement of the main house.

---

* This question is at the center of a huge controversy within the Monticello Association, whose stated purpose is to "affirm the rights of the descendants of Thomas Jefferson to burial in the . . . Monticello graveyard." According to information I could find, the Monticello Association recently voted not to admit Hemings's descendants. For a thorough investigation into the controversy, watch the PBS *Frontline* documentary "Jefferson's Blood," written and narrated by Shelby Steele, WGBH, Boston.

We toured the quarters, went into the basement, which was mostly a storage area for wood, and came out the other side, to the North Dependency, which was nothing more than horse stalls, tack room, icehouse, and carriage bay. We wandered around to the iconic back of the house again (called the West Front, as I had learned from the brochure, and what we see on the back of a nickel), and took pictures of ourselves on the steps with the famous portico and columns in the background. After that, the girls had had enough.

"Dad, can we go back down to the ticket place and buy some ice cream?" Evelyn asked.

I nodded, and off they trotted, happily leaving me to my task. I almost called them back because I wanted them to see the cramped staircases that Jefferson had built to spite the royals. The story goes that after serving as ambassador to France during the latter part of the 1780s, Jefferson, who had witnessed and applauded the storming of the Bastille, had also acquired a strong distaste for nobility, so upon his return to Monticello, he had his staircases built extra narrow, because he knew how much European monarchs loved grand staircases.

To the north of the famous West Front entrance was a towering tulip tree. It was not quite as large or as tall as the one at Mount Vernon, but it was pretty close. Again, its height described a time when the trees competed for available sunlight. I had no problem at all finding seeds on the plush carpet of green grass underneath its broad branches, and no one paid me any mind as I crouched and plucked for a good twenty minutes.

Near the tulip tree was an ancient southern catalpa. Catalpas have poetic, heart-shaped leaves, the largest leaves of any tree in North America. They're members of the legume family and have long, pencil-thin pods. I found a few, but they were empty. I could not find even one of the cottony little seeds that cram their cavity when ripe; they had long since melted away during the harsh winter months. Catalpas don't live very long, and though the tree was old, it was at best two generations removed from TJ himself.

I noticed a group of people gathering near the remnants of a huge, circular tree trunk an inch or two taller than the grass. I'd venture to say it was the largest tree stump I'd ever seen. It was located in the exact same spot on the other side of the house as the great tulip tree under which I had gathered seeds. A garden tour was just about to begin, so I stood with the loose circle of tourists awaiting the arrival of the docent. A light rain had started to fall. After a few minutes, a smiling, gray-haired, grandfatherly man appeared; he was enthusiastic, warm, and fuzzy. He began immediately with an explanation of the tree trunk.

"That massive trunk you see there is what is left of a giant tulip tree that stood on that spot since the time of Jefferson himself. Unfortunately, it had to be cut down last season due to disease. It was one of only two trees that we can verify were alive during Jefferson's time. The only other tree is that lone cypress right over there." He was pointing at a thin, spindly, pathetic specimen with a dark green hairpiece on top. "It doesn't look like much, but it's the oldest tree on the property. As for the flowers here . . ."

Before he could go off on a different vein, I had to ask, "Sir, doesn't the huge tulip tree over there on the other side of the house date back to Jefferson's time?"

He smiled, happy to show off more knowledge. "It's old, but it doesn't date back quite that far. However, it is most likely an offspring of this one here that was taken down."

He began to lead the group over to a nearby flowerbed. I followed in body but not in mind. Only when he brought us to the
sugar maple grove did I grow ears again.

"Sugar maples are not native to this region, but Jefferson, after
visiting a friend up north, thought he would like to grow them in
order to make maple syrup, so he introduced sugar maples to his
estate. He soon found out, however, that the maple sap does not
run sufficiently in this climate; it needs colder weather. Many of
the sugar maples you see here are remnants of those trees he first
imported."

The tour continued on, but I wasn't interested in the flowers
and gardens. I drifted away, gathering sugar maple keys, and then
wandered over to the pathetic cypress in search of seeds. There was
nothing there to be found but acorns and fungi. But it was while
rooting around the base of that tree that I had a brainstorm: if the
Jefferson-era tulip tree had been taken down in the fall, no doubt
there would be seeds from it still remaining in the area around the
trunk. I raced back over to where the tour had started and began to
hunt for seeds. Bingo!

In the parking lot, the girls were ensconced in the backseat of
the rental car watching episodes of an HBO sitcom. They were lick-
ing the remnants of their ice creams and laughing uproariously. I
slipped behind the wheel, and they turned the laptop so that I could
watch with them. Before I knew it, we were all watching and laughing together, a silly end to an otherwise enlightening trip, notwithstanding the distorted history.

THOMAS JEFFERSON ONCE SAID, "The tree of liberty must be
refreshed from time to time with the blood of patriots and tyrants."

A catchy phrase, and one that's been co-opted by many a recent politician, but for me it's not an apt metaphor at all. I look at liberty as more of an open road, and after visiting Monticello and Mount Vernon, I have to say that the road of liberty should be repaved from time to time with a more inclusive history.

## Gettysburg Redux

**Common chinquapin oak** *(Quercus muehlenbergii)*

CHINQUAPIN OAK BUDS

I RETURNED TO GETTYSBURG in the spring with my old friend Dave, a.k.a. Day-by-Dave, as my wife and kids call him. (It's too silly a story to explain other than to say, yes, it does come from the musical *Godspell*). Day-by-Dave is a tall drink of water, a darn good historian, a talented musician/songwriter, and a comic genius. For a living, he entertains old folks at nursing homes throughout the greater Jersey City area, singing songs, telling jokes, and dancing jigs. It's saintly work, work that only the truly inspired can perform.

We arrived late in the evening and got right down to work. We boldly walked across the muddy Triangular Field, all the way to the infamous Devil's Den, under the watchful eye of a full moon. Yes, we were breaking the law by being on National Park property after dusk—and risking a fine of five hundred dollars and/or thirty days in jail—but we were on a mission and had no time to waste. The Devil's Den is a spooky venue, especially at night. The boulders have an otherworldly quality—Martian red and shaped like unborn monsters, with all sorts of fissures, hollows, and crevices. I felt a thousand eyes watching me from all angles. We climbed around the boulders for a while like little kids, scraping our knees, scuffing our sneakers, and smudging our palms. Meanwhile, the moon had risen, and it was looming up above us like a giant white head atop the shoulders of Little Round Top, a rocky hill three hundred yards or so to the east. We decided to climb toward it.

However, as we got to the base of the infamous hill, where the service road splits in two—one road heading south toward the Wheat Fields and the other heading straight up the ridge to the summit of Little Round Top—we opted not to climb to the top. We wanted to be able to enjoy the view from the summit in sunshine the next day. It was at this point that Day-by-Dave pulled out his map and turned on the little LED headlamp he'd snapped in place on the brim of his porkpie hat. He aimed the beam at the map and began to hold forth on the history of the place:

"There was a lot of action right here where we're standing now." He looked up and made a circular motion with his head. "It was like 'capture the flag' back at the Devil's Den. The Union forces had canister guns on top of the boulders but not enough to hold it, so eventually the Rebels took it from them. It was back and forth a couple of times. Fortunately the Union forces had their artillery set up over there, on the other side of the stream. That's Plum Run." He took a hand off the map and pointed. "This whole area where we're standing is called the Valley of Death, and over where the artillery was set up, that's the place they call the Slaughter Pen."

I couldn't see his face behind the tight beam of the lamp, but I could hear his voice rising in intensity.

"The Rebels wouldn't quit. Amazing people. What was left of the Union forces fell back up the hill to Little Round Top, and that's when the infantry opened up on the Rebels trying to gain the summit; hence the name the Valley of Death. I might be wrong, but I think as battles go, it was the single most deadly fight, per capita, in the history of American warfare. Right here where we're standing."

"Let's get out of here," I said, cutting him short, suddenly getting the creeps. He folded the map and turned off the lamp. For a moment it was pitch dark. My stomach lurched.

We beat a contemplative retreat, around and through the Devil's Den and back across the mucky Triangular Field, toward where we'd parked the car. As we slogged back across the wide field—more a swamp than a field actually—Day-by-Dave continued his exposition on the battle, albeit in hushed tones. Then, about halfway across, his interpretation took an editorial turn, and he began to rail against the nation that had overcome such division only to be once again ideologically polarized. He was blaming the GOP, the corporations, the lobbyists, the media, Hollywood celebrities. And that's when he fired off one of his patented rants: "So what are we reading about or watching on television? Reality shows, nothin' but worthless crap if you ask me. How about this for a reality show: *Celebrity Colonoscopies.*"

"Celebrity what?" I stopped dead in my tracks because the mud was making a sucking-squishing sound under my feet and I thought he had said "colonoscopies."

"*Celebrity Colonoscopies.*"

I had heard him correctly.

"It would be like a modern-day sacrificial ritual. Every week a different celebrity gets the scope. Strip 'em down and lay 'em out on the operating table in their birthday suits; surgical gloves, scrubs and masks, the whole bit. Then shove that camera right up in there, give the viewers what they really want to see." In the moonlight his eyes were wild.

I felt a tickle in the pit of my stomach. He appeared before me at that moment like some Dickensian character, with his stooped shoulders exaggerated by the thick padding of his corduroy jacket, his ridiculous porkpie hat turned at a jaunty angle from the weight of the tiny clip-on headlamp, his long nose casting a ghoulish shadow, the moon and Little Round Top over his right shoulder eavesdropping, the dark and menacing mass of Big Round Top over his left shoulder. I wanted my friends, family, and even history experts along with me on these sojourns, but with Day-by-Dave, I got that *and more.*

After breakfast the next morning we headed back to Little Round Top. Upon entering the southern battlefields by car during the light of day, we were both struck by the extent of tree cutting we saw in and around Little Round Top and Big Round Top. The National Park Service was really on a tear. There were massive 150-year-old oaks lying on their sides, their golden-orange trunk flesh, round and jolly, blushing at us miserably. On the southwestern flanks of Big Round Top, an entire ten-acre swath had been clear-cut. I was horrified. At one point I couldn't bear it, and I jammed on the brakes, jumped out of the car, and hopped into the woods. I stood there in the midst of the wooden carnage shaking my head. I knelt down beside one of the felled red oaks and placed my hand on its trunk. There was a two-foot-long splinter of wood, shaped like a railroad spike, where the blade of the chainsaw had met itself unevenly in the center. I worked it loose with my hands and broke it off. Rutting around the forest floor, I could find no acorns, but I came away with part of the ancient tree to preserve.

DIRECTLY BEHIND THE ROCK LEDGE promontory poetically referred to as Little Round Top is the place where Colonel Joshua Chamberlain and the men of the Twentieth Maine famously held their position against the relentless onslaught of Alabama and Texas Rebels trying to outflank them on the second day of battle. A dirt path runs along a thin ridge into the woods from the tour road directly behind the summit. At the end of that path there is a monument that demarcates the very end of the Union lines, and where Chamberlain and his men fought so heroically. A steep drop-off from the monument leads down into gentle woods to the east. The trees there are maples, cherries, and oaks. There are no ancient trees to be found; someone must have harvested the bullet-ridden timber many decades ago.

Feeling a sort of Siren's call, I left Day-by-Dave to study the monument and walked back into the woods. I felt compelled to continue walking through the full extent of it, trying to imagine the horrors now settled into the soil below my soles. I wandered east, eventually finding myself looking at someone's backyard. The lawn was freshly cut and there was a baby blue swing set illuminated by rays of sunlight streaming through the clouds. A swing set one hundred yards behind Little Round Top.

THE LAST PLACE I GATHERED SEEDS before we went to the museum to view the artifacts (mostly rifles, swords, canons, ammunition, and surgical equipment) was the infamous Copse of Trees where Lee told Pickett to meet Longstreet with his division just before his ill-fated charge on that final day of battle. Today, a low, wrought-iron fence surrounding the half-dozen tall and stately chestnut oaks makes up what's left of the copse. These trees are the most (and perhaps only) jealously guarded trees in the entire park, because this is the one and only time that the visitors' attention is directed toward the trees. And as a result, the Copse of Trees remains above the fray, so to speak, of NPS's tree reduction program. I searched and searched, but, alas, I could not find even one precious acorn.

GETTYSBURG IS A SACRED PLACE. There is a palpable heartbeat pulsing underfoot. And when the sun goes down, the surrounding theater is alive with spirits, great and small, of the unlived lives of desperate young men. And when the liberty bell tolls, the echoes linger as if in apology. America's heart is there beating steadily on the rocky promontory of Little Round Top, on the steep grassy slopes of the East Cemetery Hill, within the boulders of the Devil's Den, in the skeletal remains of the Copse of Trees, and in the tulip trees, sycamores, maples, and oaks. Because Gettysburg was where America's heart once stopped beating.

Today, in Gettysburg, the trees still grow lush and bear fruit, the fecund soil still produces fields of wheat, corn, and barley, and the people live nearby in peace and prosperity. If you want to feel America's beating heart, then go to Gettysburg and walk through the battlefields and gather the seeds of the witness trees and maybe even meet up with a ghost or two; then you will know that "the dead shall not have died in vain—that this nation, under God, shall have [had] a new birth of freedom—and that government of the people, by the people, for the people, shall not perish from the earth."

Chestnut oak (*Quercus montana*)
American sycamore (*Platanus occidentalis*)
Honey locust (*Gleditsia triacanthos*)
Black oak (*Quercus velutina*)
American chestnut (*Castanea dentata*)

EMPTY AMERICAN
CHESTNUT SEED POD

AMERICAN CHESTNUT

## Appomattox, Virginia

From Gettysburg, Day-by-Dave and I headed south for Asheville, North Carolina, to meet up with two of our oldest and closest friends. Our route would take us through the last few miles of Pennsylvania and into Maryland, West Virginia, Virginia, Tennessee, and finally North Carolina. Driving by automobile through the eastern mountains and valleys in early May is like taking a glass-sided floral tour. Redbud, dogwood, honeysuckle, lilac, magnolia, horse chestnut, apple, cherry, locust, and tulip trees are all in various stages of bloom on both sides of the highways. To see the multicolor wilderness tickles the heart and scratches the itching soul. (In Europe, where I lived for five years, so many of the trees and forests are gone, and consequently so is the population's fundamental sense of wildness; we are profoundly different people as a result.)

Traversing the thin strip of land through northwestern Maryland, I saw the breathtaking splendiforae on either side of the highway suddenly devolve into innumerable mall-size distribution warehouses, one after the other. For twenty miles, standing where farmers' fields and pristine forests once stood, were single-story, four-sided monoliths with semi-trailers sticking out of them like spikes, and sucking the thoughts right out of our heads. We said nothing until we hit the West Virginia line, at which point Day-by-Dave began to grouse under his breath.

"Why us? What is it about us that makes *us* such good consumers? Why can't the Chinese or the Indians or the Brazilians consume like we do?"

"The media. Indoctrination. Maslow's Hierarchy of Needs," I tossed out a grocery list of nouns. He nodded in agreement.

We made it as far as Charlottesville that first day, traveling through the Virginia rain almost the entire ride. Initially we intended to pitch our tent in the woods near Monticello, so I could try to gather some more tulip tree seeds from the erstwhile giant that knew TJ personally, but the weather forced us to seek civilized shelter at the Red Roof Inn across from the University of Virginia. After checking in, we headed downtown for dinner. Much to our surprise, there were plenty of restaurants still open and an impressive selection of ethnic cuisines to boot. We ate at an *haut* diner famous for its meatloaf, which we both ordered. It was good, albeit a bit too fancy for our tastes.

Full of food and groggy from the bottle of red wine, we tried to walk it off by strolling around the historic university grounds despite the incessant drizzle. We were pleased to see that, on campus, the ancient trees all have starring roles. Each specimen we came across had its own plot of land, just like great bronze statues of vaunted alumni. We admired the trees but gathered no seeds.

By the next morning the rain had stopped and the sun had come out. We ate a big Southern-style breakfast of grits, sausage, and pancakes, and mapped out our route between bites. I decided to forego another visit to Monticello (I had enough of admissions fees to last me a lifetime) and instead we opted to visit Appomattox Courthouse, an hour to the south, deep inland along one of the state's rural routes.

SOUTH OF CHARLOTTESVILLE is horse country. Mile after mile of white picket fences gloated of an exclusive class overly preoccupied with their equines. I don't like horses. After college I worked for a few months on a ranch in Texas. I experienced firsthand how stupid and skittish those creatures are when immured inside paddocks and stables. I also got to see how some owners dote on them, and worst of all, how much better the horses are treated than some of the people who care for and train them.

Within a few dozen miles we were beyond the horse lands and into the old-growth forests. Pines and hardwoods closed in around us on both sides, dappling the sunlight and thickening the oxygen content. It was forest all the way until just outside the hamlet of

Appomattox. Around a long turn, a parking area emerged, under-lining a large historical marker. We slowed and pulled in. Giant sycamores, oaks, and maples greeted us as we stepped out of the car. Maps, charts, diagrams, and even a tape-recorded message were pro-vided along a path that led straight into a thick wood. This was the spot where Robert E. Lee had spent his final days as commander of the Army of Northern Virginia before signing the terms of surren-der with General Ulysses S. Grant. Alongside the narrow dirt path leading into the woods, a sign indicated that his last headquarters were another five hundred feet beyond.

Sure enough, we came to a clearing and another marker indi-cating the spot where Lee had camped in early April 1865. How-ever, the trees in the immediate vicinity were not a hundred and fifty years old; not even close. I stood with my hands on my hips, swiveling around and looking for big trees. Then the quietude of the little circular spot pierced my heart, and I began to fathom the history of where I stood: right where I was standing, Robert E. Lee had decided to surrender his army, and with it the whole notion of a separate Confederacy. For a Northern boy like me, whose grandpar-ents had come to this country long after 1865, the Civil War doesn't make much sense. Then I, too, had to admit a kind of defeat, real-izing that no matter how many Constitutions are written, or how eloquently they are worded, or how heroically they are defended, humankind will forever remain a contradiction, saying one thing and doing another. No less now than then. No more they than we.

Fifty yards down the path, an ancient chinquapin oak, its bulky torso looking like a man among boys, its lofty treetop sticking high above the rest in the forest canopy, caught my attention. It could have dated to the mid-1800s. My first chinquapin. I had read about the species, how it had shouldered a heavy load during much of our nation's early development. First, it was used to delineate property lines as split-rail fencing; then it was burned as fuel for steamboats and laid down to support rail lines for the intercontinental railroad; and finally, it was hewn into barrels to hold whiskey.* Not only did the size of the specimen make me smile, but something about the oblong shape of the leaves and their round, rippling lobes reminded me of hair in the Don Martin cartoons from *Mad* magazines of my youth. Under the thick carpeting of chinquapin leaves, I found countless numbers of fat, thumb-size acorns, their rhizomes literally bursting out of the shell. I filled two baggies, plus a plastic bag full of soil to plant them in back at home.

TWO MILES DOWN THE ROAD, at the McLean house, where Grant and Lee signed the terms of surrender, there is a plaque out in front with a photograph of the home as it looked shortly after the event. There were three locust trees in the front yard on that April day in 1865, and there are three locust trees in the front yard today. Even though they look eerily similar, they are not the same trees, the green-uniformed ranger on the front porch explained to us, but they are certainly related. I looked and looked for a long time and found just two tiny seeds stuck to the inside back of a dried-out seedpod. It was the smallest haul to date, but the seeds were viable.

Behind the house I found an old sycamore, maybe a hundred years old. I found some seeds and put them in a baggy nonetheless. As it was getting late, we decided to forego the house tour and just cupped our hands and looked in the windows instead. We found out from the same park ranger that the house had been disassembled,

* From Peattie's *A Natural History of North American Trees.*

brick by brick, and moved to Washington, D.C., where it stood for many years as a museum. Later (we never found out when or why) it was once again dismantled and reassembled back at its original location. Mind-boggling, the energies of man.

Later on, heading west on Route 24 toward Lynchburg and Interstate 81, just about out of the city limits of Appomattox, we noticed another historic marker alongside the road. We pulled into the parking area to investigate. Off in the distance, back about five hundred yards, we could see the McLean house at the far end of the uncut fields. Here, a massive and ancient black oak, as large as a house, and a tiny cemetery marked the spot where some of the final shots of the Civil War had been traded. The diminutive cemetery held just nine soldiers—eight Confederates and one Union, the latter unknown. Small Confederate flags and one Union Jack flag fluttered alongside the graves. It was a moving sight. The massive oak tree, as wide as it was tall, was plenty old enough and had witnessed the final moments before peace was declared. There were tiny acorns everywhere I looked. I gathered a few handfuls quietly.

## American Chestnut Foundation Research Farm

It was getting late. We made a beeline for Meadowview, Virginia, home to the American Chestnut Foundation. Day-by-Dave and I are both members of the foundation, and we had hoped to get there before five o'clock so that we might find someone to show us around. However, it was almost 7:00 P.M. by the time we arrived. Amazingly, as if he'd been waiting for us all day (we did not alert anyone that we were coming), Dr. Fred Hebard, the ACF's staff pathologist, and his loyal but smelly golden retriever appeared on the front porch just as we were pulling into the driveway.

The American Chestnut Foundation has been around since 1995. Plant scientists and nature lovers alike could not accept the fact that this once-dominant hardwood species, the American chestnut—such a crucial food source for people and animals, and one of the most serviceable woods for making furniture and musical instruments—was fated for extinction from the dastardly chestnut blight fungus *Cryphonectria parasitica*. With grants, private donations, and sponsorship from organizations such as the U.S. Forest Service, Mount Vernon, and people like Jimmy Carter, the ACF has been hard at work these many years trying to create a blight-resistant American chestnut tree, with the goal of one day restoring the tree to its native range.* The whole idea makes me want to jump for joy.

Dr. Fred, who looks like John Updike, with his angular face and wry grin, took us on a tour of the farm in his clunky, sky blue pickup truck. It's not a very big farm, about a hundred and fifty acres, but it's a beautiful setting, with monstrous Mount Rogers, Virginia's highest peak, off in the distance. He first showed us the groves of experimental trees from the earliest plantings. It was a pathetic sight. The old groves of chestnuts were more dead than alive, wracked by disease, their bark falling off, most of their branches and leaves missing, and their trunks full of festering wounds.

Then he took us to see the newer specimens, planted like cabbages in rows; none were more than a few feet tall. They, however, looked much healthier. He pointed out a couple of the more

---

* For more information or to donate, write to the American Chestnut Foundation, 160 Zillicoa Street, Suite D, Asheville, NC 28801; or go to their website, www.acf.org.

promising specimens, with their bark intact and the leaves on their branches a bold green. They did indeed look hale and hearty, and he explained as he drove us back toward the farmhouse that the ACF has back-crossed the trees with a blight-resistant Chinese species, and created a mostly blight-resistant variety that is virtually 100 percent American chestnut. The ACF plans to introduce about five hundred chestnuts to the eastern woodlands in the coming years, with the poetic vision of seeing these magnificent trees once again growing large and lavish, and feeding the hungry bears and you and me.

We gave Dr. Fred a hard time about his title, staff pathologist, but with his waggish sense of humor, he fired right back at us with some regional jokes.

"A couple of farmers, one from West Virginia and one from Virginia, had a running feud. Then one day the farmer from West Virginia got so mad he threw a stick of dynamite at the Virginia farmer's house. The Virginia farmer just picked it up, lit it, and threw it back." He laughed as loud as we did.

We spent that night in the tent behind the ACF farmhouse, Dr. Fred leaving the door open in case we needed to use the bathroom. When we awoke the next morning, the place was a beehive of activity, cars coming in and out, dogs barking, people shouting. And in the trees behind our tent was a joyous chorus of songbirds. Before departing, we went inside to thank our host. Then I tried to trade a few of my seed specimens for a couple of ACF chestnuts.

"Sorry, but I don't have enough nuts to trade," he said, frowning.

"Okay, how about this: I'll trade you a half dozen chinquapin acorns from a tree that stood right next to where Robert E. Lee camped the night before he signed the surrender at Appomattox Courthouse for two of your chestnuts?"

"Really, I'm sorry, but I've got no more chestnuts to give out," the good doctor said, shrugging innocently.

"Driving a hard bargain, huh? Here's what I'll do, I'll—"

"Look, I'd like to help, but I can't. Not yet. Soon, I hope."

I smiled and apologized, adding that if all went well, there'd be plenty of chestnuts in our future because of his good work.

**Sugar maple** *(Acer saccharum)*
**Southern catalpa** *(Catalpa bignonioides)*

SOUTHERN CATALPA
SEED and LEAF

## Asheville, North Carolina

I loved reading Thomas Wolfe—the lyrical mastery of style, the maudlin narrative of childhood ecstasies and traumas, the agonized reveries of longed-for achievements, the utopian depiction of the writer's life, and the infinite capacity for vocabulary. All of it compelled me to read every word he ever wrote. But that strong initial bond did not stand up well to the test of time, because ultimately, for me, Wolfe lacked one key ingredient: humor. The mother of a high school friend of mine, and an English teacher herself, once said to me, "There is an appalling lack of humor in the American canon of literature. Everything important that has been written could just as easily have been written with a sense of humor." She was so right. Since then, I have always applied her opinion to Wolfe.

Be that as it may, the plan for my Wolfe pilgrimage was simple: At the Asheville, North Carolina, airport at noon on Tuesday, meet up with my good friend Mothball (short for Mothballhead), who was flying in from Maine, and our other playmate, Colonel (because he presents like one) B. T. McGillicuddy, who was driving in from coastal North Carolina. Day-by-Dave and I opted to try to save time by taking Route 23 over the mountains at Johnson City, Tennessee, instead of driving another sixty miles farther south to more easily cross the peaks on Interstate 40. Day-by-Dave's 1980s road atlas had Route 23 delineated as a simple red line, i.e., a four-lane state road. Not anymore.

Twenty years and a half billion dollars later, Route 23 is now Interstate 26, an eight-lane, state-of-the-art concrete superhighway, with all the bells and whistles: de-icing systems, grooved overpasses, fog warning lights, runaway truck ramps, and a 215-foot-tall bridge. This wonder of the world cuts an enormous swath right through the heart of the Blue Ridge Mountains and forests. What a boondoggle. In America today, the road more or less traveled always gets upgraded, while the surrounding nature gets degraded.

WHEN WE PULLED INTO THE AIRPORT parking lot just a little late, there they were up ahead, Mothball and the Colonel, walking and talking and laughing like kids. The Colonel had dressed for the part: muslin short-sleeve shirt, straw cowboy hat, a pair of army green shorts exposing his birdlike legs, loafers, no socks, and a cane. Mothball, his once-red hair now graying, was an obvious northern tourist, with his heavy-duty backpack obscuring all but his Hush Puppies, blue jeans, and hoary head.

With the Colonel leading the way behind the wheel of his massive black pickup truck, we went directly to a honky-tonk along the French Broad River, south of Asheville. The Colonel had lived for years in the mountains outside of the city before moving to the coast with his mate, so he was quite familiar with all the best watering holes in the area.

Once we were inside, every other sentence out of the mouth of the sassy gal behind the bar started with the words *You boys*: "You boys want ice in them beers?" "You boys brought the rain with you, didn't cha?" "You boys don't hunt." "You boys . . ." Indeed, to be among old friends again, no matter what age, turns all men back into boys.

Ostensibly, the get-together was for them to pitch in and help me gather seeds at the Thomas Wolfe house, but our true intent was to commiserate with our dear old friend the Colonel, who had recently lost his wife and his beloved bulldog, not to mention his having undergone major back surgery. Never one to feel sorry for himself, he was nonetheless crazy and joyous, but we knew him well enough to know that on the inside he was mighty lowdown.

We yucked it up at the honky-tonk for an hour or more before the Colonel limped off his stool and pointed toward the truck with his cane: "Y'all want somethin' to eat?"

After taking us on a joy ride through the area, eventually he brought us to a Mexican joint and we lunched on deep-fried burritos and drank Negro Modelos. Afterward, he took us to a downtown hotel, where, after we checked in, we sat out on the balcony of my room, drank PBRs, listened to Day-by-Dave play his guitar, and watched life walk on by.

Asheville is one of those rare places that is both small town and big city, where the urban and rural come together in one elastic mix. In the recent past, the city was a mountain refuge for tuberculosis patients or rich northerners looking to get away from it all. Today it is on the shortlist for young graduates, professionals, and artists seeking a big-city lifestyle without all the angst and expense.

Asheville also has some amazing architecture. In the downtown business district, there is a wide range of styles, from classic three-story brick buildings to Art Deco masterpieces such as the City Hall Courthouse (built by Douglas D. Ellington and after which the Empire State Building was modeled) to the flaming redbrick Spanish Renaissance Revival Church of St. Lawrence. There are also nifty little tree-shaded parks, such as Pack Square, where people gather to paint, read, or listen to musical performances. It's a gorgeous city, but if the building and population growth continue on their present trajectory, it will soon lose that small-town charm. I hope that never happens.

Later that night, after a dinner near the hotel, we strolled through the city streets, the warm, sultry southern air kissing our cheeks and lifting our spirits. We eventually found ourselves standing in front of the Thomas Wolfe House, at 48 Spruce Street, just five blocks from our hotel. "The Old Kentucky Home" boarding-house, as Wolfe's mother named it, looked like a storybook set. The two-story Victorian structure, painted yellow and trimmed in white, with its sharply angled roof lines, dormers, wrap-around front porch, and ornamental woodwork and railings up and down, sparkled in the diffuse light of the streetlamps.

There was no one in sight as we stepped onto the front porch. There were, however, three high-backed rocking chairs lined up in a row as if someone had been expecting us. As if they'd done it every day of their lives, my three childhood pals, each one now a full-grown man with his own unique style and story, inwardly complex but outwardly cartoon-like, sat right down and rocked away. Meanwhile, I remained standing out on the front lawn, admiring the two soaring maples on either side of me.

The trees were as old as the house itself. In *Look Homeward, Angel*, Wolfe wrote about how the trees in his yard "rose gaunt and stark." That was no longer true of these two elders, as they had matured into fat, lavish organisms, full of ancient tales and wise saws. I had to get down on my hands and knees to look for maple keys in the grass. Aided by the plethora of streetlights and the brightly lit hotel across the street, I was able to see well enough to find what I was looking for. (It was the first and only time I would collect my seeds at night.) I noticed another, even older maple tree thirty yards east of the house, along the sidewalk, so I walked over to investigate and, to my delight, discovered the branches laden with clusters of helicopter keys. Unfortunately, they all dangled out of reach. I hunted around and found a long, dead branch and used it to knock loose a few bunches.

There was also a tall, thin catalpa in the backyard and I found some seedpods with seeds still inside. Later I learned that there a catalpa tree had stood in the backyard for many years, but no one could tell me if this was the same one. And all the while I gathered seeds, my three friends rocked and mocked.

I came back around to the front as Day-by-Dave began to riff on the "good ole boy" theme. He was teasing the Colonel, who had grown up with us in Connecticut but through the years had undergone a radical southernification. It was something we could never assimilate: that the Colonel had become a good ole boy while we three northerners remained accentlessly the same.

Day-by-Dave, a born actor, transformed his physiognomy from a rocking-chair Bubba into the eminent Hungarian phonetics expert Zoltan Karpathy, from George Bernard Shaw's *Pygmalion*. I looked up from my hands-and-knees labor searching for seeds just in time to see him stop rocking, jump out of his chair, point his long spindly finger at the Colonel, and boldly declare, "Za drawl ees too good! I say za Colonel ees not Sousern at all! No no no, he ees not even American! He ees . . . *Hungarian!*"

An elderly couple passing by on the sidewalk, arm in arm, stopped in their tracks and stared at the sight of Day-by-Dave pointing an accusatory finger at the Colonel on the front porch of the Thomas Wolfe Memorial Home.

The Colonel, whose laugh had a cartoonish squeak-squeak to it, squeak-squeaked and squeaked some more.

I looked at the baffled couple on the sidewalk and shrugged my shoulders.


THE NEXT MORNING, I found that the Colonel had gotten up with the chickens and had gone to visit his sister, who lived nearby. After a late breakfast, Mothball and I decided to visit the bookstore in the heart of downtown, while Day-by-Dave stayed back at the hotel to strum his guitar and wait for the Colonel to return.

At the wood-warm and inviting Malaprop's Bookstore/Café, I presented myself to the owner and explained the nature of my visit. Emoke B'Racz, an aunt-sweet woman of Hungarian extraction, had heard a little about my project from my editor and even had some suggestions of places I might visit in the area.

But it was Mothball who made the biggest impression on her. Emoke, besides being the owner of a successful bookstore in Asheville, is also a poet. And Mothball, besides being the owner of a successful bakery in Portland, Maine, is also a gifted painter. They had a lot in common.

She bought us cappuccinos in the café section of the store and self-deprecatingly recounted her thirty-year history as owner of the place. For the first twenty years of the store's existence, she pointed out, it was touch and go, but as the city of Asheville blossomed, the business burgeoned.

"But book selling, probably like bread baking, doesn't make you rich," Emoke concluded.

"Well, I'll have you know," Mothball responded with proverbial hands on hips, "that I make *thousands* of dollars a year at my bakery!" That made Emoke laugh. She then left us momentarily and returned with a copy of her book of poetry and promptly gifted it to Mothball—poet to painter, bookstore owner to bakery owner.

A couple of minutes later, after Emoke had left us to help customers, the two other cartoon characters in our troupe entered the shop, stage right. The whole atmosphere of the place changed. Where just moments before patrons had been quietly perusing the shelves for books or sedately reading newspapers or contemplatively drinking lattes, the place now ricocheted with loud jibber-jabber:

The Colonel, two steps ahead of Day-by-Dave, same costume as the day before, hobbled impatiently over to our table in his lickety-split gait. He grabbed a chair, spun it around, hung his cane off the back of it, and plopped down, elbows up on the tabletop, nearly upsetting our drinks.

He eyeballed us impishly: "Y'all been drinkin' them fancy coffees? Sheet, you like a couple o' sissy boys," he chided, doing an imitation of himself.

"Sissies? Hells bells, them two boys look more like two schoolgirls, all done up, sittin' on the bus," Day-by-Dave/Foghorn Leghorn crowed as he noisily pulled up a chair next to the Colonel. Mothball, always the first to get embarrassed, turned bright red as he took a sip of his cappuccino.

"Looky Mothballhead thar, lappin' up his café latte with that big ole tongue o' his like some Labro'dor receiver," Day-by-Dave continued.

After making a spectacle of ourselves at the bookstore and bidding adieu to a smiling Emoke, we giddy-apped over to the Thomas Wolfe Visitor Center, paid the admission fee (sigh), and waited to take the tour. Because the house tour wouldn't begin for another fifteen minutes, we had time to explore the exhibit hall in the back of the center. The small museum was full of Wolfe's personal effects from the family home and his New York City apartment, tools from his father's stonecutting shop, and enlarged sepia-tone photographs of Wolfe and his siblings from his schooldays.

As we shuffled through the mazelike hall, we came upon a day-bed behind a velvet rope. But what made that "winsome tableaux of old-fashioned days," as one of the captions put it, make my eyes sparkle was a sleek black, gold-handled cane lying across the bed. The Colonel, that rascal, leaned over the velvet rope and deftly exchanged his gnarly wooden cane, its broken handle held in place by a fraying piece of duct tape, for the noble staff on the bed. He took the cane in his hand and tossed it up in the air, twirled it like Chaplin, tipped his hat with it, and then replaced it on the bed.

Less than an hour later, the four of us stood groggily inside the charmless, bed-cluttered boardinghouse where Thomas Wolfe had suffered through childhood with his mother, Eliza—just he and she alone—while the rest of the family lived two blocks away at the Woodfin Street residence. He lived there with her from age four to fifteen, when he went off to college at the University of North Carolina–Chapel Hill in 1916. We and we alone had to endure an insufferable hour-long tour of the Old Kentucky Home, conducted by a docent who recited his monologue in monotone, with his hands held behind his back and his eyes tightly closed. He offered nothing but platitudes and frillery in his rehearsed soliloquy. Oddly, the docent failed to mention anything about the notorious childhood of a tortured genius who had suffered grievously at the hands of his dysfunctional family inside that very house, where as a boy Thomas Wolfe had witnessed his sibling's death and endured the bitter rivalry between an abusive, alcoholic father and a money-grubbing mother.

The docent droned on: "In June of 1922, the same year and month that Thomas Wolfe graduated from Chapel Hill, his father, William Oliver Wolfe, a tombstone maker and a descendant of hardy Pennsylvania Dutch farmers, and who for many years had not set foot in this house, passed away in this room and in this very bed that you see before you."

Near where the father had died a miserable, drunken, bitter death sat an entire basket of wooden canes, which proved something beyond a reasonable doubt, something that I had begun to suspect ever since embarking on my quest to visit the homes of dead legends: that there is often an abiding remnant with more of the story to tell for those who care enough to hear it. The abiding remnant in Wolfe's case was the cane: a symbol communicating to me loud and clear that the reason he lacked for humor was not because he didn't have humor but because he was disabled by his upbringing. His books, his words, his art, became the cane that bore his handicap.

It felt good to be liberated from the spectral ache of that dreary house, with its creaking floors and death-laced drapery and bone-dry woodwork. And yet I felt I had gotten to know Thomas Wolfe so much better than I did before my visit.

A whimsical recipe of one cup each of the Colonel, Mothball, and Day-by-Dave, a swig of Thomas Wolfe and his Old Kentucky Home, and a measure of a bookstore owner/poet, stirred vigorously with a wooden cane and sprinkled with catalpa and maple seeds, all tasted sweet. Make that bittersweet.

## Back Home

IT WAS NEARING THE END OF SUMMER and all the saplings had outgrown their two-sizes-too-small pots, like adolescent boys crammed into last year's winter boots. My only option was to offer them up for adoption to family, friends, and neighbors. It was not a bad idea; unfortunately, I failed to provide adequate instructions on how to properly care for them, and before too long bad news about their health and well-being started to come in. It wasn't good. All but a handful of the adoptees had bitten the dust. Case in point: the three Ken Kesey Oregon maples I gave my former English-teaching colleague Steven Smith, an Adirondack version of Kesey himself, with his brawny physique and merry prankishness. When I inquired a month after I'd gifted them to him, the poet-gone-funny wrote me this little ditty:

> *Dear Rick,*
> *I can still recall your psychedelic smirk*
> *When you gave me Kesey trees without much Kesey dirt*

*I still have a great notion*
*To create a magic potion*
*Perhaps an acid-laced Kool-Aid fertilizer will work*
*To grow the dead plants Further*

*Sorry,*
*Steven*

P.S. Make love in a tree and leave.

I learned later that he had kept the poor saplings in the refrigerator for a week before planting them.

After that, I began to de-gift them.

# Part Seven

*I wonder if anyone else has an ear so tuned and sharpened as I have, to detect the music, not of the spheres, but of earth, subtleties of major and minor chord that the wind strikes upon the tree branches. Have you ever heard the earth breathe?*

—KATE CHOPIN, MRS. MOBRY'S REASON

Southern magnolia (*Magnolia grandiflora*)
Southern live oak (*Quercus virginiana*)
Pecan (*Carya illinoensis*)

SOUTHERN LIVE OAK

## New Orleans, Louisiana

I think about America before Columbus all the time. And I always end up fast-forwarding through the centuries, from a continent of uncut forests, undammed rivers, litter-free beaches, jet plane–less skies, and vast herds of buffalo on the plains, to suburban sprawling landscapes, Army Corps of Engineered rivers, condominium-lined beaches, jet-jammed skies, and a colloidal nexus of concrete highways. Like black holes and quantum mechanics, it squiggles my brain.

The stark contrast between these two centuries makes me ask myself to what place and period in this galloping history would I, if I could travel back in time, choose to return and whom would I most like to meet. Without hesitation, my choice would be 1915 New Orleans, and the person I'd most like to meet is the young Louis Armstrong.

If our genes and surroundings condition our minds and bodies, then music conditions our hearts. In all the music that makes us who we are, there is one song that plucks our strings and beats our drum and blows our horn louder than any other. For me that song is Louis Armstrong's "When It's Sleepy Time Down South." Happy is he who knows his own song.

I had never been to New Orleans before I went there to gather seeds in October of 2009. Four years after Hurricane Katrina, I expected to find a treeless, miasmic, anarchic mess, a mere semblance of its former grandeur, floundering on the threatening banks of the overwrought Mississippi, but what I found instead was a treasure in the form of a city, beautiful beyond words and full of rich, exotic flavors and aromas—an American Xanadu.

My nephew Matthew, with the updo, would be joining me once again. Together we would travel through the Deep South, from New Orleans up into Mississippi and over to western Alabama, and back down again. Initially I had made arrangements for us to stay just one day in New Orleans, because I didn't expect to find trees there. Boy, was I wrong.

I WAS NOT PREPARED for my drive through the French Quarter. I crawled along the narrow streets, utterly enchanted by the carnival sights all around me, mindless of the road in front of me. I was snapped out of my reverie by the sight, and sound, of an angry tuba player, his huge brass bell dancing from side to side in front of my car. I had taken a wrong turn, or, rather, no turn at all. Driving north along Chartres, you find the road abruptly closes to automobile traffic directly in front of the illustrious stone edifice called The Cabildo, at Jackson Square. Cars are obliged to turn left down St. Peter's Street, and even though there is no sign indicating this, it should be self-evident, as the paved road turns into granite sidewalk and then dips down six inches into the famous square. The vendors around the area fill in the rest of the visual clues. But I, I took the road not meant to be taken, and that nearly cost me a huge fine. Fortunately, the tuba player was there, and I followed his circular gesture, made a U-turn, and got back on the road more traveled.

After maneuvering around the Quarter, I finally managed to find my hotel in the heart of the Vieux Carré, along Chartres (pronounced "charters," like the fishing excursions, and not the way the French pronounce it: *shartr*) at the Hotel Provincial. It was only about 10:00 A.M. and Matthew wasn't due to arrive until the afternoon. I quickly unpacked, grabbed my baggies and backpack, and accosted the concierge, putting it to him straight:

"Are there any old trees left in the French Quarter?"

"Old trees? Sure. There are lots of old trees down on Esplanade, just three blocks over, and of course in the park."

"The park?"

"Jackson Square, back around the corner."

He drew the route with a red pen on a map, and handed the map to me with a smile. I folded it, put it in my pocket, and set off.

What a fairy-tale city to walk in! The ancient brick and dusty stucco, the filigreed balconies, the wide wooden galleries, the sweeping stairways that reach down from the Creole town houses as if they want to shake your hand; the musty mystical aroma of spices and garlic and dirt and sweat all oxidizing and romanticizing in the moist river air. It took me just a few blocks of my rhythmic walk to understand why Louis Armstrong would get all weak in the knees whenever he began to play the song that embodies the raw pathos of his beloved birthplace: "Do You Know What It Means to Miss New Orleans."

Then I came to Esplanade, a two-lane road lined by the iconic, stately double-gallery houses featured in so many promotional photographs of the city. But the stars here are the two rows of live oaks, some more than a hundred years old, running up and down a narrow median as far as the eye can see. The oaks were planted about fifty feet apart and positioned on either side of the grassless median. The massive limbs of the older trees reached out over both sides of the avenue like an arbor and, before Katrina struck, I was told, formed a tunnel over the median itself.

My happiness over this unexpected urban paradise was tempered slightly by numerous gaps in the two rows of oaks; I suspected many had been lost during the hurricane. In some of the gaps, little oaks and scrawny palms were growing. On the thin median, acorns littered the ground. Bent over like an old farmer, I harvested to my heart's content.

For two blocks, I wandered along from old oak to older oak picking up acorns, until I came to the intersection of Bourbon and Esplanade. There I decided I'd gathered enough, put the bulging baggy in my backpack, and meandered down Bourbon Street, back toward the heart of the Quarter. It was extremely hot and sultry, somewhere in the nineties, I had been told by the front desk clerk, and getting hotter. I was sweating generously. But as I strolled merrily along Bourbon, still very much under the spell of the live oaks along the Esplanade, I became aware of a man on the other side of the street strolling merrily along, even more merrily than I, greeting everyone who passed by. He was tall, white, gray-haired, fiftyish. He never offered the same salutation twice.

"Morning." "Beautiful day for a walk." "Good to see you!" "Love that T-shirt." "Great city, i'n' it?"

He was the host of the town. I did my very best to remain abreast of him, preferring to observe rather than interact, but I had a heck of a time not passing him, because he would frequently slow unexpectedly or stop altogether, forcing me to tie my shoe, look in my backpack, or rearrange my ponytail. This comic game went on for a couple of blocks, until I saw a fascinating tree on his side of the street. I immediately angled across Bourbon.

I stooped over and began to search the ground under the tree for seeds. When I stood up, he was there watching me with his big gray eyes.

"What're ya lookin' for there, my friend?" he asked, his hands behind his back. Close up, he reminded me of a thinner version of W. C. Fields. So I told him. The hand came out from behind his back, and we shook. Then, without as much as a "That's interesting," he began filling me in on the condition of the city before and after Katrina. As the owner of a house on Dauphine Street, one block north of Bourbon, he'd been one of the first people to return to the Quarter after the storm. He gave me all the geological history of the French Quarter, how it had been built on dry land, well above sea level, many years before the city's levee systems went in, so most of the streets had only minor flooding, and much of the damage sustained in this area during the hurricane had been from wind and not water. He concluded his lecture by estimating the total loss of live oaks on Esplanade at about 30 percent.

We began to walk slowly, side by side, along Bourbon Street. He pointed out Lafitte's Blacksmith Shop, the oldest continuously run tavern in America, and shortly after that we turned down a narrow alleyway behind the St. Louis Cathedral, where I'd earlier almost gone off the road. About halfway down Pirate's Alley, he stopped in front of an old building with a dark brown plaque heavy with oxidation. The historical marker indicated that a young William Faulkner, the future Nobel laureate, had once lived in the house back in 1925, and it was where he had written his first novel, *Soldier's Pay*.* Then, without so much as a word, my tour guide pushed open a door next to the plaque and went in. I followed.

Faulkner House Books is a little jewel of a bookstore, nestled on the ground floor of the same house where Faulkner once lived. It's only one room, but it sure packs a wallop, full of rare editions by Tennessee Williams, Sherwood Anderson, and Walker Percy, and of course, books by and about William Faulkner. Joanne Sealy, one of the store's booksellers, was there. My new-found friend, Matt Easley, introduced me to her. When we told her how we'd met, she let out a guffaw and shook her head. "Well, you bumped into the right guy."

And just as if the two of them had been conspiring for years, waiting for me to come looking for authors' homes and trees, they began to make suggestions of houses I should visit and trees they knew about. Joanne pulled out a priceless little book full of names

---

* I would later learn that he started out in New Orleans at age twenty-seven, writing poetry, but his good friend and neighbor Sherwood Anderson, who lived right around the corner, across from Jackson Park, convinced him to switch to fiction, and the rest is history.

and addresses of New Orleans's most famous writers' residences.* There was John Kennedy Toole, who lived uptown, one block off St. Charles; Walker Percy, in the Milan neighborhood; William S. Burroughs's house over the river in Algiers, on Walker; Lillian Hellman, at 1718 Bretagne; Sherwood Anderson, who lived in the Pontalba Apartments, at 540-B St. Peter's Street; and Tennessee Williams's house right around the corner, off Dumaine. In fact, Joanne knew the doctor who lived there. She would make a phone call on my behalf to let him know I was coming. She was pretty sure there was a banana tree in the courtyard that Tennessee Williams either had planted himself or had written about.

It was at this point that she told me the story of Williams's boardinghouse days on Toulouse Street, and about the crazy landlady who had poured a pot of boiling water through a hole in the floor on top of one of the tenants who was naked and in bed with someone he shouldn't have been. In fact, the scene was described in a play Williams wrote entitled *Vieux Carré*. I asked if she had a copy of it that I could buy. (She did, and I bought it and read it that night.)

My head spinning, and my notebook full of names and addresses and even phone numbers, I thanked Joanne profusely and headed out the door, the ineluctable Matt Easley right on my tail. The plan was to go over to Tennessee Williams's house on Dumaine; Matt would show me which house it was. It was a five-minute walk, but on the way we passed Madame John's Legacy, the oldest building in the city, built when the Spanish ruled back in 1788. We stopped and stared. It's one of those wooden gallery buildings, painted dull green. It was all boarded up.

* Alan Brown, *Literary Levees of New Orleans*, Montgomery, Ala.: River City Publishing, 1998.

Just a few houses down is Tennessee Williams's former house. I rang the bell but no one answered. I cupped my hands over my eyes and looked down the narrow passage along the alleyway on the side of the house toward the courtyard in the back. I could see a large-leafed tree in the shadows and wondered how I would go about storing a banana seed. (I learned later that banana seeds are extremely difficult to germinate.*) I'd call again tomorrow.

With Matt as guide, I walked back toward my hotel, passing first through Jackson Square. He pointed to all of the oaks and magnolias that had survived Katrina. I was delighted to see such old and majestic trees and was determined to collect their seeds, but at that moment I was worried that my nephew had arrived and wouldn't be able to get into the room.

As we walked, Matt offered to take me around the next day to the infamous Lower Ninth Ward, to show me where the floodwaters had caused the most damage. It sounded like something I should see, but I already had a long list of names and addresses to check out and not much time to do so. Out in front of my hotel, we shook hands. I tried to thank him, but I am completely inept when it comes to thank-yous and compliments. All I could sputter was "You're awesome, man!"

Poor Matthew had been waiting for me. The front desk had insisted that he call me on my cell phone, but I don't have one. (This technological lack, so to speak, on my part would become the central topic of discourse during our seven days at close quar-

---

* The best way is to soak them in a 10 percent bleach solution for two days. Then rinse them and place them in a sterilized but moist soil medium. Over the next two weeks, they should be baked at ninety degrees for eight hours each day.

ters.) While he unpacked, I made reservations to stay another night, there being just too much to do in one day.

An hour later, Matthew, who has the biggest set of peepers since Bambi, was walking along beside me through the Vieux Carré. We had pumped a couple of cold beers down our gullets, and because I was preoccupied by the thought that we would not have enough time to visit all the places on my new list, we headed directly over to Jackson Square to gather seeds.

Jackson Square isn't that big, but what it lacks in size it makes up for in character. Like the great parks of the world, it's a people magnet and a catalyst for artists, jugglers, and mimes. In front of the three great buildings that resolve the square—the Cabildo, St. Louis Cathedral, and the Presbytère (the Cabildo's twin)—Matthew and I stood looking toward the soaring equestrian monument of Andrew Jackson smack in the center of it all. What makes Jackson Park different from most central parks is that it doesn't look restored or anachronistic; it looks authentic. Walking around it, you get the sense that it's the eighteenth century, that the Louisiana Purchase and the War of 1812 ain't even happened yet. In a world of Xbox, HDTV, mp3s, and PDAs, Jackson Square still puts asses in the park benches.

There are two monstrous live oaks directly across from the Cabildo, along St. Peter's Street, right across from Sherwood Anderson's former apartment building and a stone's throw from Faulkner's Pirate's Alley. There was absolutely no doubt in my mind that both men would have taken a break from their scribbling in the soporific swelter, walked over to the park, and sat a spell under the shade of those great convoluted branches. I noticed how there were no squirrels around, but many of the acorns had bites taken out of them. (I learned later that rats, not squirrels, had taken those bites.)

On the extreme opposite side of the park, with the caricaturist artists at work nearby, we found a magnificent magnolia laden with fist-size seedpods, the ripe red seeds exploding out of the pods like some sort of alien plant. Best of all, many of the pods had fallen to the ground, and the seeds, the size and shape of kidney beans but the color of red-hot candy, were dangling out of the pods, their little silken threads keeping them attached. We picked the area clean. At one point, a tattooed, bearded, ponytailed man noticed what we were doing, stopped, looked through the thick bars of a fence, and began talking to us. His words surprised me.

"Collecting the magnolia seeds, huh? You know how to propagate them?"

"Not really, but I know someone who does," I responded from my kneeling position.

"It's easy, man. Put them in a jar full of water for about a week, and let them ferment. The red seed coating turns to goop, and the hard seed is left. Then dry them out like tomato seeds. Same thing. Where are you gonna grow 'em?"

"New York State, near Lake Ontario."

"They'll grow there, too. I'm an organic farmer. I don't grow many trees, but I've grown magnolias. They just need plenty of water."

I looked down at a stubborn seed, and when I looked back up, the man was gone. It was one of the few times an unaffiliated party had stopped to offer advice and to inquire about the purpose of my seed gathering. Nice.

Next to the magnolia was a little redbud tree with its characteristic lustrous, mocha brown bark and delicious clusters of dark espresso brown pods dangling from low-hanging branches. I gathered a few of them.

I nudged Matthew. "Come on. Let's go over to Louis Armstrong Park; it's five blocks straight up St. Ann."

We entered the park at Congo Square, a circular area paved in cobblestones. The musical heritage of Congo Square has no equal in the world. During the latter part of the seventeenth century and the early part of the eighteenth century, Congo Square was where African American slaves would congregate to socialize, to barter and trade, to sing and dance. In other words, ground zero for American music. And next to Congo Square, to the west, are three huge sandstone edifices: the New Orleans Municipal Auditorium, the Mahalia Jackson Theater of the Performing Arts, and the Sewage and Water Board Building. (The juxtaposition of the sewage building to the theaters captures the higgledy-piggledy politics of New Orleans.)

A hundred yards or more in the opposite direction is a perfectly hideous statue of Louis Armstrong. It's a giant bronze of Pops,* ten feet tall, holding a coronet in one hand and his signature handkerchief in the other. It doesn't look anything like him. Below the statue sits a little putrefying lagoon with walkways and arching bridges. It looked more like a cheesy miniature golf course than an interpretive walk. Awful. But according to the signs, the lagoon is slated to be the future site of the New Orleans Jazz National Historical Park, and, one hopes, a more fitting tribute to the world's greatest musician and to the birthplace of jazz will be the end result.

All around the eclectic park, live oak trees cover huge circular sections of space. There is one enormous one, older than any tree

---

* Armstrong was known as Stachmo and Pops—the latter nickname I like even better than the former because it was the name Wynton Marsalis so lovingly referred to him by in the Ken Burns's documentary *Jazz*.

I've experienced so far in the city. It stands between Congo Square and Sachmo's statue and must be close to two hundred years old. The sights and sounds that ancient forest father must have seen and heard in its lifetime ignite the imagination. It made me think of Walt Whitman's poem "I Saw in Louisiana a Live-Oak Growing,"* but Whitman's famous poem is about a tree sitting all by itself, "utter[ing] joyous leaves." He wondered how it could be so joyous living all alone like that; so he took away a branch of leaves with some moss wrapped around it as a token of its indomitable spirit. Few people know that Walt Whitman lived for a short period of time in 1848 in New Orleans, when he worked as a young newspaperman. A recent PBS biography of the poet posits that the Crescent City was actually the inspiration for the writing of the twelve poems that went on to become his earth-shattering masterpiece *Leaves of Grass*.†

The live oak in Congo Square has lived the opposite life of Whitman's "live-oak," uttering its joyous leaves for two centuries surrounded by its own family and friends and the greatest music the world has ever known. Had Walt Whitman seen this tree instead of the other one, he wouldn't have taken away leaves and moss, he would have gathered the acorns, planted them, and then instead of "sound[ing] his barbaric YAWP over the roofs of the world,"‡ he would have danced and sung instead.

It was early afternoon the next day. We had been unsuccessful in gaining access to Tennessee Williams's home with the

---

* From Book V, "Calamus," of *Leaves of Grass*.
† For more about this, watch Mark Zwonitzer's riveting new biography of Whitman made for the PBS series *American Experience*.
‡ From "Song of Myself."

banana tree in the courtyard, so after an al fresco lunch in Jackson Park, we decided to check out William Burroughs's former home, across the river.

One of my favorite photographs of Jack Kerouac is a headshot of him wearing a newsboy cap, taken in Algiers. I had always thought that the Algiers in the caption meant Algiers, the capital of Algeria. Wrong. It was Algiers, Louisiana, directly across the Mississippi from the French Quarter. It sticks out like a fat thumb as the mighty river curves like a sad mouth around its point. You can take a ferry over from Canal Street, but the front desk clerk at our hotel advised against it. We drove over.

I knew very little about William S. Burroughs. Someone had given me a biography of him that I only skimmed.* Nor had I ever read *Naked Lunch*. My only frame of reference for Burroughs came from Kerouac. It didn't matter, because Matthew knew all about him:

"Now, which character was Burroughs in *On the Road?*" I asked without embarrassment.

"Old Bull Lee," he said as he sat in the passenger seat of the car, sketching a caricature of me in profile in his notepad.

"I thought that was Herbert Huncke."

"No, no, that was Burroughs. You didn't know that?"

"You'd be surprised how much I don't know. All I remember about that character is that he moved out of New Orleans because the bars were dull and the beer was too expensive, and he was a heroin addict with a wife and kids."

"He wasn't just a heroin addict. He had read everything and studied everything and traveled everywhere; he was like the wise

* *Literary Outlaw: The Life and Times of William S. Burroughs* by Ted Morgan, New York: Avon Books, 1990.

old sage of the group. But what he was doing in Algiers was experimenting with self-analysis through drugs." He began to draw again.

"Oh, is that what he was doing?"

"You have to remember that drugs back then were new; they didn't even know how addictive or harmful they were."

"Didn't he come from an extremely privileged background and graduate from Harvard?" I was full of middle-aged cynicism, but all ears. At this point in the conversation, we were crossing over the Greater New Orleans Bridge, with the New Orleans skyline over our left shoulders and the caffe latte–colored Mississippi two hundred feet below our tires. There were large barges all over the river, and way off in the distance, mountains of billowing thunderheads floated above the horizon like heavenly piles of shaving cream. We both stopped talking and took in the sights until we were off the bridge and cruising along the boulevard in Algiers.

Matthew was back at his drawing, filling in the little details around my head. Something about the ponytail and the shape of my nose made me look like a squirrel. I returned to our conversation:

"Didn't Burroughs murder his wife?"

"You know the story?" he asked, not looking up.

"Refresh my memory."

"He shot her in the head in a game of William Tell. They were in Mexico at a party, and in front of a bunch of people. She put a glass on her head, and he missed and killed her. They were both really drunk."

"I would imagine."

"But he said later that it was more like a mercy killing because she was so tired of living, you know, and such a bad drug addict."

"Did he go to jail?"

"I'm not sure."

His voice trailed off as our attention was diverted by the sights around us. We were driving slowly along a four-lane avenue with a wide median, but virtually no trees planted on it. On both sides of the street, abandoned houses with boarded-up windows and Fore-closure signs pasted to the doors described a neighborhood of bro-ken lives. Matthew had closed his sketchbook and put it on the dashboard, and was studying the area intensely through the wind-shield. At an intersection, his head double-jerked to the right.

"I just saw a sign for Wagner Street."

At the next stop sign, I turned right. Burroughs's house was down two blocks. I pulled up directly in front of the shotgun plantation-style house. I put the car in Park and cut the engine. Right outside the passenger-side window, an impressive copper-colored historical plaque with fat white Times Roman font read:

> ## WILLIAM S. BURROUGHS
>
> ### Residence from 1948–1949 of
> ### *William S. Burroughs*
> #### WORLD RENOWNED AUTHOR OF
> #### *Naked Lunch, Junky, Queer*
> #### AND MANY OTHER WORKS

"So, did he go to jail?" I looked down from the plaque and into Matthew's huge brown eyes, wanting an answer to the question be-fore we got out of the car.

"I don't know. I don't think so." Then he crinkled up his brow. "I'm really surprised that you don't know this stuff; he's a pretty major figure, especially for writers."

"Yeah, well, you're right. He is one of the literary lions, but in the end, it all comes down to feelings."

"Feelings?"

"Like Maya Angelou said, 'People will forget what you said and did, but they won't forget how you made them feel.'"

"How did Burroughs make you feel?"

"Well . . . there's some pretty ugly situations out there and people like Burroughs, and even Angelou herself, like to rehash it all. We can't connect to everything we read, not that it isn't valid."

"But isn't that what art is supposed to do, show us all sides and perspectives so that we can become more compassionate and more intelligent?"

"Of course it is, but you still can't deny your feelings. There's this ridiculous notion out there that great art is the direct result of a fucked-up childhood, or poverty, or physical or psychological abuse. That's not it at all. You can't reject where you came from. But that's why Kerouac is so loved, because he was loved as a child. A lot of times, artists will substitute the love they never got as children for the love of their art, but it's not the same. Do you know what I'm trying to say?"

"I think so."

"I'm the product of a happy childhood. So are you. That's how we feel about the world. But enough of this talk. Let's find some seeds."

Burroughs's neighborhood is close to the river, but you would never know it. The area, made up mostly of small single-story homes, was completely devoid of human activity except for an occasional passing car. Every other lot was empty. There were precious few trees around, and these were young, twenty, thirty feet high, many grow-ing up like weeds along fence lines. There were only shrubs in front and alongside Burroughs's former house. It looked like the area had suffered from major flooding during Katrina to be so bereft of older trees. (I asked about this an hour later, at our visit to the Garden District Bookstore, and was told that Algiers had incurred only minor damage during Katrina.) The whole setting was vacuous.

The house was a long single-story affair with a wrap-around porch, door-size windows on all three sides, and fat, square columns supporting the roof's hefty overhang. We circumnavigated the place slowly, Matthew clicking away with his thirty-five millimeter at the interesting white house from all angles. We circled around behind it, and I couldn't help but notice that it looked like it was seaworthy. To a Northerner used to wide houses built on stone or brick foundations, the long and narrow single-story shotgun houses of the South, built three feet off the ground on wooden posts, look like ocean-bound vessels. Perhaps that's the point: when you live along the Mississippi, you had better be ready.

Two blocks over, within sight of the Burroughs house, in the backyard of a brick house ringed by an imposing spiked fence and menacing dogs glaring at us in the yard, we came across an ancient live oak. As we searched the area outside the fence for acorns, we became uncomfortably aware that a teenager on a bicycle, riding up and back and up and back, was watching our every move. It was slim pickings under that tree—just three acorns—leading me to feel that Burroughs had had very little contact with beauty.

Two blocks in the opposite direction, we came upon an old pecan tree next to a drainage ditch. There were pecans all over the ground, and we helped ourselves, filling two baggies full to the brim. Matthew snapped plenty of pictures of the tree, but I could tell he was feeling as uncomfortable and disconnected as I was.

"Let's get out of here," I said.

He didn't respond but started loping back toward the car with his head down, deep in thought.

Before hopping into the vehicle, we stood with our hands on the roof of the car looking at the erstwhile Burroughs home and searching for some sort of connection. Down the street a dog started barking maniacally.

"Well, he only lived here for a year," I commented, as if to excuse the brevity of our visit.

Matthew didn't say anything.

"Come on, let's go back to the dull and expensive bars in New Orleans."

"Yeah," he agreed.

THAT NIGHT, LYING IN BED, I couldn't get to sleep because I kept thinking about that live oak tree in Congo Square, being there, front and center, for that singular moment in American musical history, which got me thinking about Whitman's live oak tree standing all alone in the middle of an open space—the diametric opposite. He and I had both perceived the same joyous utterances, he from leaves and I from the tree's proximity to the amazing cultural ferment of that period.

I mulled over my live oak vision until sleep surrounded me, and in the morning, I wrote my own sublime poem about the tree:

I SAW in Congo Square a live-oak growing,
Surrounded by a crush of black folks, bartering and singing
    in the marketplace,
With soulful companions, it once stood uttering its joyous
    song in leaves,
And its look, majestic, regal, proud, made me think of young
    America,

But I wondered how it could utter joyous leaves standing so
    many years without its rowdy musicians near,

And I gathered up its acorns and locked them in my Baggy,
    together with a little N'Orleans dross,

And brought them away, and I have placed them upon my
    windowsill;

They are not there to remind me of my dearly beloved family,

(For lately I think of little else but them)

Yet it remains to me an inspired token, and makes me think
    of jazz music;

For all that, and though the live-oak glistens there in Congo
    Square still,

Uttering joyous leaves all its life with so many friends and
    lovers near and far, I know very well I must live and do
    the same.*

---

\* The original poem from Whitman's *Leaves of Grass* reads as follows:

*I SAW in Louisiana a live-oak growing,*
*All alone stood it, and the moss hung down from the branches;*
*Without any companion it grew there, uttering joyous leaves of dark green,*
*And its look, rude, unbending, lusty, made me think of myself;*
*But I wonder'd how it could utter joyous leaves, standing alone there,*
    *without its friend, its lover near—for I knew I could not;*
*And I broke off a twig with a certain number of leaves upon it, and twined*
    *around it a little moss,*
*And brought it away—and I have placed it in sight in my room;*
*It is not needed to remind me as of my own dear friends, (For I believe*
    *lately I think of little else than of them;)*
*Yet it remains to me a curious token—it makes me think of manly love;*
*For all that, and though the live-oak glistens there in Louisiana, solitary, in*
    *a wide flat space,*
*Uttering joyous leaves all its life, without a friend, a lover, near,*
*I know very well I could not.*

# Eudora Welty

**Water oak** *(Quercus nigra)*
**Southern live oak** *(Quercus virginiana)*
**Red pine** *(Pinus resinosa)*

WATER OAK ACORN

IT'S A LONG WAY FROM William S. Burroughs to Eudora Welty. To go from the gnarly, opiate-addicted, avant-garde, nonlinear Beat novelist to the sweet, genteel, beloved, domestic aunty of the short story is a long and winding road. Only in a nation of such infinite possibilities could two writers born contemporaneously in the same region of the country create such diametrically opposite forms of the same art. But of the two, my heart belongs to Eudora.

I actually encountered Eudora Welty in person when I was a college freshman. I'll never forget it. My literature professor, an eccentric character of sixty, with a shock of wild white hair, a flushed face as red as a maraschino cherry, and a high soprano voice that cracked every third word, walked into the classroom with an elderly woman on his arm.

"Looks like Markraft finally got a date," the classmate next to me whispered. I almost burst out laughing.

The old lady shuffled in, leaning heavily on our professor's bony arm. She looked like she was fresh out of a nursing home in her decades-out-of-fashion dress. She had ears two sizes too big, buck-teeth, extraterrestrial hands, and the most penetrating eyes I'd ever seen. Like a lighthouse beacon, those perspicacious peepers swiveled on their perch, scattering thoughts and sucking air out of every head and chest they made contact with. They wiped the smile off my face.

Ominously, her eyes settled on an unsuspecting student in the back of the room. An upperclassman, a girl, sat by an open window smoking a cigarette. It was the late seventies; you could smoke in a classroom back then.

"Put out that cigarette!" the old woman squawked. The voice was thorny and the tone malevolent.

The girl took a long drag and shook her head, blowing a big cloud up toward the ceiling. "No, we can smoke in here if we want to. It's our right."

"Fine, then. I won't read," the woman said as she folded her arms stubbornly across her sunken chest and plopped down in a chair.

A brief staring match ensued, and finally, with a puff and a huff, the co-ed snubbed out her butt, grabbed her books, and left the room.

At that point, our professor intervened, his voice cracking up and down about accommodating invited guests, especially one as esteemed at Miss Welty. Eudora Welty! Some students in the class actually gasped. (I had not read Welty yet, much to my loss.)

Sitting facing us with a book in her lap like a kindergarten teacher, Miss Welty began to read from one of her stories, entitled "Why I Live at the P.O." She really got into the reading. It was "Papa-Daddy" this and "SSSStella-Rondo" that, every sibilant she read hissing like a rattlesnake. I was entranced.

Then, out of the blue, her voice began to crack, and lo and behold, two viscous bulges appeared at the corners of her eyes. She was crying! She dropped the book down in her lap, pulled out a handkerchief, wiped her eyes, and then blew her nose. It was a long, slow, wet blow.

"I mussst apologizzze. I often ressspond to my own wordsss," she drawled with a self-amusing but gracious tone. Then, with a sigh, she picked the book back up and finished reading her story. I confess I didn't get it at the time: crying over her own words?

Cut to 1996. My first novel, *Life in the Rainbow*, had just been published and I was on a little promotional tour in the Midwest. I was up at the lectern reading in a bookstore in Milwaukee. It was one of my first public readings. There were maybe twenty-five people gathered as I read from the chapter entitled "Beware the Eyes of Marge."

Suddenly, my voice cracked, followed instantly by tears in my eyes that blurred the words on the page. I was forced to stop because . . . Papa-Daddy, don't you know, I was responding to my own words!


MATTHEW AND I DROVE OUT of New Orleans on twenty miles of raised causeway, twenty feet above the Louisiana bayous and end-less Lake Pontchartrain. As one crosses into Mississippi on I-55, the

Lower Mississippi Delta looks and feels more like a Caribbean country than a part of North America. Up above, the dynamic cloud
formations threaten tropical squalls, while on the ground, the tall
trees all have fluted boles and wet feet; and in between the two, giant white birds with long legs and elongated necks fly low and slow.
Not until we were halfway to Jackson and well north of the Gulf of
Mexico did it feel like we were back on terra firma.

With tornado warnings coming at us via the radio and a furry,
purple-pink-hued cloud bank bearing down on us from the west,
we pulled into downtown Jackson. It was lunchtime, and despite
the threatening weather, people were out on the streets eating their
lunches and enjoying the sultry air. Like many American cities,
Jackson is a hodgepodge of modern monoliths with a smattering of
Greek Revival and Federal-style homes in between. It's particularly
accentuated in Jackson because the buildings are so spread out.

I pulled up to a curb and asked a man in white shirtsleeves sitting on a granite stoop eating his bagged lunch about where the
Welty home was. He was able to direct me to the general location.

In the time it took us to find the house—no more than ten minutes—the ominous clouds had passed, albeit not without some scary
wind gusts, and the sun had come out, its numinous, golden rays of
light falling directly on the National Historic Landmark Tudor Revival home at 1119 Pinehurst Street. It is located in the midst of an
upscale neighborhood with similar style homes all around. Directly
across the street is the demure-looking campus of Belhaven College, with its main quad spread out in full view of the Welty home.
The day we were there, students meandered along the walkways and
played Frisbee out on the lawn. Massive live oaks stood out along
the perimeter of the campus.

We parked below yet another copper-colored historic plaque

(this one told of how Miss Welty had lived here for seventy-six years) and disembarked. There were soaring red pines to the right, ancient live oaks to the left, and shrubs all around the base of the house. Even with all that verdure out front, I could feel an energy emanating from the back of the house. There were no signs indicating that we couldn't venture there, so, without the slightest hesitation, we marched right around to the backyard.

What a delightful place! There were flowers of all shapes and sizes and colors and origins, maintained in cursive, dull-edged beds. (I should say *borders*, because a notation found in Miss Welty's mother's garden journal read, "Beds—no. Borders—yes.") The garden is two levels, both about the same size, roughly thirty feet in diameter. The upper level is perennials, the lower level roses. What I liked so much about the milieu was how natural it all felt. It wasn't overly showy or too meticulously maintained. It was quite wild, in fact, with some of the greenery, dare I say, overgrown. Unlike the precision landscaping and gardens at Monticello and Mount Vernon, with their excessive use of mulch, razor-sharp edging, and symmetrical rows, beds and shapes, this garden was strictly about colors and perfume, and not about show. Just one look around and I knew in an instant that Miss Welty did much of her writing in the garden, and every day of the week she had fresh-cut, sweet-smelling flowers on her table.

But gardens and flowers were not what I had come for. The entire time I had been milling about the garden, I was aware of a soaring black oak, one hundred feet tall, in the neighbor's backyard. (That house has since been sold to the Welty estate and is used as an education and visitors center.) There was no fence or divider between the properties, so I strolled over and stood under the great specimen, staring up into its branches, the first of which jutted out perpendicular to the ground, thirty-five feet up. This wondrous beast had observed Miss Welty every day of her life, digging, pruning, and smelling her roses. And, fortuitously, the frightening winds that had preceded us had knocked down several small branches that lay at my feet, laden with ripe acorns.

"Matthew, come look at these acorns."

Matthew, who was examining the trees down the slope in the woodland area twenty yards on, bounded over to me like a deer. I placed in his big mitt a couple of acorns, which he studied intently, delicately tickling the fuzz with the tips of his fingers. As I was bent over putting the second baggy of acorns in my backpack, a young woman appeared at our side. She was a few years older than Matthew, short, brunette, fashionable, with black-rimmed glasses.

"Hello, we were just wondering if you are planning to take the house tour, because we're scheduled to give one in fifteen minutes." She had no Southern accent at all.

"Sure," I said. I was delighted by the question, because I thought that she had come to scold me for collecting seeds.

We compliantly followed the pretty young docent into the house next door—the Education and Visitors Center—paid the admission fee, and were promptly left alone to tour the small museum on our own.

It was typical of many of the museums I had encountered, i.e., plenty of black-and-white photographs, heirlooms, and select quotations in big bold fonts mounted on the wall. We were eventually waved into a small back room of the house and shown a fifteen-minute film of Miss Welty's life. The old gal was sure having some fun with me, because the film ended with her reading from her inimitable short story "Why I Live at the P.O."

Next we toured the house where Miss Welty lived for most of

her life.* But before we went in the house, the young docent pointed out a young oak tree on the front lawn. She explained that it stood where a much larger and older water oak had stood for many years, and was just a sapling when Miss Welty's father bought the house in 1925. Apparently a few years back, the old oak had developed some sort of disease, and the curator deemed it a detriment to the estate and the other trees on the property, so they cut it down and replaced it with another water oak. We were told that Miss Welty dearly loved the old oak. I was glad to hear she was not alive when they did away with it, but at the same time I felt that pressure on my chest knowing that time was ticking for so many of America's witness trees.

The interior of the house was as light, commodious, and pleas-ant a living space as one could ever hope to inhabit. The living room, with its comfortable couches, cushioned chairs, and red brick fireplace, was oriented toward the large picture window that looked onto the lush quad of the campus across the street. We were told that Miss Welty put fresh flowers on the cocktail table in front of the couch every morning. The house was not air-conditioned; how-ever, its east–west orientation was endowed with cool cross-breezes during the summer, so doors and windows were often left open. Books were ubiquitous, lying on the couch, resting on the mantel-piece, stacked on the cocktail table, placed on the piano stool, and lined up on the shelves.

On the dining room table was a display of Miss Welty's hand-written notes. She wrote her works by hand, then spread her scrib-

---

* She was born across town, at 741 North Congress Street. The family moved to 1119 Pinehurst Street in 1925. She lived in the house until her death on July 23, 2001, at age ninety-two.

blings out on the table and set the passages in order with Scotch tape. There were books everywhere in that room, too. I noticed a framed letter on the wall written by Miss Welty and addressed to her mother. It was from Yaddo. In it she complains of how uncomfortable and distracted she feels at the retreat, and how she would much prefer to be home, sitting at the dining room table playing cards. I chuckled to myself, knowing just how she felt.

Next we were led into the kitchen. It was a very small space, ten by twelve feet, which looked out onto her beloved garden. The antediluvian appliances could have been used for a 1950s advertisement, right down to the clock on the wall. Simple, basic, serviceable: that was Miss Welty's style. We were told that she did not allow guests into her kitchen, and that her mother loved to bake bread there.

A downstairs bathroom was also fifty years out of date, with its black-and-white tile floor, white porcelain tub (no shower), sink, and toilet. After that, I didn't need to see or hear anymore. I understood the author well enough. Her life was and still is an open book. She didn't need to travel to exotic ports of call or live on the edge of a cliff or in some faraway city or pump drugs into her veins or any of that nonsense. All she needed was to be at home with her loved ones and her garden. That's all her exquisite imagination required. In *The Optimist's Daughter*, she writes, "For life, any life, she had to believe, was nothing but the continuity of its love."

You could feel that love everywhere, inside the house and especially outside in the garden.

# Willie Morris and
# Tennessee Williams Redux

**Southern magnolia** (*Magnolia grandiflora*)
**Pecan** (*Carya illinoensis*)
**Swamp chestnut oak, a.k.a. basket oak** (*Quercus michauxii*)

BASKET OAK
LEAF and SEED

## Yazoo City, Mississippi

Highway 49 from Jackson is a straight two-lane highway that angles north by northwest through the heart of the Mississippi flatlands toward the great river. Forlorn cotton fields line both sides of the road almost the entire way, and behind them run endless forests of red pine, dark and monotonous. Every now and then, a derelict plantation stares out at the lonely fields behind dislocated columns and a jaundiced facade.

We floated into Yazoo City down Grand Avenue under a dreary, late afternoon sky, past the good, the bad, and the ugly. "Yazoo, far from being the ludicrous name that others would take it, always meant for me something dark, a little blood-crazy, and violent," wrote Willie Morris in the introduction to his autobiography *North Toward Home*. He also goes on to say that the word comes from the Cherokee and means "death."

Middle-class homes along a stately, tree-lined avenue quickly devolved into decaying single-story homes once we passed over the railroad tracks. Before we knew it, we were in the center of an utterly defunct downtown business district. The majority of the three-story-tall brick edifices, most in excellent condition, lay empty. There were a few businesses, but they were far out of keeping with traditional Main Street–type shops: a tattoo parlor and a used appliance shop, for example. To my eyes, the brick of all the buildings had an odd glossiness and extra-ruddiness to them, as if flushed from too much whiskey or embarrassment. (I later learned that the entire town had burned to the ground in 1904 and was entirely rebuilt within two years.) Two of the buildings toward the end of the three-block span were painted outrageous Day-Glo colors, and because there were no cars on the road, we simply stopped in the middle of the street to look at them. "Coming Soon" one building's sign announced of a musical coffeehouse due to try its luck. Matthew, the consummate shutterbug, hopped out, knelt down, and snapped a few photos. It all looked like some artifact from early in the last century, perfectly preserved like the buildings of Pompeii. We were so taken by it all that we turned around and drove through again.

It was three in the afternoon. We hadn't eaten since breakfast, so we made for a restaurant back at the beginning of the business district. It was an ice-cream parlor that doubled as a sandwich shop.

No other patrons were around, and as a result, we received a great deal of attention from the woman behind the counter. She was a middle-aged white woman with a craggy face, a dead tooth, and straw-colored hair, wearing a green short-sleeve Izod shirt with the restaurant's logo on it. She had the most perfect Southern accent, the first Southern drawl I noticed in the people I met down South this time.

She made our sandwiches with tender loving care, and as she passed them over the counter to us, I casually asked her if she had ever heard of Willie Morris or knew where he used to live. No, she had never heard of Willie Morris, but right on cue, another woman, with the same green Izod uniform, appeared from a back room just as I was asking the question. She was shorter than the craggy-faced woman, also white, with dyed brown hair and a permanent smile plastered on top of a mouth that never stopped moving. She let me know right away that she was the owner, but unlike the other woman, she had no Southern accent. She knew who Willie Morris was, but she did not know which house he had grown up in. Without as much as a "But I can find out," she was on her cell phone making inquiries, talking a blue streak.

Matthew and I hungrily made our way over to a round table next to the street-side window and began to inhale our food. After a few minutes, the owner sidled over to our table and launched into a description of Morris's house, its color, the distance from the restaurant, the surrounding area, the local landmarks, the street names, and the people who lived nearby. Before I could thank her, she was into a full-blown history of Yazoo City. Fortunately we had our sandwiches to eat, which precluded our having to respond at any point. For twenty minutes, we sat there just nodding our heads and chewing our food.

In her deluge of words was one bit of lore that piqued our interest: the Yazoo witch. Local legend has it that a witch who was
believed to have murdered a young boy was chased into a swamp by
a group of town elders and drowned in quicksand. But before she
went under, she vowed to return to wreak vengeance. Twenty years
to the day after her drowning, the entire city burned to the ground
on May 25, 1904.* The sandwich shop owner also told us one tidbit
about Willie Morris that I hadn't known: he was buried out in the
city cemetery next to the witch's grave, as per his request!

A half hour later, back in the car, we found Morris's house
smack-dab on Grand Avenue; we had passed by it on our way into
town. It was much smaller and humbler than I had imagined: a
simple Cape Cod affair exactly like the house I had grown up in.
This one was painted dull green, with two windows on either side of
a demure front door and a two-step front stoop made of brick with a
little overhanging portico above. Sticking out of the roof were two
dollhouse-size dormers, and all around, the place was overgrown
with bushes and trees that were shorter than the house itself. There
was nothing on the property that dated back even a couple of decades. However, out on the curb directly in front of the house was
a magnificent magnolia, its army green leaves and branches laden
with buds ripe with blood red seeds. We hunkered down and picked
up the scarlet drops until we felt replete.

Around the corner, on the side street next to the house, we
found a half dozen elderly pecan trees dating back a hundred years.
The houses along that street matched the trees themselves, as both
were unkempt, with broken branches and missing roof tiles, excori-

* For the complete story of the Yazoo City witch, read chapter 1 of Willie
Morris's book Good Ole Boy.

ated bark and moss-covered siding, and zillions of thumb-shaped pecans and a child's playthings scattered in the yards. We filled our baggies in no time, and were paid no never-mind by the cars that drove by.

Back at the Morris house, I was hoping to find the elm tree that young Willie and his ten-year-old friends had sat up in for hours in a prank gone awry as described in *Good Ole Boy*, but there was no elm tree back there. I did, however, find an old locust tree on its last legs. Among the rusty cans, bottles, and used condoms in that alleyway, I was delighted to discover a handful of seedpods that the squirrels had overlooked. It was a bonus round, and with the sun beginning to set, I felt lucky.

As I loaded my haul into the trunk and glanced over at Morris's childhood house, I was struck by the thought that such an accomplished person, such a worldly man—a Rhodes scholar, editor-in-chief of *Harper's* magazine, and award-winning author— had grown up in a crazy nowhere place like Yazoo City. For me, it was the wry testament to success: to grow so far beyond where you came from that going back home is stranger than going forward.

Matthew wanted to visit the cemetery to see where Morris and the Yazoo witch were buried, but I had to say no to that, on account of the growing darkness—and my phobia of cemeteries.

Readers often discover an author for whom they have a strong affinity; the feeling is described as something magical. I think *magical* is too strong a word. I tend to believe it is a simple matter of reader and author thinking a lot alike. Fifty years before I had my epiphany in Lincoln's home looking at a photograph of him standing next to a basswood tree, Willie Morris, just a young boy of ten at the time, had the exact same epiphany sitting in a public library leafing through a history book of Yazoo City. He came upon a photograph, taken seventy-five years before, of an old man stand-ing behind Morris's very own elementary school under an oak tree. The picture made Morris leap out of his seat and race out of the library and down the road to see that tree.

"I stood where the old man had stood, on the precise spot . . . the whole business, the tree and the old man, made me feel a little dizzy," he wrote in chapter 3 of *Good Ole Boy*.

And that's just how I felt.

We headed north toward another author's home.

## Clarksdale, Mississippi

Even before I knew that Tennessee Williams had grown up in Clarksdale and that the town was the source of many of his charac-ters and settings and themes, the place held a mythical fascination for me. During my days working as a nurse's aide in a mental hos-pital in Milwaukee, I learned that some of my black, middle-aged female colleagues hailed from Clarksdale. I used to love to sit and listen to them talk. The colorful tales they told, the food they de-scribed, just the way they spoke, sent me.

"Richard," began Dorothy, the angelic, forty-something, so-black-she-was-purple-black aide I worked with, her silvery front tooth smile a blinding joy.

"There's a story about an old uncle of mine, an old sharecropper living south of town with his wife and grandchildren. One morn-ing he woke up and heard a terrible roar outside his window. He walked out on the front porch and there he saw a tornado coming straight for him and his little house. He grabbed himself the first thing he could get his hands on, a piece of plywood, and when that tornado reached his front stoop, why he raised it up sideways over the top of his head, stepped forward, and with both hands sliced right down into the middle of that tornado. And what do you think happened?"

"He was killed?"

"No! He split that thing in two! One side went this way; the other side that way; and the whole thing just fizzled right out into nothing. My own cousin saw him do it with his own two eyes."

"Wow!" was my only possible response. And it was heartfelt.

CLARKSDALE IS THE HEART of the Mississippi Delta. Its history is synonymous with the infamous (slavery, sharecropping, Emmett Till, Ike Turner) as well as the mythic (the Mound Builders, the Great Migration, Sam Cooke, and Muddy Waters). It is the birthplace of the Delta blues and the childhood home of Tennessee Williams. Like all restive prodigies of small towns who are emboldened rather than broken by the parochial attitudes they grew up around, those from Clarksdale had an extra jolt of contrary motivation: segregation. Even today you can feel the lingering haze of black is black and white is white and never the twain shall meet.* Like Yazoo City, the train tracks separate the black side from the white side; the only difference in Clarksdale is that those rail lines symbolize not only the division between the races, but also the way to Chicago and other northern cities: the American Promised Land.†

The Delta Blues Museum is housed in the old Illinois Central

---

* Rudyard Kipling's "The Ballad of East and West" is where the phrase "*and never the twain shall meet*" comes from.
† Clarksdale is featured in the award-winning history book by Nicholas Lehman, *The Promised Land: The Great Black Migration and How It Changed America.*

Railroad passenger depot in downtown Clarksdale. The depot was saved from demolition by a vintage guitar dealer from New Jersey named Skip Henderson,* who, with the help of local businesses and a grant from the federal government, restored the depot and donated it to the county, which in turn transformed it into the Delta Blues Museum. In recent years, Billy Gibbons of ZZ Top has helped bring the museum much-needed notoriety. And the actor Morgan Freeman owns the saloon across the street from the museum; it's called the Ground Zero Blues Club.

It was mid-morning, overcast and sprinkling, and only a few visitors were parked in the huge parking lot in front of the museum/depot, which sat amid a bank, a hotel, a few shops, warehouses, and, sadly, swaths of empty lots. We paid our admission and entered. This museum, like any museum, was a collection of artifacts, but in this case, we were surrounded by lively and unusual things: zoot suits, fancy shoes, guitars of all shapes and sizes, banjos, harmonicas, LPs, 45s, washboards and buckets, even the remnants of the shack Muddy Waters lived in as a boy. Set up in the back of the space, the hut, with its wide, worm-eaten boards, looks more like an archeological discovery from pre-Columbian times than a dwelling from twentieth-century America. The museum also contained a casket, with a grotesque female effigy inside, made out of Mississippi mud. There was another large "sculpture" next to it: a square-shaped skull

---

* Raymond "Skip" Henderson organized the Mount Zion Fund, a nonprofit group that supports rural churches in Mississippi and memorializes past musicians from the area by providing their graves with headstones. The inspiration behind the MZF happened in 1989, when Henderson endeavored to raise money for the Mount Zion Church to keep it out of foreclosure and to place a cenotaph in the church's cemetery in honor of Robert Johnson, the great blues musician who is buried there.

with teeth purposely missing. Matthew was smitten by the grue-some folk art pieces and stood for a long time contemplating them.

To me, the Delta Blues Museum was still a museum: that is, a place I longed to escape. The idea of a music museum is, on the surface, as illogical as an architecture, literature, or film museum: that's what cities, libraries, and movie theaters are for. QED: the only real music museum is a concert hall or a juke joint. However, I admit that perhaps the best way to honor the bluesmen who have left this sphere is a museum, and the Delta Blues Museum in Clarksdale is doing a vital job keeping memories alive, and attracting tourists and much-needed revenue to an economically depressed area, while providing essential education about one of America's original art forms. And I did find something in the music museum that suited my fancy: postcards of bluesmen, a score of them.

But it was trees that I had come to find, specifically Tennessee Williams's trees. I had an address of St. George's Episcopal Church and Rectory, where the Pulitzer Prize–winning playwright had lived as a young boy with his grandparents, mother, and sister. I knew it was near downtown, but I was tickled pink to discover from the young admissions clerk at the museum that it was "right over there": that is, you could see the church and Williams's house from the steps of the museum. We hopped in the car and drove around the block, parking right in front of the rectory, which is adjacent to the classical Episcopal church, with its understated spire, soft red brick, and stained-glass windows.

We stepped out of the car literally on top of a bronze plaque, set into the concrete sidewalk slab, of Tennessee Williams. The marker is engraved with a caricature of the playwright in the right-hand corner, the raised type describing his connection to the area and his literary achievements, all contained within an outline of the state of Mississippi. It was an elegant memorial, and we stood above it, the toes of our shoes encircling the edges, and read it.

I must confess that I am not a huge Tennessee Williams fan. I don't frequent the theater, nor do I like to read tragedies. But in researching Williams's early life, I became fascinated by his powerful connection to Clarksdale. What impressed me most was how many of the city locals over the years have been able to point out specific people, places, and themes in Williams's works that were true to life. There really were people in Clarksdale named Stella, Blanche, and Brick.

Three ancient oak trees stood directly in front of the rectory, shooting skyward from the curb and eighty feet into the air. All three were at least a hundred years old. Their singular presence accentuated the fact that there were precious few trees of any consequence anywhere in the surrounding area. These were an awesome sight and reminded me of ruins, like pillars of antiquity from Gilgamesh's legendary walls of Uruk. I got right to work gathering acorns. Under the oldest and largest of the trees, I found only one acorn, but it was the biggest acorn I'd ever seen, as large and fat as my big toe.

At one point, as we were gathering, a man came bounding out of Williams's former home and down the steps toward a truck parked out on the street. He wore a Boston Red Sox cap, a Red Sox parka, and a smile. He looked like he was straight out of Kenmore Square and not the heart of the Delta.

"Finding what you need?" he asked, without a hint of Southern accent.

"Indeed," I said.

"Well, we aim to please."

He began to walk toward his truck, but I couldn't resist asking him, "Boston Red Sox? We're a long way from Fenway Park."

"Red Sox Nation knows no boundaries," he boasted, and with a little shrug, off he went, proving that even in Clarksdale, there's a lot going on just below the surface.


I WORRY THAT WHEN WE GO as tourists to Clarksdale, Mississippi, in search of authentic roots, in doing so we preserve the past in amber instead of keeping it alive in the here and now. We should also honor the past by listening to new artists, and bringing new music, art, and words to life in their interpretations today. It's an intelligence that must be experienced.

Honey locust (*Gleditsia triacanthos*)
Shumard oak (*Quercus shumardii*)
Osage orange (*Maclura pomifera*)
Eastern redcedar (*Juniperus virginiana*)
Southern magnolia (*Magnolia grandiflora*)

OSAGE ORANGE

THE RIDE FROM CLARKSDALE to Oxford is an hour and fifteen minutes, straight across the northern part of the state, along Route 278. The landscape changes abruptly at the halfway point, from the dry brown flats of the Delta cotton fields to the lush green umbrage of the hilly hardwood forests.

We stopped in a teeny town called Marks to get gas. As Matthew filled the tank, I went in to the convenience store to buy some nuts. A group of men was sitting around a booth drinking coffee and talking about the Alabama versus Ole Miss football game set to start within the hour. As I stood there holding my bag of peanuts, I tried to listen in, but I couldn't understand a word of what they were saying, which got me thinking, here I was standing in line in my own country, yet I felt every bit as foreign as when I lived in Asia and Europe.

## Oxford, Mississippi

Oxford was mayhem! People were everywhere, carrying seat cushions, banners, and pennants, everyone dressed in either Alabama crimson or Ole Miss red, white, and blue. I saw a dozen blood red sweatshirts with "BAMA" written across the front in bold white capital letters, and just as many with the state flag of Mississippi, which looks like a cross between the French tricolor and the Confederate flag. The traffic was bumper to bumper but without any edge to it, unlike New York City traffic.

The city center of Oxford is a classic square around which sit antebellum structures made of fiery red brick and trimmed out with columns and porches. If there were an American downtown that could double as a movie set, Oxford is the place. We wanted to walk around town and visit the famous Square Books, but there was nowhere to park, so we decided to go directly over to Faulkner's home at Rowan Oak instead.

At the end of an upscale neighborhood, and in the middle of the woods a mile from downtown and the football stadium, we found it. As we bumped along the rutted-out dirt road to the visitor parking lot, we saw no cars with Ole Miss banners. Apparently the folks of Oxford revere Faulkner so much that, even during a classic Saturday showdown, his visitors' lot remains sacrosanct.

When we got out of the car, we heard a hissing sound. (I should say Matthew heard a hissing sound; I constantly hear hissing on account of my tinnitus.) We stood there nonplussed, Matthew listening to the hissing and I watching him listening to the hissing. I finally knelt down and started feeling around the tire until something jagged sliced my fingertip. Wouldn't you know it? We had a screw in our tire. I looked at my watch. It was 2:30 P.M. Suddenly the ground began to shake and there erupted a deafening, living roar, the likes of which I had never before heard. We both jumped. Of course: the football game had started.

We decided to go looking for a place that could plug the tire while we still had enough air in it to drive. We rode all over town looking for a garage that was open, but no luck. We found a Goodyear tire place that had a small note in the door. Closed. As I was walking away, shaking my head at Matthew, a car pulled in next to us. The driver got out of his car and smiled at me. He was a well-dressed man in his thirties, and his whole family was in his spanking-new SUV.

"Can I help you?" he asked.

"Yeah, I've got a screw in my tire. I'm looking for a shop that can plug it."

"Oh boy. We closed two hours ago. The whole town is shut down because of the game. Why don't you come on in, and I'll call around and see who's open."

What a nice guy. He must have called a dozen places. Nothing was open. Nothing. I thanked him and assured him we'd be all right. It was no big deal, other than the fact that it was Saturday and getting someone to plug the tire might have to wait until Monday. There was one of those ridiculous temporary spare tires in the trunk that would probably get us to our next destination. So we did the only thing we could do: we went back to Faulkner's with the remaining air we had left in the tire to carry out our mission.

We parked in the same spot, and at the exact moment I exited the car, another earth-shaking roar went up: touchdown for the hometown, I assumed. It was a bizarre juxtaposition, standing there between the two realms: the spooky mansion of a literary genius to my right and the volcanic excitement of tens of thousands of fervid fans at a modern-day gladiatorial event to my left. The powerful lights of the stadium glowed just over the treetops, adding an otherworldly ambience to the tableau. I wondered if Faulkner, when he was alive, could hear the crowd at the football games from his house while he was busy writing.

With the seed-gathering gear on my back, we hiked along a muddy woodland trail toward the great manor.

Faulkner was fascinated by the old secluded antebellum home, called "the Bailey Place" when he bought it in 1930. He renamed it Rowan Oak a year later, after a Danish legend, hoping perhaps that the name would offer some sort of protection from the outside world. The legend goes that if a rowan oak (a.k.a. mountain ash) is found growing out of another tree, witches have no power over it, since it does not grow on the ground. People who found such a tree would cut branches off it, shape them into a cross, and place the icon over their front door in an effort to ward off evil spirits. Faulkner clearly believed in the protective powers of the trees around him, and he lived in the house for more than thirty years, until his death in

1962. No doubt he was also trying to ward off intruders wanting to give him their two cents.*

Visiting Rowan Oak, it is easy to understand that his house was the principal setting behind many of Faulkner's novels, most notably *Light in August*, which was originally called *Dark House*. On all four sides, ninety acres of dark woods, as haunting and provocative as the author's works themselves, press in on the mansion, adding a Gothic claustrophobia to the setting. An alleyway of ancient, striated cedars, taller than the house, line the walkway up to the Doric columns of the front entrance, blocking out all light and evoking a chilly foreboding in the visitor's heart. The Greek Revival mansion, built by Colonel Sheegog in 1840, when Oxford was little more than a frontier outpost, looks every bit its age. Numerous shack-like outbuildings—suggestive of an ignoble age when slave and slaveholder, left alone by the outside world, lived their parasitic lives fitfully—are visible nearby.

But Rowan Oak is also an arborist's delight, with the most impressive array of tree species I'd come across since my visit to Mount Vernon and Monticello— magnolia, locust, oak, pecan, walnut, maple, Osage orange—many of them situated on the grounds like tributes to mythological characters. And wherever we went, the great white house, with its long and hollow windows like eyes, loomed in the background, watching us suspiciously. Around the

---

* Faulkner was postmaster of the University of Mississippi post office for three years. He hated the job and would ignore patrons and on occasion throw mail away. After he resigned from the job, he commented about his experience: "I reckon I'll be at the beck and call of folks with money all my life, but thank God I won't ever again have to be at the beck and call of every son of a bitch who's got two cents to buy a stamp."

back of the house, behind an outbuilding and out of sight of the mansion, Matthew and I found an amazing tree specimen. Its trunk was sliced open and spiraled like a slaughtered cow's carcass, its bark dusty and rust-colored, its branches twisted and droopy. We stood looking at it for a long time, Matthew taking lots of pictures. I could not identify the leaves and assumed it was an Osage orange, which I knew about but had never experienced. Eventually we drifted away from it, toward the deep woods close by.

We entered the woods along a thin path and were soon stunned at what we discovered a few yards in. At the edge of a precipitous drop-off, above a narrow ravine that sliced diagonally through a heavily wooded section, was a huge oak tree, the biggest I'd yet encountered, not in height but in girth. Its trunk was so wide that Matthew and I together could not reach around it with our arms and touch. One of its massive branches had recently broken off, and it lay wedged against the enormous bole like a gangplank. I scrambled up it and leaned against the colossus. There was no doubt that this oak had been on Faulkner's radar and possibly was the inspiration for his countless words and thoughts and poems.* The ground was littered with its huge acorns, and for the next twenty minutes I was completely absorbed gathering as many as I could find.

Sweating and dizzy from stuffing numerous baggies with acorns, I looked around to discover that Matthew had disappeared. I called out. He didn't answer. Thinking that he probably had gone back to the house, I wandered up that way. At the palatial front door, I pulled on the door handle and walked right in, coming face-to-face with a tall, effervescent young woman in her thirties who turned

---

* The first piece Faulkner ever published, a poem entitled "L'Après-Midi d'un Faune," begins "Ah, I peep through the trees . . ."

out to be a poet in the Ole Miss graduate program. I asked her if she had seen my nephew; she hadn't. We then struck up a conversation. I revealed to her my mission, which delighted her to no end. She started writing down names of garden consultants and natural historians associated with Rowan Oak who knew infinitely more about the trees than she did. And as she was writing, I happened to mention our tire plight. She didn't hesitate and got right on her cell phone and called up her boyfriend, who, she then informed me, was coming over to fix the tire himself. And right at that moment, Matthew entered the house holding a light green, softball-size version of a human brain.

The Osage orange is one of nature's most bizarre creations. The heavy, waxy fruit is full of milky sacs. Its only use today is as an insect repellent, but back in 1934, President Roosevelt used the tree almost exclusively in his "Great Plains Shelterbelt" WPA project, to help prevent soil erosion in the nation's dust bowl, because the hearty trees offer an excellent windbreak. And because of their thorns, Texas ranchers used Osage orange trees along their property lines to keep cattle penned in before the advent of barbed wire. Indians liked to make bows and clubs out of the tree's sturdy, elastic wood.

Holding the Osage orange in his hand as if it were Faulkner's pickled brain, Matthew and I took a house tour. Déjà vu: Faulkner's home reminded me exactly of Emerson's, only fifty years newer. This one was, of course, much larger and more solidly put together; however, the austerity and general ambience of the dark furnishings, musty bedrooms, extravagant wallpaper, and oil paintings were all a repeat of the Concord house. But because there was no burden to the visitor of the requisite docent-led tour, we were out in fifteen minutes, the highlight of our tour being the room where Faulkner had scribbled the outline of a fable on a bedroom wall. (I once covered all four walls of a bedroom with quotes and vocabulary words, to the horror of my landlord.)

The angelic graduate student followed us to the front door and told us to meet her and her boyfriend back at the entrance in a half hour, which was closing time. With time to burn, Matthew and I decided to seek out more seeds. I took two steps from the front door and met a locust tree. I did my best Spud Webb impersonation and jumped inches in the air to knock down a few seedpods before noticing some pods gratuitously scattered on the ground nearby. Next, Matthew led me to the other side of the property, where he had found the Osage orange. Under a spindly mass of branches where the woods and lawn met, there was an entire tribe of Osage fruits. I crawled in under the branches and got to work deciding which specimens I would keep. I found three that were nice: round and weighing a pound or so. I wrapped them in plastic bags and dumped them into the backpack.

When we returned to the steps of Faulkner's mansion, our savior had arrived. Dave Hardin, in his late forties, with reddish-blond hair in a ponytail and hands and a complexion that described a man who had never taken a shortcut in his life. With enthusiasm equal to his lady friend's, he heartily shook my hand. Then, with no more than an exchange of names, he held up the tire plug kit he'd just purchased for the task and asked me to lead the way to the stricken vehicle.

He attempted to plug the tire where the car was parked, but he realized he needed more purchase, as well as access to air power, so he and I hopped into the car (amazingly, the tire still had enough air in it to get us where we needed to go) and drove to a nearby filling station, while Matthew and the docent followed us in her car.

Dave refused any assistance and removed the tire and then the screw, plugged the hole, filled the tire with air, and put it back on all in the time it takes two people to get to know one another. As he pulled and pushed and plugged, we talked. Turns out, Dave is a well-known singer-songwriter throughout the South. And when he'd heard about my seed project, he revealed a startling coincidence: his most famous song is a tune he wrote called "The Tree," in honor of Julia Butterfly Hill, the woman who lived in a 1,500-year-old, 180-foot-tall redwood for two years in order to save it from the loggers' saws. I knew all about "Luna," the name Hill had given her beloved redwood, because it was on my original list of trees to visit and take away seeds from.

When the tire was back in place, good as new, I offered to take Dave and the docent out to dinner, but they had other plans. I tried to pay him. He wouldn't take my money. I finally insisted that I buy the tire repair kit back from him in case we had another mishap, which he reluctantly accepted. As they rode off into the sunset, Matthew and I stood there waving and smiling at one another, basking in our good karma.

With the Ole Miss versus Alabama game still going on, we figured we had a window of opportunity to get some chow before the whole town came undone. We got some sandwiches and sodas at a deli and headed back to Rowan Oaks. In the soft twilight of the late afternoon, the woods felt mysterious and alive as we found our way through them and back onto the Rowan Oak property. All was quiet, which meant that things were not going well for the home team.

There is a great magnolia tree rising from the center of a circular garden just where the cedar-lined walkway begins fifty yards from the front of the house. I hadn't noticed it before. It was almost too dark to find seeds, but I managed to do so nonetheless. There were plenty of ripe red seeds on display, and I gathered up a whole bunch and put them in my backpack.

The sun had set. I glanced around the property. The trees were casting long, distorted shadows across the lawn; the sky above was a congealed, coppery slush. I stood directly in front of the house, at the far end of the walkway, between the two rows of ancient cedars that led down to the mansion's Grecian façade. The soaring columns, bone white, reminded me of four hideous fangs; the steps a sort of makeshift altar; and the void beyond, where the front door stood, was like the very entrance to the River Styx. It was chilling—a perfect emblem, especially in that rubicund twilight, of the phantoms that must have gnawed and fermented inside Faulkner's mind and heart. Phantoms that still linger at Rowan Oak.

**Water oak** *(Quercus nigra)*
**Southern magnolia** *(Magnolia grandiflora)*

MAGNOLIA TREE
SEED POD

## Tuscumbia, Alabama

We drove through the dark and the pouring rain from Oxford, Mississippi, to Tuscumbia, Alabama, birthplace of Helen Keller. At Tupelo, we found the Natchez Trace Trail and followed it north through the low-lying hills. This spectacular parkway, built in the 1930s by FDR's Civilian Conservation Corps* "traces" the old graz-

---

* The Civilian Conservation Corps (CCC) was a public works relief program created and instituted by President Franklin Delano Roosevelt for unemployed men that provided a vocational training through useful work related to conservation and the development of natural resources from 1933 to 1942.

ing route of the eastern buffalo that once migrated between the lush pastures of Mississippi and Alabama to the salt deposits of the southern Appalachians. At night, it is a scary and spectacular drive as the road roller-coasters up, down, and around, punctuated by wildlife surprises around some bends. During it, Matthew and I kept repeating to each other like a litany how lucky we were to be rolling along on four healthy tires. Thank you, Dave Hardin.

A bit fried from the drive, we pulled into downtown Tuscumbia around about 10:00 P.M. and looked for libation and then sleep. We passed more than a couple of signs for "Ivy Green, Birthplace of Helen Keller," but no signs for hotels or motels. Outside of town we found a small motel and checked in.

THE NEXT MORNING WAS SUNDAY. It was a particularly quiet morning with no wind, an odd sky, and thin cloud cover. As we drove from the motel back into town, we noticed people of all ages and sizes dressed in their Sunday best crowding into the innumerable churches along Main Street. Tuscumbia is a churchgoing town. We followed the cheery signs to "Ivy Green, Birthplace of Helen Keller" and, without much ado, arrived at our destination. All we had to do was enter a very formal entranceway, and go up the one-hundred-meter-long driveway leading to the bright historic home—but two huge iron gates, twelve feet high, barred our way. The place was closed.

"Wouldn't you know it. My last and final stop and it's closed. We can't stay another day, because I won't be able to catch my flight tomorrow morning, and neither will you," I grumbled to Matthew.

We stood holding the bars of the gate, gazing longingly at the fabled home beyond our reach. The huge front lawn was chock-full of an odd assortment of tree species; most of them were giant hundred-year-old specimens: oaks and willows and magnolias. A cyclone fence circled the perimeter. There was no way to get onto the property. The property at Ivy Green is huge, at least for a home within city limits: its dimensions I guessed to be about a football field wide and several fields deep.

To my small relief, I spied some towering trees on the east side of the house that looked close enough to the fence to offer their branches up to some seed-gathering possibilities. So we started to walk in that direction. Along Keller Lane we found an old oak leaning over the fence. I searched along the sidewalk but found only a few viable acorns; most had been either cleaned away by lawn crews or eaten by squirrels. As we continued along the fence line, drawing ever closer to Keller's home, we heard loud voices coming from the house, and an instant later, as we drew abreast of the storybook mansion, we discovered an open gate. It was an obvious invitation. We walked in.

If harps or trumpets had begun to play, it wouldn't have surprised me in the least. Besides my father, Helen Keller was my first hero in life. Her spirit, her will, and her strength of character were the bedrock upon which I rested my faith and hope. In a world corrupt and nonsensical, her purity and optimism righted all wrongs and changed bad into good. As a young boy, I was afflicted with a nasty case of hyperactivity disorder, and as a result I lagged far behind my peers in reading, writing, and 'rithmetic, causing no end of worry to my family. I especially couldn't sit still long enough to read even one page of the printed word. So my parents got me a tutor, even though they couldn't afford it. (My dad, at the time, was working in a factory that made electric pencil sharpeners.)

I remember my tutor vividly. She was an ancient gray-haired fossil, and she lived in a tall, spooky old house that reeked of the dry, smoky smell of books, just like she did. Oftentimes we would sit side by side outdoors, under the shade trees beside her house of a sunny summer's day, and like Annie Sullivan, she would hold my fingers on the page and move them along the glossy surface of the musty books as she read the words to me. I was perhaps eight years old at the time. Then one day, just like Helen Keller, I had an epiphany, but it wasn't water from the pump that opened my eyes to the power of words; it was, ironically, Helen Keller herself. I couldn't believe it—rather, I wouldn't believe it—as she read from *The Story of My Life*, that a young, deaf, mute, and blind girl had written those beautiful words. It was unfathomable to me that a person so disabled could be aware of things and understand them the way she did, let alone read and write better than I could. I was so taken aback by that fact that I had to bring the book home and read it for myself.

*The Story of My Life* was the first book I ever remember reading, and Helen Keller, more than any other author, instilled in me a love for and belief in the power of the written word

I STOOD THERE DIRECTLY IN FRONT of Ivy Green, Helen Keller's home, with a smile on my face. I just couldn't believe it—there *I* was and there *it* was. The house looked so bright and warm and inviting, as if I'd lived there in a past life. The strange loud voices coming from behind the house made me a little uneasy, and in the back of my mind I had an unsettling feeling that the gate might have been inadvertently left open. But that worrisome sentiment quickly dissolved as I got to work gathering seeds from among the multitude scattered about the area.

I had recently pored over a copy of Keller's book and underlined all the passages that mentioned the trees she had interacted with as a child: a butternut behind her house, mimosas in the front, a wild cherry down the block. Bent over and gathering with great élan, dizzy from the bounty around me, and just feet from Keller's house, I wasn't focusing on the details but on the delight.

Who knows how long I greedily gathered and harvested there out in front of her house. Fifteen minutes, a half hour, an hour? I was aroused from my blissful state by Matthew, who'd come bounding around the house, calling my name:

"Uncle Rick, the police are here!"

"Huh?" I held three baggies in my hand; my ponytail had come undone, so my hair covered most of my face except my eyes, and my hands were stained blood red from harvesting magnolia seeds. I also must point out that I was wearing an extra-large tie-dye T-shirt with a huge peace sign across the front. In sum, I was a close facsimile to Charles Manson, albeit some inches taller, with a pushed-in nose and an affinity for trees and books rather than hallucinogens and homicidal violence.

I swiveled around on my spot and looked to the right; at the end of the sprawling front lawn, I saw a police cruiser parked behind our car. In front of me, through the trees and beyond the fence, I saw another cruiser, and behind me I turned to see another police car driving slowly down the west-side alleyway. We were surrounded.

"How do you know they're here for us? There're other people here, too," I said as Matthew came leaping over to me with his head down and a tight look on his face.

"Those aren't people," he said ominously as he came to rest at my side. "That's a tape recording playing over and over again. It's in a little theater area in the garden out back. Someone must have left it on." He took one step closer to me. "Cops make me really nervous."

"Relax, guy, the gate was open," I reassured him.

"So what could they arrest us for? Reverse vandalism?"

Three cops appeared from around the sides of the house—one from the east and two from the west—at the same time. Oddly, they were dressed in three different uniforms. They approached in choreographed movements, not in step but in rhythm. They came to rest at the same time, a few feet from us. The lone cop directly in front of me was a big young burly dude, 250 pounds of buzz-cut authority, with a great round face, jowls, and dark circles under his eyes. As for the two other cops, the older one was in his late fifties, short, spindly, leather-faced, and mustachioed; and next to him stood the glossy, copper-colored version of Terminator: tall, dark sunglasses, no lips, muscular boa constrictor arms folded across a barrel chest. At that moment, it looked as if our karma had run dry.

"May I see your identifications please," Buzz-cut snarled, straight-faced, eyeing us suspiciously: first me, then Matthew, then me again.

"Sure," I replied.

Matthew had his passport out like a magician, hopping over and handing it to him lickety-split, while I struggled to pull my driver's license from its sheath.

"Got it!" I exclaimed as it finally came loose. I waved it cavalierly in the air as I walked it over to him. He snatched it out of my hand with his great big paws. No words were exchanged between us. I glanced back at Terminator, whose stance and expression hadn't changed a whit. The spindly, leather-faced guy was shielding his eyes from the sun, looking up into the sky, avoiding eye contact with me.

With our documents in his possession, Buzz-cut squelched his radio and read the vital stats out loud to a dispatch operator, our names, addresses, and birth dates bouncing off of Ivy Green's walls.

An odd wind rustled the treetops, and a moment later, a magnolia cone thudded to the ground inches from my feet.

As I bent over to pick it up, I heard a deep voice say, with a tickle in his voice, "Oswego?"

I straightened up and looked back around at Terminator.

"Don't tell me you're from Oswego?" I addressed him.

"Cortland."

"Cortland, New York? The Red Dragons. Division Three National Champions!"

Even from where I stood, I could discern a wrinkle on his metallic lips, suggestive of a smile.

But hope was dashed when Buzz-cut growled, "Well, gentlemen, you're trespassing on private property." The indictment twirled there like a hand grenade with the pin pulled out. I looked over at Matthew, who was studying his shoes.

Buzz-cut spoke again: "What made you think it was okay to disregard the closed signs and enter the grounds?"

"Well, first of all, I didn't see any sign that said it was closed. Second, the gate was open, and third, we heard voices and thought a tour was being conducted." I said this in all earnestness, without a hint of impudence.

At that moment, a titmouse came flitting over my head and landed somewhere out of sight up in the magnolia tree. It began to sing, repeating the same refrain, over and over: *seeds, seed, seeds.*

Buzz-cut took a deep breath, and then, when he looked back at me, his threatening expression and body posture had softened. He smirked a little, and as he did, he said, "Let me give y'all some friendly advice. Don't be walkin' around on private property on a Sunday morning in that getup and not expect people to notice you.

You're in Alabama, and people here notice, you understand?" his accent resonating musically.

He handed back our IDs, then gestured toward the open gate. We walked together over to the fence and out onto the sidewalk.

"Y'all have a nice day. And make sure to drive within the posted speed limit."

"Thank you," I said as we turned and started walking down the sidewalk. Then I stopped and turned back to look at him.

"This is a wonderful place. The people of this town should be so proud. Helen Keller is my hero," I added.

He nodded, earnestly appreciating my words.

Matthew and I walked in silence back toward the car.

At the great entrance gate, I looked up at the house. I didn't see any cops or their cars. I had an odd feeling that something was different.

Echoing across the yard, I heard that little titmouse repeating over and over again its same refrain: *seeds, seed, seeds.*

THE DAY I RETURNED from my adventures down South there was an e-mail message on my computer. It was from a man named Brian Sayers from Clarence, New York, president of the New York State Arborists, whom I had contacted and spoken to a month or so before about my seed project. He had left me hanging about his decision to help me out. At long last, here was his answer:

*Dear Richard:*

*Sorry for the delay in getting back to you, but we have been working on some sort of plan to take over the care and propagation of your seedlings and seeds. We plan to build a greenhouse on some land that we are going to clear out right on our five-acre property.*

*However, before we actually begin that process we need some things from you as follows:*

1. A list of the trees (species, etc.)

2. A list of their origin, including documentation if you have it.

3. An okay from you that we can do as we wish with these plants. (We plan to start a program where people can "adopt" a tree for a small amount and then they would be able to "walk through" our grove of trees. We might even work out something whereby such an "adopter" would also get a copy of your book.) We expect also that, should we be successful in developing some of the seeds into trees, we could eventually sell them.

4. Finally, all of this is dependent upon our assessment of the viability of what you have. That is, we will want to see the seedlings to make sure that they are likely to survive.

Anyhow, please get back to me with your thoughts and whatever information you can provide. Obviously then, the more provenance, the better.

Brian

I nearly fell over backward in my chair. Needless to say, I provided that provenance and soon afterward he came to my house to take a look at my seeds and indoor grove. I gave him the tour. Smiling and shaking his head the whole while, he took photographs, scratched down some notes, and picked up seedlings to read the names I'd scribbled on pieces of masking tape stuck on the front of the pots. What was clearly evident to me by the look in his eyes and the smile on his face was that Brian Sayers was as excited about it all as I was. At the end of the tour, both of us reflecting the same boyish enthusiasm, we shook joyous hands, sealing the deal. I would deliver half of everything I had to him in a few weeks, once he had everything prepared.

Of all the circumstances along this journey of mine, it was this turn of events at the last possible moment that most assured me that this cockamamie idea of mine had grown into something meaningful and long-lasting, that the trees would live on for others to touch and see and, someday, to climb in, dream from, dance around, and write about.

Dear Reader,

It is with both hope and trepidation that I imagine you turning the last page of my narrative and saying, "Hey, what about Toni Morrison and Emily Dickinson!? What about Steinbeck and Hemingway?!" And likely many more.

With all my heart, I say, I am truly sorry. I ran out of time. I could've traveled forever . . . and I intend to, and to keep adding to this book via the modern world's other ubiquitous medium, the Internet. I will post from more travels, but much more important, I would love for you to add to this journey, to tell me and others where you have been, what trees you have encountered, and of course, what seeds you have gathered. Keep the spirit of this book going online; I have built a site called LiterarySeeds.com, and I truly hope you'll use it to share your thoughts and sightings and photographs with me.

I did think you'd like to see what was on my original list of people and places to visit but didn't get to. I must confess that the journey I *ended up taking was not nearly as literary as this list implies. I wanted to give credit where credit was due, and for that reason movie and television stars who contributed to my early ecstasies figured in the original list. Likewise, jazz music has been my greatest passion, so many a jazz great was also included. All in all, the wondrous artists, figures, and places in this original list inflamed my spirit. Here is that list not yet accomplished:*

## LITERATURE

- Amherst, Mass.—Emily Dickinson
- Baltimore, Md.—Edgar Allan Poe
- Baraboo, Wisc.—Aldo Leopold, author of the classic *A Sand County Almanac*
- Brooklyn, N.Y.—Betty Smith
- Chicago—Studs Terkel
- Clyde, Ohio—Sherwood Anderson
- Hempstead, N.Y.—Walt Whitman
- Indianapolis, Ind., and Schenectady, N.Y.—Kurt Vonnegut
- Natchez, Miss.—Richard Wright
- New Canaan, Conn.—Maxwell Perkins
- Oak Park, Ill., and Key West, Fla.—Ernest Hemingway
- Pine Grove, Pa.—Conrad Richter, author of *The Light in the Forest* and *The Tree*
- Sag Harbor, N.Y.—John Steinbeck
- Salem, Mass.—Nathaniel Hawthorne
- West Park, N.Y.—John Burroughs

## HISTORICAL FIGURES

- Auburn, N.Y.—Harriet Tubman
- Gloverville, N.Y.—Elizabeth Cady Stanton

- Hyde Park, N.Y.—Franklin and Eleanor Roosevelt
- Nova, Ohio—John Chapman, a.k.a. Johnny Appleseed
- Philadelphia, Pa.—Benjamin Franklin
- Rochester, N.Y.—Susan B. Anthony
- Swartekill, N.Y.—Sojourner Truth and John Burroughs

## PLACES

- Central Park
- Sites along the Lewis and Clark Trail
- Little Big Horn
- Pearl Harbor and Wheeler Field (where my uncle Vincent was killed on December 7, 1941)
- Williamsburg and Jamestown

## MUSIC AND MOVIES

- Baltimore, Md.—Billie Holiday
- Florence, Ala.—W. C. Handy
- Grand Rapids, Minn.—Judy Garland
- New York, N.Y. (Yorkville section)—Bert Lahr
- New York, N.Y.—Huntz Hall and Leo Gorcey
- Pittsburgh, Pa.—Fred Rogers, a.k.a. Mr. Rogers
- Queens, N.Y.—Louis Armstrong and Rodney Dangerfield
- St. Louis, Mo.—Miles Davis
- Windsor, Vt.—Bob Keeshan, a.k.a. Captain Kangaroo

## Acknowledgments

Writing a book is like climbing Mount Everest: it cannot be accomplished alone. That said, it is still not nearly as difficult a task as finding words to thank those who made it all possible.

Stealing a line from another Great One, I would like to say to my better half, Mary, "Baby, you're the greatest!" To my daughters, Katherine and Evelyn, who provided just the right touch of love, antagonism, and camaraderie all along the way: Thanks, losers!

I would like to express my heart-throbbing, knees-to-the-ground, hands-clasped-in-front-of-me gratitude to Carl Lennertz, my dear friend and editor, whose immaculate leadership, passion, love, grace, ecstasy, vision, guidance, and wisdom made a dream come true. Without him this book would not have been possible.

I would like to extend my calloused hand to my awesome nephew Matthew Ferrer, whose curiosity, creativity, and praying-mantis-like powers of observation perfectly complemented my ADHD/rapid-eye-movement perspective. I would also like to thank my beloved sister, Debbie Horan Ferrer, whose care, artistry, and savoir-faire have always been the greatest of all gifts. Debbie and Matt also lovingly drew the beautiful illustrations inside this book. To my parents, Yolanda Horan and Richard V. Horan, Sr. (R.I.P.), for their love and munificence since day one, and all of my extended family for their love and support through the years. To my in-laws, Ray and Barb Buckley, whose generous support and providence have provided untold serenity.

To my oldest and dearest friends, David Case (a.k.a. Day-by-Dave), Matthew James (a.k.a. Mothballhead), and Brendan McAuliffe (a.k.a. Colonel B. T. McGuillicuddy), without whose genius, friendship, and hysterical laughter life itself would be reduced to nothing more than a pitiful little fart; to Richard Mihulka (a.k.a. Krakow), who taught me the true meaning of trees; to Diane Drugge and Tom Powers, whose wisdom and encouragement early on made all the difference; to Chip Fleischer, Michael Moore, and Larry McMurtry, who provided me with the opportunities of a lifetime; to Al Nayer, who proved to me beyond any doubt that creativity is the primal magic; to Wallace (Steven Wallace), whose extraordinary intelligence, gentility, and courage "made the flag on the mast to wave"; to Nathan Carter for his generous hospitality; to Brian Sayers, my Dudley Do-Right, who came along at the penultimate moment to save the seeds and the saplings and to make everything all right; to my agent, Helen Zimmerman, who was ever ready with helpful insights and much-needed advice in all the right places; to Michael Krohnen, who expressed the meaning and merit of my work with his beatific smile; to Tass Bey, the mystical world healer, who provided key resource materials and rejuvenating karma at precise moments along the way; to Nancy Pfeiffer, for all her help and advice; to John Slagg, an American hero, whose primary source

World War II stories, told in his incomparable Brooklynese, took my breath away; to Phyllis Algeo of Nova, Ohio, for her charitable donation in providing me with seeds from the last living apple tree planted by Johnny Appleseed; to Tom Fels, for his anecdotes about Shirley Jackson; to Ken Lehman of Pine Grove, Pennsylvania, who took the time to tell me as well as show me all about the life of Conrad Richter; to all of the volunteer docents who provided me with invaluable tidbits of information; to Emoke B'Racz and Paul Yamazaki, who were critical fonts of information; to Steve Smith and Kathie Hangac, whose professionalism, humor, and camaraderie were a great comfort to me at the onset of my adventure; to my arch nemesis, the Eastern grey squirrel (*Sciurus carolinensis*)—I'll see you in Hell, varmints; to the writers, athletes, musicians, historical figures, alive and dead, who so generously provided me with the seeds I humbly sought, both literal and metaphoric; and last but not least, to all the trees that have provided the vital wood flesh for millions of magical books throughout the ages: Thank you!

## About the author

## About the book

Insights,
Interviews
& More . . .

## Read on

# Meet Richard Horan

RICHARD HORAN is a novelist, an ESL teacher, and a nonfiction book reviewer for the *San Francisco Chronicle*, *Christian Science Monitor*, *Washington Times*, and other publications. His novel *Goose Music* was a finalist for the Great Lakes Fiction Award and winner of *ForeWord* magazine's Bronze Medal for Book of the Year in Fiction. He lives in Oswego, New York.

He will be adding true tales of more author visits at literaryseeds.com, and encourages you to go there and add your own stories of books and trees, seeds and favorite authors. ∾

Catherine Horan

# A Conversation with Betty Smith's Daughter

### Ailanthus, a.k.a. Tree of Heaven (*Ailanthus altissima*)

The first name on my list for seed gathering was Betty Smith, author of *A Tree Grows in Brooklyn*. My pipe dream was to find, still growing in Brooklyn, the tree that had inspired her story. However, my hopes were quickly dashed after a phone conversation with her daughter, Nancy Pfeiffer, alive and well at eighty-seven. She wistfully explained that all of her mother's trees were gone, for one reason or another; nevertheless, she had a few interesting anecdotes to offer about the trees her mother had planted. In the end, the treasures I gathered from the estate of the late Betty Smith came in the form not of tree seeds but of tender memories retold by friends and family about an esteemed author's love affair with a much-maligned species of tree.

It should be pointed out that the central metaphor of Betty *Smith's A Tree Grows in Brooklyn* is the notorious ailanthus tree, a.k.a. tree of heaven, also derisively referred to as the "tree of hell" and the "weed tree," because of its miraculous ability to thrive in inhospitable environments and to vigorously re-sprout when cut down. (In college I had my own little gardening business, so I have many ▶

> 66 My pipe dream was to find, still growing in Brooklyn, the tree that had inspired her story. 99

3

a memory of battling this insufferable weed.)

Ailanthus trees are an invasive species, and eradication programs have been attempted nonstop almost from the tree's first arrival in the United States from mainland China around the middle of the eighteenth century. In present-day China, it is still highly prized as an ornamental tree, but it also continues to be used in traditional medicine and as a host for silkworms. Ailanthus can be found growing all over America—in abandoned lots, along highways, and coming right up out of cracks in sidewalks. However, it rarely lives more than fifty years, so any chance of my finding Smith's original ailanthus tree still growing in Brooklyn was out of the question.

But Pfeiffer told me about the ailanthus tree that her mother planted in the walled-in garden behind her home in Chapel Hill, where Smith lived almost her entire life and where she is buried. Back in 1945, when 20th Century Fox came out with the movie version of Smith's book (directed by her former Yale classmate Elia Kazan), someone had the clever idea to send ailanthus saplings out to various critics as part of a publicity campaign. Pfeiffer doesn't recall how many were sent out, and she certainly has no idea where or

> ❝ Ailanthus can be found growing all over America—in abandoned lots, along highways, and coming right up out of cracks in sidewalks. ❞

if any of them are still growing today. However, she sent me a photograph of her niece (Betty Smith's granddaughter) sitting in the walled-in garden with an ailanthus in the background. Pfeiffer is quite sure that the tree is one of the saplings from that early publicity campaign. Later on, however, they had to take the tree down when it threatened to topple the garden wall.*

Betty Smith and her family owned a beachside cottage on the Outer Banks of North Carolina, and they took shoots from the aforementioned ailanthus and planted it around that house. Then, in 1993, the cottage and an ailanthus tree from one of those shoots had to be moved back from the shore because of erosion. The tree continued to grow tall until the house was sold in 2002. Since then, the house and tree have been torn down and replaced by a large rental unit.

Pfeiffer did tell me about a living tree that was planted at the Leonard Street Library in the Williamsburg section of Brooklyn, the same library branch Smith immortalizes in her book, and where the book's ▶

66 A living tree . . . was planted at the Leonard Street Library in the Williamsburg section of Brooklyn, the same library branch Smith immortalizes in her book. 99

---

* Through Google Images, one can find photos of Betty Smith, including a good picture with this very ailanthus tree in the background.

protagonist, Francie Smith, goes to escape the hustle and bustle of the Brooklyn streets. (The building is still located at 81 Devoe Street in Williamsburg.) On January 17, 2007, to commemorate the thirty-fifth anniversary of Betty Smith's death, a tree was planted there in Smith's honor. It was not an ailanthus, but rather an *Amelanchier*, also called serviceberry, juneberry, or wild plum. The tree, along with a plaque and a proclamation, was presented by a World War II veteran from Smith's old neighborhood, John Slagg, who while fighting the Japanese in the Pacific Theater, wrote to Smith to tell her how reading her book was like "taking a furlough in proxy," because the book evoked vivid memories of his beloved hometown. Smith wrote him back, and the two continued a correspondence throughout the war.*

Nancy Pfeiffer gave me a little background on the writing of her mother's famous book,† and shortly

66 John Slagg, . . . while fighting the Japanese in the Pacific Theater, wrote to Smith to tell her how reading her book was like 'taking a furlough in proxy,' because the book evoked vivid memories of his beloved hometown. 99

_____

* A write-up of that Brooklyn ceremony can be found at the following link: www.nycgovparks .org/sub_newsroom/daily_plants/daily_plant_ main.php?id=20462.

† An interesting footnote to the writing of *A Tree Grows in Brooklyn* is the fact that Betty Smith

thereafter ended our phone conversation by reading to me the prologue of the first edition of *A Tree Grows in Brooklyn*. Her mellifluous schoolteacher voice, even over the phone, nearly brought tears to my eyes:

> There's a tree that grows in Brooklyn. Some people call it the Tree of Heaven. No matter where its seed falls, it makes a tree, which struggles to reach the sky. It grows in boarded-up lots and out of neglected rubbish heaps. It grows up out of cellar gratings. It is the only tree that grows out of cement. It grows ▶

❝ There's a tree that grows in Brooklyn. . . . No matter where its seed falls, it makes a tree, which struggles to reach the sky. ❞

attributes its inspiration to another author in this book. She tells the story on the back of the book's jacket cover, written in 1943: "Six years ago I was living in Brooklyn and working in a Federal Theatre show in New York City. I was held up one night on account of dress rehearsal. Walking to the subway, I passed a still-open bookstore. I knew I couldn't afford it, but I bought a book anyhow. I took it to bed with me and began reading it. I finished it at dawn. The book inspired me, because before I went to sleep, I penciled a brief, half-page outline on the last page and headed it 'Notes on a Novel I'll Write Someday.' . . . I had absolutely forgotten I had ever written that outline. Yet, six years later in the writing of the novel, I followed that outline faithfully. The book? Thomas Wolfe's *Of Time and the River*."

lushly . . . survives without sun, water, and seemingly without earth. It would be considered beautiful except that there are so many of it.

I certainly had a new appreciation for a tree that had, up to now, been an old nemesis. ᕦ

# Quotations on Trees from Literature and History

"Even if I knew that tomorrow the world would go to pieces, I would still plant my apple tree."   —Martin Luther

"To have a child, to plant a tree, to write a book."               —Emile Zola

"The trees shall be my books."
—Shakespeare, in *As You Like It*, III.ii, 5

"Let us cross over the river, and rest under the trees."          —last words of Thomas Jonathan "Stonewall" Jackson

"Trees cause more pollution than automobiles do."        —Ronald Reagan

"Trees outstrip most people in the extent and depth of their work for the public good."
          —Sara Ebenreck, *American Forests*

"You can't be suspicious of a tree, or accuse a bird or a squirrel of subversion or challenge the ideology of a violet."
—Hal Borland, *Sundial of the Seasons*

"Evolution did not intend trees to grow singly. Far more than ourselves they are social creatures, and no more natural as isolated specimens than man is as a marooned sailor or hermit."
          —John Fowles, *The Tree*

"The creation of a thousand forests is in one acorn."
          —Ralph Waldo Emerson ▶

**The creation of a thousand forests is in one acorn.**

9

"I frequently tramped eight or ten miles through the deepest snow to keep an appointment with a beech-tree, or a yellow birch, or an old acquaintance among the pines."
—Henry David Thoreau

"You must not know too much or be too precise or scientific about birds and trees and flowers and watercraft; a certain free-margin, and even vagueness—ignorance, credulity—helps your enjoyment of these things."
—Walt Whitman

"A few minutes ago every tree was excited, bowing to the roaring storm, waving, swirling, tossing their branches in glorious enthusiasm like worship. But though to the outer ear these trees are now silent, their songs never cease."
—John Muir

"A fool sees not the same tree that a wise man sees." —William Blake

"A hypocrite is the kind of politician who would cut down a redwood tree, then mount the stump and make a speech for conservation."
—Adlai Stevenson

"A stricken tree, a living thing, so beautiful, so dignified, so admirable in its potential longevity, is, next to man, perhaps the most touching of wounded objects." —Edna Ferber

66 Though to the outer ear these trees are now silent, their songs never cease. 99

"A sure cure for seasickness is to sit under a tree."        —Spike Milligan

"It is remarkable how closely the history of the apple tree is connected with that of man."
                —Henry David Thoreau

"A tree against the sky possesses the same interest, the same character, the same expression as the figure of a human."        —painter Georges Rouault

"A tree growing out of the ground is as wonderful today as it ever was. It does not need to adopt new and startling methods."
                —painter Robert Henri

"A tree is an incomprehensible mystery."        —artist Jim Woodring

"A woodland in full color is awesome as a forest fire, in magnitude at least, but a single tree is like a dancing tongue of flame to warm the heart."        —Hal Borland

"All things share the same breath—the beast, the tree, the man . . . the air shares its spirit with all the life it supports."        —Chief Seattle

"He who plants a tree, / Plants a hope."        —Lucy Larcom, in the poem "Plant a Tree"

"And I say the sacred hoop of my people was one of the many hoops ▶

> ❝ A sure cure for seasickness is to sit under a tree. ❞

that made one circle, wide as daylight and as starlight, and in the center grew one mighty flowering tree to shelter all the children of one mother and one father." —Black Elk

"Break open a cherry tree and there are no flowers, but the spring breeze brings forth myriad blossoms." —Ikkyu Sojun

"Character is like a tree and reputation like a shadow. The shadow is what we think of it; the tree is the real thing." —Abraham Lincoln

"Even if one tree falls down it wouldn't affect the entire forest." —Chen Shui-bian

"Every crag and gnarled tree and lonely valley has its own strange and graceful legend attached to it." —writer Douglas Hyde

"For in the true nature of things, if we rightly consider, every green tree is far more glorious than if it were made of gold and silver." —Martin Luther

"I didn't want to tell the tree or weed what it was. I wanted it to tell me something and through me express its meaning in nature." —photographer Wynn Bullock

"I often lay on that bench looking up into the tree, past the trunk and up into the branches. It was particularly

**❝** I didn't want to tell the tree or weed what it was. I wanted it to tell me something and through me express its meaning in nature. **❞**

fine at night with the stars above the tree."                    —Georgia O'Keeffe

"I said to the almond tree, 'Friend, speak to me of God,' and the almond tree blossomed."   —Nikos Kazantzakis

"I think that I shall never see a billboard lovely as a tree. Perhaps, unless the billboards fall, I'll never see a tree at all."            —Ogden Nash

"I think that if you shake the tree, you ought to be around when the fruit falls to pick it up."      —Mary Cassatt

"I was in my yard and thought that the tree was a living being. We take trees for granted. We don't believe they are as much alive as we are."
                    —Ziggy Marley

"If a tree dies, plant another in its place."            —Carolus Linnaeus

"If you're not a tree hugger, then you're a what, a tree hater?"
                    —Douglas Coupland

"In the perception of a tree we can distinguish the act of experiencing, or perceiving, from the thing experienced, or perceived."
                    —philosopher Samuel Alexander

"Never say there is nothing beautiful in the world anymore. There is always something to make you wonder in the shape of a tree, the trembling of a leaf."
                    —Albert Schweitzer ►

❝ Never say there is nothing beautiful in the world anymore. There is always something to make you wonder in the shape of a tree, the trembling of a leaf. ❞

### Quotations on Trees from Literature and History (*continued*)

"When the destructive analysis of day is done, and all that is truly important becomes whole and sound again. When man reassembles his fragmentary self and grows with the calm of a tree."

—Antoine de Saint-Exupéry

"Someone's sitting in the shade today because someone planted a tree a long time ago."　—Warren Buffett

"Poems are made by fools like me, But only God can make a tree."

—Joyce Kilmer

"In the slanting sun of late afternoon the shadows of great branches reached across the river, and the trees took the river in their arms."

—Norman Maclean

"I never saw a discontented tree. They grip the ground as though they liked it, and though fast rooted they travel about as far as we do."

—John Muir

❝ I never saw a discontented tree. ❞

# Books on Trees

THESE ARE MY BIBLES:

Arbor Day Foundation. Illus. Karina I. Helm. *What Tree Is That? A Guide to the More Common Trees Found in North America.* Lincoln, Neb.: Arbor Day Foundation, 2009.

Fairchild, Jill. *Trees: A Celebration.* New York: Weidenfeld and Nicolson, 1989.

Fowles, John, and Frank Horvat. *The Tree.* 1st U.S. ed. Boston: Little Brown, 1979.

Giono, Jean. *The Man Who Planted Trees.* Chelsea, Vt.: Chelsea Green, 1985.

Keeler, Harriet Louise. *Our Native Trees and How to Identify Them: A Popular Study of Their Habits and Their Peculiarities.* Kent State University Press, facsimile of 1900 edition, 2005.

Linford, Jenny. *The Tree: Wonder of the Natural World.* Bath, UK: Parragon, 2006.

Peattie, Donald Culross. *A Natural History of Eastern and Central North American Trees.* 2nd ed. Boston and New York: Riverside Press, 1964.

————. *A Natural History of North American Trees.* Boston and New York: Houghton Mifflin, 2007.

Preston, Richard. *The Wild Trees: A Story of Passion and Daring.* New York: Random House, 2007.

Sibley, David Allen. *The Sibley Guide to Trees.* New York: Knopf, 2009. ▶

## Books on Trees *(continued)*

Williams, Michael D. *Identifying Trees: An All-Season Guide to Eastern North America*. Mechanicsburg, Pa.: Stackpole Books, 2007.

Zim, Herbert S., and Alexander C. Martin. Illus. Dorthea and Sy Barlowe. *Trees: A Guide to Familiar American Trees*. A Golden Nature Guide. New York: Simon and Schuster, 1952. ᴄᴏ

Don't miss the next book by your favorite author. Sign up now for AuthorTracker by visiting www.AuthorTracker.com.